FOCUS ON

First Certificate

LONGMAN

SUE O'CONNELL

Addison Wesley Longman Limited
Edinburgh Gate, Harlow,
Essex. CM20 2JE, England
and Associated Companies throughout the world.

First published 1987 by William Collins Sons & Company Ltd
Second edition published 1993 by Thomas Nelson and Sons Ltd
This third edition published 1996 by Addison Wesley Longman Ltd
Second impression 1996

ISBN 0 175 56997 5

Set in 11/14.5pt Adobe Minion and
10.5/13.5pt Monotype GillSans Light

Printed in Spain by Gráficas Estella

Acknowledgements

Picture Research by Simon James Collier, The Okai Collier
Company Ltd

Action Plus Photos: p41, p48, p267 Allsort: p267
Gareth Boden Photography: p92, p262, p266 Stuart Boreham
Photography: p62, p67 Bristol Zoo: p188, p226 Britstock: p4 (top
right), p 260 Bubbles Photo Library: p209 (top left) J Allan Cash
Photo Library: p87 (bottom right), p147 (left), p194, p209 (top
right), p261 Bruce Coleman Photo Library/Andy Purcell: p204
(tortoise) Bruce Coleman Photo Library/Hans Reinhard: p204
(canary) Express Newspapers: p148 The Ronald Grant Archive:
p258 The Image Bank: p196 (left), p266 London Express News: p87
(top left, bottom left) The Military Picture Library: p80
Network Photographers/Peter Jordan: p204 (snake)
Network Photographers/Gerald Sioen: p196 (right)
Network Photographers/Barry Lewis: p26 The Observer
Newspaper: p87 (top right) Sue O Connell: p209 (bottom) Pictor
International Limited: p42, p155 (middle right), p222, p261, p262,
p264, p266 The Press Association: p181 Private Eye p140 Chris
Ridgers Photography: p166 (top, top centre) The Sunday Times:
p30 The Sunday Times/Peter Watson p65, p71 The Telegraph
Colour Library: p4 (middle bottom), p141, p155, p163 (left), p204
(goldfish), p260 Tony Stone Images: p4 (middle, bottom right, top
left, bottom left), p37, p45, p54, p73, p138, p143, p147 (right),
p155, p163 (middle right), p166 (bottom centre, bottom), p169
(all), p202, p204 (mouse, cat), p209 (top centre), p219, p260, p261,
p262, p264, p267 You Magazine: p49, p89, p101.

Illustrated by Andy Hammond, Biz Hull, Kevin Jones Associates,
Stephen Morris, Tim Slade

We are grateful to the following for permission to reproduce copyright
material:

AA Membership for the adapted article 'Young Drivers, what every
parent should know.' by Claire Evans from *AA Magazine,* Issue 12
(Spring 1995); Anna Coote for the adapted article from 'Equal at Work'
; BBC Worldwide Publishing for adapted extracts from the article
'Space Invaders' by Mike Johnson from *BBC Good Food Guide
Magazine,* Christmas/January 1995, and for the article 'Beat the
Teacher' by Clive Doig; The Bristol Journal; Caliban Books for the
article 'The Pools Winners' by Peter Razzell and Stephen Smith; The
Central Office of Information for the articles 'If you have to complain'
and 'You're already well equipped to prevent crime'; The Consumers'
Association for the articles 'A few golden rules', 'Beware Supermarket
Selling', Do you need a car at all?', 'Use your oven sparingly', and 'Buy in
Bulk'; The Countryside Commission for 'The Country Code' and 'The
countryside Access Charter'; The Daily Mirror for extracts from the
articles 'Just a normal day?' by Marjorie Proops and 'Granny, 70, holds
up bank'; Focus Magazine for 'Keeping a Watch on your Lifestyle'
Introduction by Caroline Green from *Focus Magazine,* No. 5, April
1993; Friends of the Earth; Robert Harding Syndication for adapted
extracts from the articles 'Saturday Night, Sunday Morning' by Rebecca
Cripps from *Marie Claire,* June 1995 and 'The Meteorologist' by
Rebecca Cripps from *Marie Claire,* June 1994; Harper and Row/The
Good Health Guide for the article 'For me, being healthy is...';
HarperCollins Publishers for the puzzles from *Graded English Puzzles
No 6',* by Lewis Jones; The Health Education Council for extracts from
the articles 'Cuts, bruises, bites and burns' from *Minor illnesses,* and
'Eating well'; Hobsons Publishing Plc for an adapted article from *Excel
at Interviews* by Patricia McBride; Living Magazine; The Mail on
Sunday Magazine for the extract from the article 'Vive la Différence';
The National magazine Co Ltd for extracts abridged from the article
'Not Just a Load of Rubbish' by Sharon Maxwell Magnus from *Good
Housekeeping,* September 1988 © National Magazine Company; The
Observer magazine for the extract from the article 'Hard Track to
Africa' by Trisha Greenhalgh and the article 'The Rudiments of
Wisdom' by Tim Hunkin; Private Eye for two cartoons; The Publishing
Team for adapted articles from 'Ice Times' from *Prime Time* Magazine,
20 October 1990; Random House UK for the extracts from 'Slow Boats
to China' by Gavin Young published by Hutchinson; Salamander Books
for the extract from 'In the Heart of Borneo' by Redmond O'Hanlon;
Solo Syndication Ltd for the articles 'What's the big idea?' by Lee
Wilson from *You Magazine,* 15.4.94, 'Christina's call of the wild' by
Christina Dodwell from *You Magazine* 26.8.84 and 'It is better than you
know what' from *You Magazine* 27.11.88; South West News Services for
adapted extracts from the article 'Scruff Justice' by Ken Elks from the
Sunday Express 28.3.93; The Sunday Express for the adapted extracts
'Freezing' by Mark Elston Dew, 'I can't travel without', ' Waiter for a
Week' by Danny Danzinger, 'Have you ever wanted to try someone
else's job' by Danny Danzinger and 'Young skater' by Robin Cousins
from *The Sunday Express Magazine* ; Times Newspapers Ltd for extracts
from the articles 'An inch above the collar, an inch below the knee' by
Nicky Maitlis and the articles by Geoff Capes, Sally Oppenheim,
Rosalind Plowright and Bill Sirs from *The Sunday Times Magazine,* the
extracts from the articles 'First Read the Small Print' by Mela Brown,
'The Big Hitch' by David Wickers and '7 banks a day are robbed in LA'
by John Barnes from *The Sunday Times,* and the extracts from the
articles 'Adventure Travel' by Ronald Faux and 'Dear travel agent' by
Fank Barrett from *The Times,* © Times Newspapers Ltd; Wayland
Publishers Ltd for the extract from the article 'Waste age man' by
Jonathan Holliman; Woman Magazine for the extract from the article
by Mervyn Edgecombe.

We have unfortunately been unable to trace the copyright holder of the
article 'What children really think - working mothers' by Joyce Robins
from *Living Magazine,* October 1985 and would appreciate any
information which would enable us to do so.

Contents

Lead-in   What sort of holiday would you choose as a break from studying or working?

❶   Look at the pictures below and think about the kind of holidays they represent. Choose two that you would prefer and think about the reasons why you would enjoy them. Think also of one thing about each holiday which you are not so keen on!

❷   Work with a partner. Ask each other about your choices and say what you like about them, and what you are not so fond of. Use the following exchange as an example.

A   Which of the holidays would you enjoy most?
B   Well, I'd prefer …
A   What do you like especially about …
B   I really enjoy …
A   Is there anything you don't like about …
B   Well, I don't like … very much.

❸ Now check the Functions Bank on page 105. How many of the expressions did you use or hear? Make a note of the ones you didn't use and try to include them next time.

❹ Change partners and discuss your choices again.

❺ Report back to the class what your second partner told you.

Text 1 ❶ Read the article.

I CAN'T TRAVEL WITHOUT …

What are the things you can't do without when you go away?

| A | **Patrick Lichfield,** |

the photographer, never goes far without the Olympus Pearlcorder dictating machine which lets him catch up with his correspondence wherever he is. The tiny tapes are either posted to his secretary, Felicity, or he gives them to someone to bring back. The quality is very good but there are often some interesting background noises.

| B | **Mel Calman,** |

the cartoonist, jokes about filling his suitcase with tranquillisers and three different kinds of toothbrushes after recent, expensive dental treatment, but it is his diary and sketch-book that are always with him when he is on the move. 'I don't keep a diary except when I'm away. I start a new one each trip now since I lost irreplaceable notes on two previous trips on a bus in the States.'

| C | **Richard Branson,** |

who recently launched Virgin Atlantic Airways, believes in travelling light. 'Suntan lotion for my nose and my notebooks which are my lifeline. But I will always sling in a pack of cards. I love a game of cards, particularly bridge, canasta or spades, but I'm not a gambler.'

From *The Sunday Express Magazine*

| D | **Barry Norman,** |

the film critic, never travels anywhere without his credit card. 'The days of anyone being stranded abroad are now over. I remember once, before credit cards were common, the *Daily Mail* sent me to Italy at a moment's notice. It was a bank holiday, I had no money and the banks were shut. There I was in Milan on a beautiful sunny day sitting in my hotel because it was the only place I could eat or drink because I could sign for it.'

| E | **Frank Muir,** |

the TV scriptwriter and humorist, never sets off on a journey without packing his Swiss army penknife. 'It does everything,' he says. 'It has about 140 things that come out. It opens bottles, gets things out of horses' hooves, it has scissors, screwdrivers, tweezers. I never go anywhere without it and I have never used it.'

❷ Choose from the five sections (A–E) to answer these questions and write the letters in the boxes.

Who likes to take as little luggage as possible? 1 ☐

Who likes to keep a record of his travels? 2 ☐

Who takes something he hasn't tested? 3 ☐

Which two people seem to take their work with them when they travel? 4 ☐ 5 ☐

Which two people take something to avoid bad experiences they've had in the past? 6 ☐ 7 ☐

Who takes the strangest thing, in your opinion?

Who takes the most useful thing, in your opinion?

5

Communication activity 1

Work in pairs. Think of one thing **you** always take with you when you travel, but don't tell your partner what it is.

Try to find out what your partner always takes by asking questions like:

Is it useful?   *Can you carry it in your pocket?*   *Does it cost a lot of money?*

STUDY BOX 1   Phrasal verb *catch*

… a machine 'which lets him **catch up with** his correspondence' (Text 1)

catch on – become popular.	*I think our new song will really* **catch on***.*
catch on – understand.	*I explained it to him but he didn't seem to* **catch on***.*
catch up with – succeed in reaching.	*Hurry or you'll never* **catch up with** *the rest.*
catch up with – bring up to date.	*I've got a lot of work to* **catch up with***.*

Focus on writing 1 *Capital letters and punctuation*

CAPITAL
LETTERS

1   Here are some of the times when we use capital letters in English. Find examples of each of the following in Text 1.

With the names of

1 people   ....

2 companies   ....

3 products   ....

4 newspapers   ....

5 countries   ....

6 cities/towns   ....

With

7 nationalities   ....

8 some abbreviations ....

2   These are the other main times when capital letters are used. Choose two examples for each group from the list below.

1 With the first word and also the main words in the titles of books, films, plays and works of art   ....

2 With areas/regions (but not with *east, west,* etc., on their own)

....

3 With the names of streets and other parts of a town   ....

4 With rivers/mountains and other geographical features   ....

5 With the names of planets (but not with *the earth, sun* or *moon*)   ....

6 With days, months, festivals and historical periods (but not with seasons)

....

7 With the names of professions when they are used as titles (but not when used generally)

....

Christmas, the Middle East, South Australia, Jupiter, the Amazon,
Doctor White, the Middle Ages, The Mona Lisa, Wall Street, Mars,
the Pacific Ocean, The Merchant of Venice, Trafalgar Square, Professor Smith.

PUNCTUATION ❸ Here are the main punctuation marks. What are their names?

1 .   2 ,   3 ?   4 !   5 '   6 " "

❹ Now match each punctuation mark with its use.

1 an apostrophe
2 a question mark
3 a full stop
4 an exclamation mark
5 a comma
6 quotation marks

a to separate items in a list
   or
   to mark a pause in a sentence before you
   add more information
b to show a letter has been left out
   or
   to show possession
c to show direct speech
d to end a sentence
e to show a question
f to show surprise or emphasis

❺ Add capital letters and punctuation marks where necessary in these short texts.

1 i havent told you where were going this summer have i well weve decided to go to nepal in july

2 ken read an article about it in a sunday newspaper you see and he was so enthusiastic that i said why dont we go

3 well be flying to kathmandu and then touring the east of the country

4 itll be a chance to see mount everest although we certainly wont be climbing it

5 by the way im going to a lecture at the library next friday professor sweeting will be talking about his recent trip to the himalayas would you like to come too

Focus on grammar I   Review of the present tenses

The **present continuous** tense refers to **temporary** situations, and actions **that are happening now**.

The **present simple** tense refers to **more permanent** situations, and actions **that are repeated**.

Look at the examples below, and discuss with a partner why the present simple is used in two of the sentences and the present continuous in the others.

I start a new diary on each trip.
Oh no! It's starting to rain.

He's away. I believe he's travelling in South East Asia.
He never travels anywhere without his credit card.

EXERCISE I   Choose the correct form of the verb to complete the following sentences:

a   The kettle .... Please switch it off.
     Water .... at 100 degrees centigrade.   **boil**
b   I .... with friends until I can find a flat of my own.
     I .... in a small village about five miles from here.   **live**
c   He .... tennis three days a week.
     John isn't here. He .... football.   **play**
d   Look, it .... You'd better take your umbrella.
     People say it .... more in Manchester than anywhere else.   **rain**
e   We usually .... the children at bedtime.
     Oh no! The children .... the cat!   **bath**

THE PRESENT SIMPLE

FORM

I speak	
She speaks	Italian
They speak	

Negative: I don't speak Italian very well.
Question: Do you speak Italian at all?

USE   The present simple is used in (complete the examples in your own words):

1   a   habitual or repeated actions and situations. *For example:*
            He often runs in races but rarely ....
     b   situations that never change; for example, scientific facts. *For example:*
            Hot air rises while cool air ....
2   future plans with particular reference to journeys and timetables. *For example:*
        The train .... at every station on the way to London.
3   time clauses introduced by **when, as soon as, after, if**, etc. *For example:*
        I'll phone you as soon as I arrive.

THE PRESENT CONTINUOUS

FORM

I am	
She is	listening
They are	

Negative: You aren't listening!
Question: Are you listening?

USE   The present continuous is used to talk about (complete the examples in your own words):

1   a   actions and situations happening at the moment of speaking. *For example:*
            The telephone .... Please answer it.
     b   temporary situations. *For example:*
            I .... in an ice cream factory to pay my college fees.
2   future plans – an expression of future plans is usually needed to avoid confusion. *For example:*
        We're taking the boat to Calais but .... the rest of the way by train.
3   annoying habits (with **always, continually, constantly**, etc.) *For example:*
        You are always criticising the way I speak.

▶ Some verbs are not usually used in the continuous form. The most common are:

wish	believe	hear	seem	mean
want	feel	see	understand	belong
like	suppose	smell	consist of	remember
hate	know	notice	contain	

▶ Some other verbs which are also normally used in the simple form may be used in the continuous form, but with a change of meaning. *For example:*

I expect you are hungry. (= I am sure)
I'm expecting a visit from the doctor. (= I am waiting for)

The most common ones apart from *expect* are:

think   see   look   hold   have

EXERCISE 2   Complete these ten sentences using each of the five verbs in the list above twice, once in the continuous form and once in the simple form of the present tense. Notice the change in meaning.

a   I .... for the contact lens that I dropped on the floor.
b   He's a real animal-lover and he .... two cats, a tortoise and some goldfish.
c   Don't disturb him! He ....
d   This jug .... exactly one litre of liquid.
e   You .... like your father in this photograph.
f   I .... how to do it now. Thanks for showing me.
g   Tell me what you .... of your new teacher.
h   Who .... you .... at the club tonight?
i   My parents .... a wonderful time in America, I hear.
j   Who .... the baby in that photograph?

EXERCISE 3   Complete the sentences below by putting the verb in brackets into the most suitable form of the present simple or present continuous.

a   'What .... you .... (do) this summer?' 'We .... (spend) a week with friends in Greece.'
b   Oil and water .... (not, mix). Oil .... (float) on top of water.
c   Why .... you .... (cook) those carrots? You .... (know) Helen .... (eat) only raw vegetables.
d   I .... (not, understand) what he .... (say). .... he .... (speak) English or German?
e   I .... (normally, go) to a keep-fit class on Wednesday evenings but tomorrow I can't because I .... (work) late.
f   I .... (know) what you .... (mean) but I .... (not, agree) with you.
g   We have a system in this house. I .... (do) the housework, he .... (cook) the meals, and we both .... (give) the orders!

Text 2

❶ Look at the headline below and say what you think the article is going to be about.

❷ Read through the first paragraph to find out if you are right.

❸ There are four gaps in the text. Each one should contain a quotation. Choose a quotation from the list (A–D) below to fill each gap. Write the correct letter in the space.

> **A** 'No, she was angry because the cows used to stop and look in at her as they went past the window.'
>
> **B** 'particularly suitable for families with children'
>
> **C** 'they should try and sort it out with a holiday company representative there and then.'
>
> **D** 'The fact that their hotel is next to a road. How do they expect to get to their hotel if it's not next to a road?'

From an article by Frank Barrett in *The Times*

Dear travel agent, please stop the cows staring at me …

For the next few weeks, tour operators will be sorting through the annual deluge of complaints. Ron Wheal, head of customer relations for Britain's biggest holiday company, which took more than a million abroad this summer, says, 'Holidaymakers are complaining about petty, silly little things.' Such as? **1 [ ]**.

Perhaps one of the most common complaints is that the holiday fails to live up to the brochure promises. A family from Berkshire with two young children were attracted by a two-week package in a three-star hotel that was described as 'friendly' and **2 [ ]**. It offered 'cots, baby minding, high chairs and early suppers'. When they arrived, the hotel was not up to three-star standard, the staff were rude and the promised facilities for children were practically non-existent.

An initial complaint which had been sent to the holiday company by the family was answered with an 'ex-gratia' payment of £30. With the help of a consumer magazine, the family issued a summons claiming £500 – which the holiday company eventually met in full.

One of the big travel successes of recent years has been the 'gite' holiday; a gite is

self-catering accommodation in France, often on a farm. The director of the Gite de France's London office recently received a telephone call from one client furious about the cows that passed in front of her gite. Was she complaining about the mess? **3 [ ]**.

Britain's biggest seller of long-distance holidays says that the majority of its complaints come from people who have chosen the wrong sort of holiday. People who fail to do their research could find themselves in the Caribbean during the hurricane season.

Mr Wheal says that if someone really wants action over a spoilt holiday, **4 [ ]**. Those who complain to the tour operator on their return and are unhappy with the response can take their case to the Association of British Travel Agents (ABTA) which will provide conciliation facilities free of charge.

❹ Now read the article again and mark the following statements as either true or false. Underline the word or phrase which gives you your answer.

		True	False
1	Ron Wheal thinks that most of the complaints his company receives are reasonable.	☐	☐
2	The most frequent complaint is that a holiday is of a lower standard than expected.	☐	☐
3	The family from Berkshire expected that someone would be available to look after their young children.	☐	☐
4	The first thing they did was to write a letter of complaint to the company.	☐	☐

5 The company paid £500 as soon as they received the letter.   ☐   ☐
6 If you stay at a gite, you have to prepare your own meals.   ☐   ☐
7 The long-distance holiday company suggests that holidaymakers should
   find out about the area they intend to visit.   ☐   ☐
8 Mr Wheal suggests that people with complaints should contact ABTA as
   soon as they return home.   ☐   ☐

When you have finished, compare your answers with another student's.

VOCABULARY MATCHING ❺ **Find the word or phrase in the text which means the same as the following:**

1 large quantity (usually of water) (paragraph 1)   ....
2 unimportant (1)   ....
3 holiday including travel and accommodation (2)   ....
4 beds for small children (2)   ....
5 almost unavailable (2)   ....
6 sent out an order to appear in court (3)   ....
7 paid completely (3)   ....
8 very angry (4)   ....
9 storm with strong wind (5)   ....
10 a service which helps to bring agreement
   between two people or groups of people (6)   ....

DISCUSSION POINTS ❻ **Work with another student and find out if they:**

1 have ever had a journey or holiday when something went wrong. If so, what?
2 have ever complained to a travel agent, tour company or hotel. If so, why?
3 have ever complained in a restaurant. If so, why?
4 have ever wanted to complain but felt too embarrassed. If so, when?
5 would prefer to complain in person, by telephone or in writing, and why.

❼ **Report back any interesting stories you have heard, and discuss these questions:**

1 What can a customer hope to achieve by complaining?
2 Is the customer always right to complain if they are dissatisfied with service?

LANGUAGE CHECK: PREPOSITIONS ❽ **Complete the following sentences with the correct prepositions. All ten prepositions come from Text 2. (If you need some help, choose answers from the list after the exercise. Each preposition should be used once only.)**

1 Many people were attracted .... the shop's special opening offers.
2 The insurance company has agreed to meet our claim .... full.
3 The shop repaired the clock completely free .... charge.
4 The course was described .... suitable .... complete beginners.
5 .... his return to England, he set about trying to find a job.
6 I didn't think his work was .... to standard so I asked him to do it again.
7 He made a search of the cellar .... the help of a torch.
8 The neighbours are always complaining .... us .... our dog.

| *on* | *for* | *as* | *of* | *with* | *to* | *about* | *in* | *by* | *up* |

Focus on listening I

You are going to hear a conversation in a travel agent's shop. The customer is interested in going to the Greek island of Crete.

Four hotels are discussed. These are:

The Concord   The Royal   The Atlantic   The Plaza

For questions 1–4, write the name of the hotel next to the picture which matches the description you hear.

THE HOTEL

For questions 5–8, fill in the missing information about flights to Crete in the spaces.

THE FLIGHT

5 Days: Friday and ....

6 Time: Third week in ....

7 Price: From £159 to ....

8 Insurance: The most expensive: *£14.25*

The cheapest: ....

Focus on grammar 2   Relative clauses

Look at these two examples from Text 2:

a   People who fail to do their research could find themselves in the Caribbean during the hurricane season.

b   Ron Wheal works for Britain's biggest holiday company, which took more than a million abroad this summer.

In sentence (a), the relative clause in green is essential to the meaning of the sentence. Not everybody would have the problem. The relative clause tells us **which** people could go to the Caribbean at the wrong time. This is an example of a **defining relative clause**.

In sentence (b), the relative clause in green is not essential to the meaning of the sentence. We know which holiday company Ron Wheal works for (the biggest). The relative clause gives us some **additional information** about the company. This is an example of a **non-defining relative clause**.

There are differences of grammar and punctuation between the two types of clause.

EXERCISE I   Say whether the following are **defining** or **non-defining** relative clauses.

a   The majority of complaints are from people who have chosen the wrong sort of holiday.

b   We stayed in our usual hotel, which had just been redecorated.

c   My mother, who is 60 today, has just come back from Australia.

d   The letter that I've been waiting for has just arrived.

DEFINING RELATIVE CLAUSES

MAIN POINTS ▶ Commas are not used to separate the relative clause from the rest of the sentence. (See sentences (a) and (d) in Exercise I above).

▶ **That** is often used instead of **who** or **which**, especially in speech. *For example:*
One client was furious about the cows that passed in front of her gite.

▶ If the relative pronoun is the object of the clause, it can be omitted.
Compare: *That's the bus which goes to the station.* (subject – pronoun cannot be omitted)
The bus which I caught didn't go to the station.
= The bus I caught didn't go to the station. (object – pronoun can be omitted)
The woman I told you about lives in that house.
= The woman that I told you about lives in that house.

SUMMARY

	People	Things
Subject	who, that	which, that
Object	who, that, whom	which, that
Possessive	whose	

OTHER
POINTS

▶ **That** is usually used after superlatives (*the biggest*, *the best*, etc.) and also after *all, only, any(thing), every(thing), some(thing), no(thing), none, little few, much, many.* For example:

> There's something *that* I ought to tell you.
> 1976 was the hottest summer *that* we have ever had.

If it is the object of the relative clause, *that* can be omitted.

▶ **Whose** is the possessive relative pronoun. It can be used for people and things. For example:

> My neighbour is a man *whose* hobby is playing the drums.
> That's the car *whose* engine blew up.

▶ **Whom** is grammatically correct as the object of a relative clause (people only), but it is very formal and is not often used in modern English.

> Compare: (Formal) *He's a man for whom I have the greatest admiration.*
> (Less formal) *He's a man (who/that) I have the greatest admiration for.*

EXERCISE 2   Column A has the first half of ten sentences. Column B contains the second half, but they are not in the correct order. Match the two halves and then link them with relative pronouns **who**, **which**, **that**, or **whose** to make complete sentences. *For example:*

1   All the people who/that have met him say he's awful.   (f)

	Column A		Column B
1	All the people …	a	sits next to me is always cheating in tests.
2	Can you take the suit …	b	you lent me has some very good articles in it.
3	She's the best friend …	c	we had never been to before.
4	The boy …	d	wife works in the library?
5	What's the name of the man …	e	is hanging in the cupboard to the cleaners?
6	I've lost the new pen …	f	have met him say he's awful.
7	Don't tell anybody …	g	anybody could ever have.
8	We decided to go to a restaurant …	h	car you scratched is walking this way.
9	The man …	i	I bought this morning.
10	The magazine …	j	you meet where I am!

When you have finished, check your answers with another student.
In which sentences can the relative pronoun be omitted? (See third main point.)

EXERCISE 3   Join the pairs of sentences below, using a relative pronoun where necessary. Begin the new sentence with the part which is in green. (You may need to change **a** to **the** in some cases.) *For example:*

> I'm reading *a book*. It has two pages missing.
> The book (that) I'm reading has two pages missing.

a   We used to live in a house. It's just been sold.
b   An old lady lives across the road. She's got eight cats.
c   You were looking for a friend. He's just come in.
d   My grandmother left me an old chair in her will. It's worth a fortune!
e   I bought my watch at a local shop. I can't remember its name.
f   The writer lives in New York. His latest book was published on Tuesday.
g   A neighbour has been to Sao Paulo. He says he's never seen anything like it.

h   I gave Helen a blouse for her birthday. It's worn out already.
i   The student has gone to university. He came top in maths at school.
j   Several people went to Paris this spring. None of them complained about the hotel.

NON-DEFINING RELATIVE CLAUSES

MAIN POINTS ▶ Commas are usually used to separate the relative clause from the rest of the sentence.

▶ **That** cannot be used instead of **who** or **which**.

▶ **Who** or **which** cannot be omitted.

EXERCISE 4   Give some additional information with a relative clause beginning **who**, **which** or **whose** in the following sentences.
a   Wimbledon, ... , is in south London.
b   He's hoping to be chosen for the next Olympic Games, ...
c   The Prime Minister, ... , will face an election soon.
d   Every schoolchild has heard of Columbus, ...
e   Mount Everest, ... , is the highest mountain in the world.

EXERCISE 5   Put commas in the following sentences where necessary. In which of the sentences could the relative pronoun be omitted?
a   A corkscrew is a device which removes corks from bottles.
b   I've just read his third novel which is his best.
c   The person who I spoke to yesterday was very rude.
d   They gave their car which was very old to their son.
e   Take the road which is signposted to York.
f   The book which I recommended to you is out of print.
g   I met your friend Jane who wants to be a pop singer.
h   The man who was supposed to meet me didn't turn up.

STUDY BOX 2   Phrasal verb *live*

'... the holiday fails to *live up to* the brochure promises' (Text 2)

live on – have as food or income.   *I don't know how he manages to **live on** the salary he gets.*
live through – survive despite difficulty.   *He's **lived through** two major wars.*
live up to – reach the expected standard.   See example above.

Communication activity 2

VOCABULARY ❶
AND
DEFINITIONS

1 Look at these ways of defining things and describing their use:

It's	a thing	that...
	an instrument	that you use for + -ing
	a tool	to + inf
	a device	for + -ing
They're things		

2 Now look at the pictures on page 17. For example:
In square 1C there's a picture of a spade.
A spade is a tool that you use for digging in the garden.

In square 1E there's an alarm clock.
An alarm clock is a device that wakes you up in the morning.

In square 1B there's a bucket.
A bucket is a thing for carrying water (in).

3 Now practise naming and defining the other objects in the top two rows (lines 1 and 2). If you're not sure of a word, ask your teacher.

4 Work in pairs using the objects in the remaining rows (lines 3–8). Choose an object and define it, without telling your partner what it is. Then let your partner guess the object. Continue, taking it in turns to define and guess.

GAME ❷ You need to work in groups of 3–5. Sit round a table if possible.

PREPARATION (FOR EACH GROUP)
Equipment:
You will need 3 sets of slips of paper:
First set: 5 slips of paper with the letters A–E written on them.
Second set: 8 slips of paper with numbers 1–8 written on them.
Third set: 8 slips with the names of the types of holiday from page 4 written on them.

Language:
Before you begin, turn to the Functions Bank (page 108) and look at the language for Expressing Need and Use. Refer to it again during the game, if you like, but don't read from the page. Feel free to express your ideas in other ways too!

HOW TO PLAY

1 Lay the slips of paper with the types of holidays on them face down.
2 Each player takes one. This represents his/her holiday for the game.
3 Then lay the two sets of papers with numbers and letters on them face down.
4 The first player selects first a letter, and then a number from the two piles. He/she then finds the picture which matches. For example: C7 is a camera.
5 The first player must say why the object will be useful on his/her holiday.
6 The rest of the group can accept or challenge the suggested use. If they are satisfied, the player has won a point. If they are not satisfied, no point is won.

7   The player returns the letter and number to the piles, and mixes them. A second player
chooses and the game continues.

The winner in each group is the player with the most points.

	A	B	C	D	E

STUDY BOX 3   Adjectives + prepositions

'*furious about* the cows' (Text 2)   '*unhappy with* the response' (Text 2)

| furious, angry, annoyed, upset | *about* something
with someone *for* doing something | happy, unhappy pleased, delighted, bored, fed up | *with* something |

interested *in*,   fond *of*,   keen *on*,   excited *about*,   surprised *at/by*,   attracted *by*

Focus on listening 2

❶   The eight pictures below show things to do with fastening or carrying. Write the correct names underneath. The first letter and the number of letters are given to help you. If you don't know them all, see if your neighbour can help.

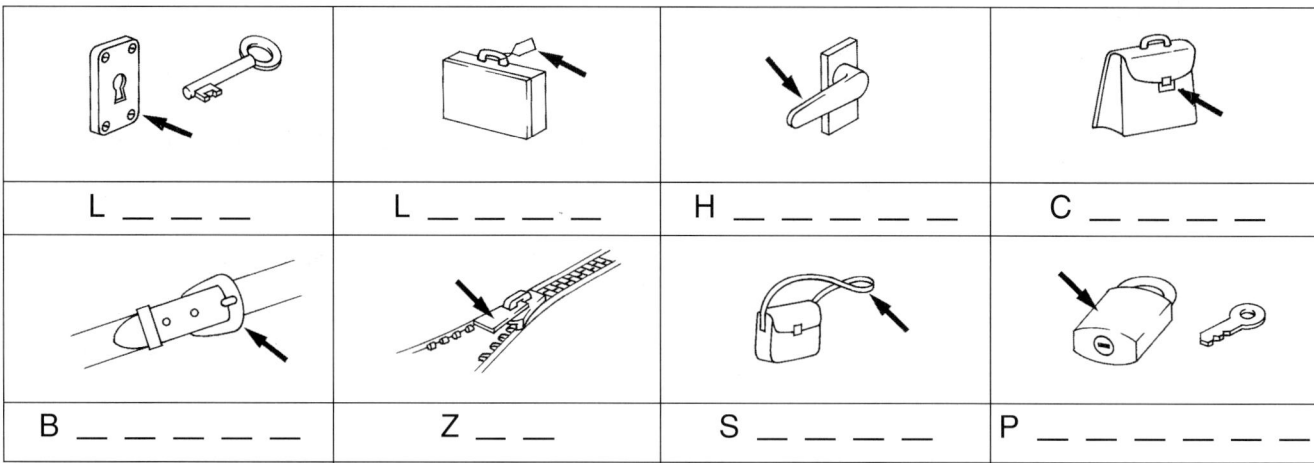

| L _ _ _ | L _ _ _ _ _ | H _ _ _ _ _ _ | C _ _ _ _ |
| B _ _ _ _ _ | Z _ _ | S _ _ _ _ | P _ _ _ _ _ _ |

❷   You are going to hear a short radio programme which gives information about suitcases. Before you listen, look at the three questions below and the table opposite very carefully. Then, while you listen, fill in the missing information.

1   The main disadvantages of leather suitcases are that they are both .... and ....

2   Modern materials used in making suitcases combine lightness and ....

3   Four-wheeled suitcases have the disadvantage that they are more likely .... than two-wheeled suitcases.

4   Complete the table below:

	Riviera	Windsor	Tornado	Mayfair
Length	67cm	68cm	75cm	
Material *(see below)				aluminium
Fastening/security	zip + padlock			2 locks
Number of wheels		2		
Strap or handle for pushing/pulling		strap		
Price			£109.50	
Tester's verdict	good value for money			

Choose from the following materials: SOFT – vinyl, nylon, PVC; RIGID – polypropylene, ABS, aluminium

Focus on writing 2 *Description*   WRITING BANK: PAGE 117

You are going to write a short piece introducing another student. First you will need to interview your subject to find out the important facts.

❶   **Work in pairs or small groups to prepare a list of questions on these topics:**
name
home town
family
school/college/university/work
plans/hopes for the future
reasons for studying English
likes/dislikes about studying English
hobbies and special interests
tastes in music/films/reading

❷   **Choose a new partner to work with. Take it in turns to ask questions and note down the answers. Be ready to ask extra questions to find out more details about what your partner tells you.**

❸   **You need to write three paragraphs.**
1   Decide how to divide the list of topics above into three groups, one group for each paragraph.
2   Think about the grammar you have studied in this unit, present tenses and relative pronouns, and try to put this into practice.

Here is an example of how you could begin:

X comes from .... but at the moment she is living in .... Her parents live in a small house in a suburb of .... with her younger sister, Y, who is 11 and their pet dog called .... She goes to .... College where she is studying ....

Language review

Choose the word or phrase (A, B, C or D) which best completes each sentence.
All the correct answers come from texts in this unit.

1 Judging by the smell, this can seems to be filled .... petrol.
  A by **B** from **C** of **D** with

2 I don't get much chance to read books .... when I'm on holiday.
  A only **B** except **C** just **D** until

3 If you've got a student card you can get into the exhibition free of ....
  A cost **B** price **C** charge **D** expense

4 You must be ready to leave at a moment's .... in case there's an emergency.
  A notice **B** call **C** advice **D** instruction

5 He's always complaining .... the noise the neighbours make.
  A for **B** from **C** of **D** about

6 Don't forget to put .... with your address on them on all your suitcases.
  A notices **B** tickets **C** labels **D** badges

7 It's hard for an actor to make enough money to ....
  A live with **B** live through **C** live up to **D** live on

8 I'd be no good at First Aid because I can't .... the sight of blood.
  A have **B** bear **C** look **D** resist

9 My wife and I are very keen .... Scottish dancing.
  A on **B** of **C** in **D** about

10 He's a good friend and he never .... to send me a birthday card each year.
  A ignores **B** stops **C** fails **D** misses

11 There's always a lot of office work to .... after the holiday.
  A take over from **B** get away with **C** catch up with **D** set out on

12 After he had finished his medical course, he .... research into the causes of heart disease.
  A did **B** made **C** took **D** followed

13 The bank robber was described by the police .... dark-haired and in his late twenties.
  A for **B** as **C** like **D** with

14 I've found the dishwasher so useful that I don't think I could .... without it now.
  A go **B** pass **C** get **D** do

15 I only bought the book because I was .... by its cover.
  A interested **B** attracted **C** invited **D** pleased

2 ▶ Other people's jobs

Lead-in 1

The drawings below represent ten different jobs.

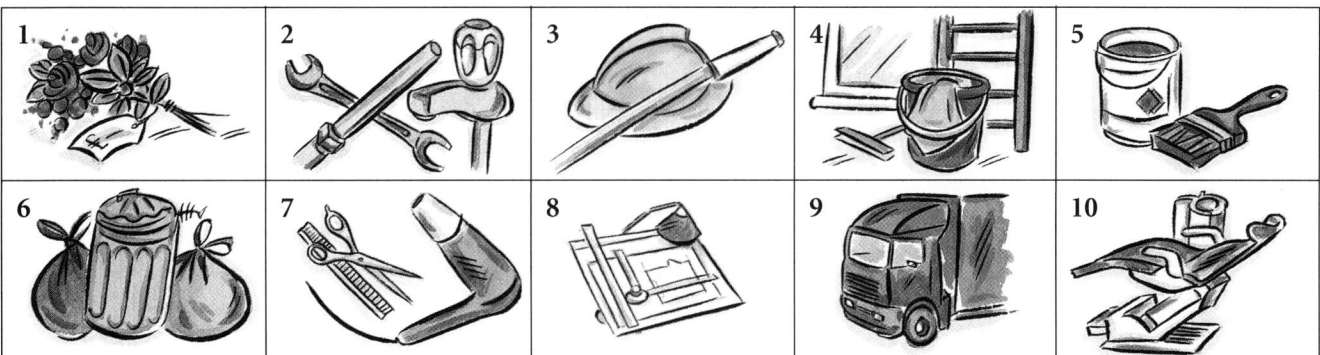

1 Work with a partner to decide what the ten jobs are.

2 Now discuss:

Which job … a) needs the most training? b) is the most useful?
c) is the best paid? d) is the least pleasant? e) is the most satisfying?
f) is the hardest?

Lead-in 2

Have you ever wanted to try someone else's job?

The writer, Danny Danziger, recently spent a week working in each of four different jobs to see what they were like. Below are short extracts from the four articles he wrote about his experiences.

1 Read the four extracts and try to guess what job he is describing in each one. Discuss your ideas with another student.

From *The Sunday Express Magazine*

A

Alan never seemed to get bored by the same old questions. But he did confide to me, 'No-one should do this job more than three years, because after a while you look at the people, and they're not people, they're the broken tap in room 23 or the lost wallet in room 7 or the couple who want to fly home because they're not having fun.'

B

The third gallery was the Time Measurement exhibit. Water clocks, sun-dials, sand glasses, watches and chronometers. I saw my life ticking by, second by micro-second.

Working in a more popular gallery you might be approached more frequently, but the range of questions is unvarying. People only want to know the same thing. 'Where's the nearest toilet/lift/cup of tea?'

C

During the week I went to bed early so I would not appear too awful in the morning light, and each day started with an agony of indecision as I wondered what to wear. I never lost my embarrassment at meeting people whose prime interest was in my physical appearance.

D

The pace starts off leisurely enough. With my crisp white apron and valet's jacket I would feel cool and confident. It's quiet enough at 12.15 to notice the famous faces who are lunching. By one o'clock, the place is jumping. As fast as tables are vacated new faces are slipping in. No time to enjoy the thrill of a film star lighting a big cigar … the sous-chef is screaming that the food for table 166 is getting cold.

❷ These are the four places where he was working. Can you match the place with the extract, and add the name of the job?

Place	Extract	Job
Photographic studio		
Museum		
Restaurant		
Holiday resort		

Again, check your answers with another student.

❸ Choose from the four extracts (A–D) to answer these questions and write the letters in the boxes.

In which job did Danny have to wear special clothes? | 1 | |

In which job did he have to work the fastest? | 2 | |

Which job made him feel most anxious? | 3 | |

Which jobs involved dealing with people's problems? | 4 | | 5 | |

Which job did the writer seem to find most boring? | 6 | |

In which job did Danny find the customers especially interesting? | 7 | |

Which job did he discuss with an experienced worker? | 8 | |

DISCUSSION POINTS ❹

1 **Individually decide:**
  a which of the four jobs you would choose to do if you had to, and why.
  b which you would **least** like to do, and why.

2 **With a partner discuss your answers to question 1.**

3 **Here are some advantages and disadvantages for Job A – the travel representative.**

Advantages	Disadvantages
opportunity to travel	losing touch with friends at home
practising foreign languages	dealing with difficult clients
meeting people	low pay

With your partner write down three advantages and three disadvantages for the other three jobs.

DISAGREEING ❺

Expressing a different point of view

Look at the table below:

Yes, I agree, I know, (perhaps) You're right,	but	on the other hand … even so … what about …? don't forget that …

For example, you could discuss the travel representative like this.

A   As a travel representative, you'd have plenty of opportunity to travel.

B   – Yes, but on the other hand you'd probably lose touch with all your friends at home.
– I know, but what about all the difficult clients you'd have to deal with?
– I agree, but don't forget that you'd have to deal with some very awkward people!
– Perhaps you're right, but even so it's not a very well-paid job.

Change your partner and discuss the other three jobs. Take it in turns to talk about advantages and disadvantages. Use your notes and try to include some of the expressions above.

6   Imagine you had the chance to work for one week only in any job of your choice. Which job would it be, and why?

Focus on listening I

Fill in the information you hear in the spaces below.

1   ## COURSES AND CAREER OPPORTUNITIES
1   'Start' course: Dates 7–11 May;   Cost ....
2   Young Engineer of the Year Competition: closing date: ....   prize: ....

2   ## LOCAL JOB OPPORTUNITIES

TAUNTON

Job Description ...*Trainee sales person*

Number of Vacancies *1*

❑ Part Time   ☑ Full Time

Wages/Salary ...*£ 3,000 a year*

Age ....

Additional information ....

....

WELLS

Job Description ....*Groom*

Number of Vacancies ....

❑ Part Time   ❑ Full Time

Wages/Salary ....

Age ...*Open*

Additional information ...*Experience is*

necessary

WARMLEY

Job Description ....

Number of Vacancies *20*

❑ Part Time   ❑ Full Time

Wages/Salary ....

Age ...*Over 16*

Additional information ....

....

EASTON

Job Description ...*Trainee baker*

Number of Vacancies *1*

❑ Part Time   ☑ Full Time

Wages/Salary ....

Age ...*Open*

Additional information ....

....

Focus on grammar 1   Adjectives and adverbs

USE

EXERCISE 1   Complete the story by putting one word from the list below in each space.

complete	closely	terribly	straight	nervous	helpfully	previous
confident	carefully	firmly	modern	quickly	unfortunately	loud

I still remember the first lesson I ever gave. I had planned it very .... (1) but as the time to start approached, I began to feel .... (2) .... (3). There were .... (4) voices coming from the classroom but when I opened the door, the noise died down .... (5) and by the time I reached the front of the room, there was .... (6) silence. I introduced myself in what I hoped was a .... (7) voice and then turned to write my name on the board. It was a .... (8) whiteboard and the .... (9) teacher's notes hadn't been cleaned off. A pupil pointed .... (10) to the board cleaner and explained that I had to press .... (11) on a button on the top to release a spray of water. .... (12) I didn't look at it .... (13) enough and when I pressed the button a jet of water went .... (14) into my eye!

Now, with a partner, read the story again, underline all the adjectives and put a circle round all the adverbs.

ADJECTIVES   **Adjectives** give information about nouns and are used

1   before nouns. *For example: A* confident *voice.*
2   with certain verbs. *For example: I began to feel* nervous.
    Some common verbs in this group are **be, seem, appear, look, feel, sound, taste.**
    For example:
        The test seemed easy.   *You look rather* tired.   *This coffee tastes* horrible.

ADVERBS   **Adverbs** give information about verbs and adjectives. *For example:*
    I had planned it very carefully.
    I began to feel terribly *nervous.* (also: *awfully, extremely, etc.*)

FORMATION

EXERCISE 2   The following table shows how adverbs are formed from adjectives. Fill in the missing examples.

	regular		no change	change of spelling		irregular	
patient	patiently		straight	happy	happily	good	well
wise	....		hard	sensible	....		
sudden	....		fast	helpful	....		
			late	true	....		

Note   Be careful with some adjectives that end in *-ly*. They cannot be used as adverbs. Use a similar adverb or adverb phrase. *For example:*
    He gave me a friendly smile.   *He smiled at me in a friendly way.*

Now use **silly, ugly** and **lovely** in similar sentences of your own. Use a different verb in each sentence.

THE COMPARISON OF ADJECTIVES AND ADVERBS

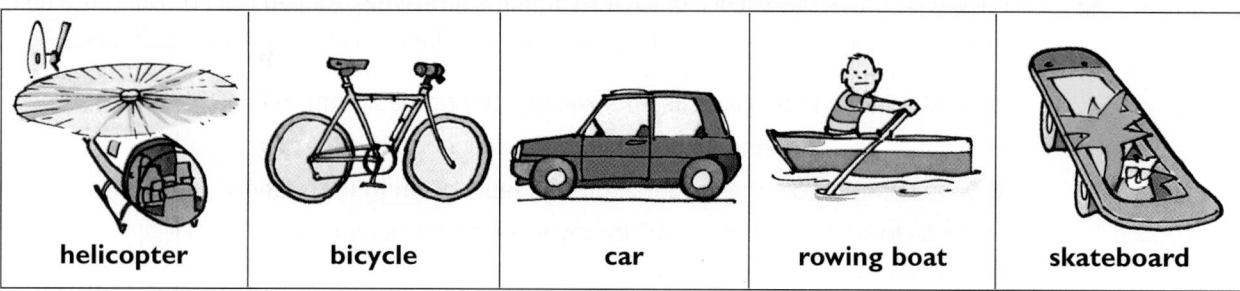

| helicopter | bicycle | car | rowing boat | skateboard |

EXERCISE 3   Look at the pictures above and complete these sentences. Check your answers with a partner. You may disagree!

A .... is cheaper than a ....

A .... is more convenient than a ....

A .... can be parked less easily than a ....

The least reliable method of transport is a ....

	Comparative	Superlative
Adjectives of one syllable: cheap	... er than	(the) ...est
Adjectives of two or more syllables: convenient Adverbs: easily	more ... than less ... than	(the) most ... (the) least ...

Irregular Forms: good
     bad
     far (distance)
     (time)
	better
	worse
	farther
	further
		(the) best
		(the) worst
		(the) farthest
		(the) furthest

Now make sentences of your own about the pictures using these words:

safely   expensive   comfortable   quickly   economically   hard

For example, you could begin like this:

You can go ...   It's .... to learn to use ...
        get about ...   repair ...
        travel ...   steer ...

EXERCISE 4   Put the adjective or adverb in brackets into the form which best suits the meaning of the sentence.

a   In your opinion, what is (stressful) aspect of being a doctor?

b   Who is (useful) to society, a policeman or a social worker?

c   I think women drive (carefully) than men.

d   Please talk a bit (quietly). You're disturbing everyone.

e   He feels much (fit) since he stopped smoking.

f   There's nothing (annoying) than losing one's door key.

g   Michael prefers to be alone. He is (sociable) person in the office.

h   He did not do very well, but at least he tried (hard) than last time.

i   That really is (bad) food I've ever eaten!

j   I bought her (expensive) present I could afford.

Text 1 *Waiter for a week*

❶ In this text, the first sentence of each paragraph is missing. As you read through the text, choose from the sentences (A–E) below and write the correct sentence in each space.

> **A** Hell, I rather imagine, is like the kitchen of that restaurant.
>
> **B** I spent as much time as possible in the dining room itself.
>
> **C** The commis takes the orders from the table down to the kitchen.
>
> **D** I was to be a commis waiter* for my week at the restaurant.
>
> **E** I reported for work at 11 a.m.

*an apprentice or trainee waiter

1

There are 50 waiters. Commis waiters and waiters work as a team. The waiter is the front man, taking orders, chatting to the customers; the commis, rather less glamorously, runs to the kitchen to bring up the orders and assist in serving them at the table. Although the commis will actually do more physical work, they share the tips equally. All in all this is fair, as it must be pointed out that the senior waiter is actually responsible for keeping a running account of the bills and if he makes a mistake, or undercharges, the fault is rectified through his wage packet. It's an important working relationship.

2

That may sound like a relaxed time to start the day, but the hours, I was soon to learn, are hell. The last client at lunchtime may not leave until half past three, or later, and the evening shift starts at 6 p.m. What can you do in 2 1/2 hours, especially if you don't happen to live in central London? Once or twice I didn't get home until 4 a.m. The hours, it was generally agreed, are the worst thing about waitering.

3

He places the order for hot food under the nose of the sous-chef who is shouting out orders to the cooks, while orders for cold dishes and salad go to a separate counter, and desserts are from yet another area. The kitchen is two flights of stairs away from the restaurant. The commis then comes up to see if any more orders have been taken while the previous one is being prepared. At the same time, dishes have to be cleared or put on the table, glasses refilled, ashtrays emptied, and somehow there always seems to be a new table with six or eight new orders to be filled – two flights away in the kitchen.

4

Yelling chefs, endless banging of pots and crockery, steaming casseroles, hissing frying pans, men with red shining faces, trays with loads heavy enough to break your wrists. And running. Always running. Up and down, down and up. And since everyone is running, and always with loaded trays, you need the co-ordination of a gymnast to stay out of trouble.

5

I noticed that wearing a uniform somehow transformed me into a role. It wasn't play-acting. Customers become sir or madam. Deference, a quality I usually lack, became the order of the day. I became very sensitive about the way I was treated. I hated being summoned by the click of the finger or the bend of the index finger. It was hurtful if conversation deliberately stopped as I served the meal, and yet unkind if it continued as if I didn't exist. I began to notice if people said please and thank you, and then whether they looked at me when they said it.

From *The Sunday Express Magazine*

❷ Now answer these questions.
1 What exactly did the writer's job involve?
2 What seems to be the worst part of a waiter's job?
3 What made his job more difficult?
4 What did he dislike about the customers' behaviour?

❸ There are a number of quite difficult words in the text but you should be able to work out what they mean from the context. Choose the most likely meaning (A, B or C) for the following words or expressions:

1 *glamorously* (line 6): A glamorous job is
   A an active, energetic one.
   B an exciting, attractive one.
   C a difficult one.

2 *rectified* (line 16): '… the fault is rectified through his wage packet' means
   A the money is taken from his earnings.
   B he has to pay a fine for his mistake.
   C he must pay back the money to the customer.

3 *yelling* (line 49):
   A working
   B singing
   C shouting

4 *co-ordination* (line 58):
   A skill
   B courage
   C strength

5 *deference* (line 64):
   A being tidy
   B showing respect to people
   C fighting back

6 *the order of the day* (line 65):
   A the most popular dish of the day
   B the programme of work for the day
   C the normal way of behaving

7 *summoned* (line 68):
   A answered
   B touched
   C called

❹ **Say whether the following statements are true or false, and why.**

		True	False
1	A commis waiter has to be careful to add up bills correctly.	☐	☐
2	The senior waiter earns more in tips than the commis waiter.	☐	☐
3	It was hard for the waiter to make use of his free time.	☐	☐
4	The commis waiter has to wait in the kitchen while the food is prepared.	☐	☐
5	The kitchen was extremely noisy.	☐	☐
6	There was a danger that waiters would crash into each other.	☐	☐
7	The writer normally finds it easy to be respectful to people.	☐	☐
8	He felt that some customers behaved rudely to him.	☐	☐

DISCUSSION POINTS ❺

1 a The writer didn't like customers to click their fingers to call for service. How do you normally call a waiter in your country? Do you know any different methods of attracting a waiter's attention in other countries?

  b Why did the writer feel hurt when conversations stopped as he served a meal? Do you stop speaking while a waiter is serving you, or do you carry on?

  c Do you like a waiter to be extremely polite to you or do you prefer more casual service?

2 a When is it normal to give tips in your country? Which people do you always tip, and which do you tip if the service was especially good?

  b Do you approve of tipping, or do you think it should be stopped? Why?

  c Have you ever refused to tip someone who expected a tip? If so, what happened?

Focus on grammar 2   The simple past

USE

The simple past tense refers to actions or situations which began and ended in the past. There is no connection with present time. It has two main uses:

▶ It refers to a definite time or period of time in the past. *For example:*
  I bought *this car last July.*
  It snowed *three times last week.*

There are many ways of expressing a definite time in the past. Look at the following examples.
He went *to America in 1984.*
                    two years ago.
                    when he was a student.
                    during his last year at college.

EXERCISE 1

Complete the following sentences by choosing the correct word from the list below. There may be more than one possible answer.

at	in	when	for	before	on	ago	during	after	until

a He got married .... 1985.
b He was President .... the period 1964–1967.
c How long .... did you last see him?
d The fire started .... 6 o'clock.
e I was ill .... three months.
f They had to use candles .... there was a power cut.
g He read a book .... he fell asleep.
h She left Spain .... four years.
i Fortunately they left the building .... the bomb exploded.
j Didn't you see the match .... Saturday?

Note

The time is not always mentioned but it is still clear that the action or situation is now ended. *For example:*

I opened *the door,* looked *out into the darkness and* saw *the same face again. Then I …*

► The simple past tense refers to past habit. *For example:*
I worked in London for three years.
She lived abroad for most of her life.
He smoked twenty cigarettes a day as a student.

EXERCISE 2   Complete these sentences:

a   When I was at school I ....

b   If he behaved badly when he was a child, his mother ....

c   A hundred years ago people ....

d   I hate sport now but when I was younger ....

e   At school which subjects .... ?

FORM 1   **Regular verbs:**   Infinitive + **-ed.**
For example: work – work**ed**

There is a change in the spelling of the simple past form of **some** regular verbs.
For example: fit – fit**ted**

Complete the following table.

dance	danced	stop	stopped	prefer	preferred	try	tried
argue	....	tap	....	occur	....	apply	....
use	....	rot	....	travel	....	study	....

FORM 2   **Irregular verbs.**

There are some rules, but as they are quite complicated the best approach is just to learn the irregular forms.

Fill in the gaps in the table below and compare your answers with a partner.

Infinitive	Past	Past participle	Infinitive	Past	Past participle
....	became	....	....	....	heard
bite	....	....	....	laid	....
....	....	broken	....	lost	....
....	caught	....	put	....	....
....	....	chosen	....	rode	....
cost	....	....	....	....	shot
....	drove	....	steal	....	....
fall	....	....	....	....	taught
....	....	felt	tear	....	....
fly	....	....	....	wrote	....

Communication activity *Working can be a health hazard*

Stress is the mental strain which we feel when we have to cope with difficult, unpleasant or dangerous situations.

Some jobs involve a lot of stress because of the nature of the work. A construction worker, for example, working on a new building high above the ground, is in constant danger. What special stresses would be suffered by:

1   a traffic warden?   2   a prison officer?

Some jobs are stressful because of the circumstances. You may enjoy your job but if the new boss is bad-tempered and criticises everything you do, you will probably suffer from stress too, after a time.

Other jobs are much more relaxed. It's hard to imagine a gardener suffering from serious stress. What other low-stress jobs can you think of?

Stress can cause high blood pressure and lead to mental illness or heart disease. It also causes problems for employers like strikes and accidents.

Recently, a British university made a study of a number of different jobs to see how much stress workers suffered. Here is a list of 26 of the jobs they studied.

actor	film producer	miner	pop musician
architect	firefighter	museum worker	postman/woman
bus driver	professional footballer	nurse	salesperson, shop assistant
dentist	hairdresser	pilot (civil)	secretary
doctor	journalist	police officer	soldier
engineer	librarian	politician	teacher
farmer	manager (commerce)		

Work with a partner to:
1   Decide which job involves by far the **most**, and which by far the **least** stress.
2   Put the other 24 jobs in three groups according to whether they have high, medium or low stress.

When you have finished, compare your answers with another pair and discuss your reasons. Finally, turn to page 228 for a complete list of results.

STUDY BOX 1   Expressions with *do* and *make*

'... if he **makes a mistake** ...' (Text 1)
'... the commis will actually **do** more physical **work**' (Text 1)

MAKE

money	a complaint	a mistake
war	an inquiry	a charge
certain	an excuse	a discovery
sure	an offer	use of
a journey	the bed	fun of
a trip	a choice	room for

DO

good	homework	a favour
harm	housework	a test
damage	one's best	an experiment
business	one's duty	the washing-up
work	one's bit	

Text 2

❶ Describe these people and their clothes. Match each picture to one of the headings (A-D) in the text. Where do you think each person works and what do they do?

❷ Find this information from the texts (A–D) as quickly as possible.

1 Who spends most money on clothes?
2 Who spends least money on clothes?
3 Whose employer provides them with a coat?
4 Whose employer has the most detailed dress requirements?

Child psychiatrist   A

Tony Kaplan, of the Tavistock Clinic.

Dress requirements Psychiatrists should dress to inspire confidence, and wear a tie and preferably a jacket.

Annual expenditure on work clothes £300.

No dress allowance

His views Since my patients are children I dress to feel comfortable and put them at their ease. Children often have a mental image of doctors – dressed in stiff white coats, 'grown up' clothes – and associated with this is the idea of terror and pain. So it's very reassuring for them to see a 'doctor' in casual and colourful clothes who appears friendly and in touch with their needs.

Obviously in a teaching hospital, and other professional contexts, I would be more formal. At my first job I arrived in clean jeans, trainers and an earring and it took two years before anyone told me my dress was inappropriate.

School pupil   B

Samantha Wood, sixth former at Chatham South Secondary Modern School, Kent.

Dress requirements The sixth form as a whole can either elect to wear their own clothes or choose three colours. We've all opted for the three-colour system; this year it's black, white and beige for girls (worn with flat shoes and sensible earrings); black, burgundy and grey for boys. There are strict uniform requirements for the rest of the school.

Annual expenditure on school clothes £170 (with several items passed down to Sam in her family, or hand-knitted).

Dress allowance

Her parents buy her school clothes.

Her views I prefer knowing exactly what colours I'm going to wear to school. If I had free choice I would get bored of my clothes, especially if I didn't have anything different to wear outside school when I went off to meet friends.

Barrister   C

Ann Mallalieu.

Dress requirements Written rules, laid down by the Bar Council: 'Suits and dresses should be of dark colour. Dresses or blouses should be long-sleeved and high to the neck, and white or of other unemphatic appearance. Collars should be white and shoes black.'

Annual expenditure on work clothes £700.

No dress allowance

Her views Although 'suits and dresses should be of dark colour' implies a choice, I have been advised that 'my suit be no lighter than my gown', which is black! Your wig must cover your hair as far as possible. Basically, if you're a woman, you must look as much like a man as you can.

If you wear the wrong clothes, either the judge says he won't hear you, so you are told to go and change; or, more commonly, a senior barrister taps you on the shoulder in the robe room where you're changing and says: 'That won't do.'

Bouncer   D

Alex Condon, night security man (they prefer not to be called bouncers) at Stringfellows nightclub.

Dress requirements Dinner jacket and bow tie at all times. Well groomed and well turned out, so that he is above criticism himself when refusing someone entry to the club.

Annual expenditure on work clothes £750.

Dress allowance

Any damage to his clothing while at work is paid for by management, though they don't buy your suits initially. They do supply a heavy overcoat in the winter.

His views As a security man on the door, I am one of the first staff members people see when they arrive at Stringfellows. So obviously there is a certain pressure on me to create a good impression – smart, tidy and polite.

I don't wear any gold when I'm working: you get trouble from time to time and earrings and chains can easily get caught. As for shoes, it has to be Doc Martens; I'm standing in one place for at least seven hours at a time, and my feet tend to know about it first if I feel uncomfortable.

❸ Now read the texts more carefully to answer these questions. Write the correct letter (A, B, C or D) in each box. The first one is done as an example.

Who

was able to choose between two different dress rules?	1	B
needs to wear comfortable shoes?	2	
wore the wrong clothes for their first job?	3	
is not allowed to work if they are dressed incorrectly?	4	
chooses not to wear gold jewellery?	5	
sometimes wears second-hand or home-made clothes?	6	
has to dress like a member of the opposite sex?	7	
would dress more formally in a different situation?	8	

❹ **Answer these questions by choosing the correct answer (A, B, C or D).**

1 Tony Kaplan tries to dress so that his patients
  A know he's a doctor.
  B are impressed.
  C feel relaxed.
  D think he's fashionable.

2 Samantha Wood is happy with the dress requirements at her school because
  A she would be bored if she had to wear a school uniform.
  B she likes to wear different clothes at school and in her spare time.
  C she is free to wear whatever clothes she chooses.
  D she loves wearing bright colours.

3 Ann Mallalieu seems annoyed that she
  A has to wear a wig.
  B doesn't receive a dress allowance.
  C isn't allowed to wear any make-up.
  D cannot dress in a feminine way.

4 Alex Condon has to dress so that customers
  A feel afraid of him.
  B can't criticise his appearance.
  C know how they should dress themselves.
  D feel welcome when they arrive.

Focus on grammar 3   The past continuous

FORM   *was ....ing/were ....ing*

USE   The past continuous tense describes actions and situations which are unfinished at a particular point in the past. We have no information about the exact starting and finishing time. *For example:*

  When I woke up, the sun was shining through the window and someone was making breakfast.

In diagram form the sentence looks like this:

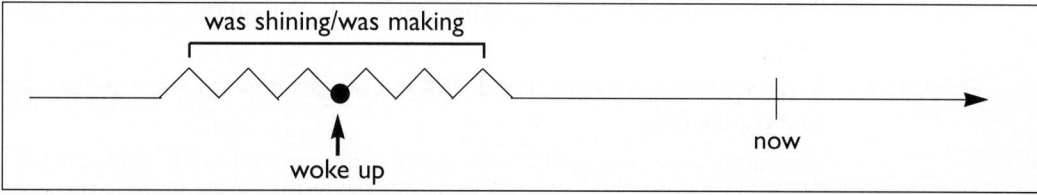

The main function of the past continuous is, therefore, to provide the background to specific events in the past, and these are the most common uses:

1 To refer to longer actions which are interrupted by shorter actions. *For example:*
  The taxi arrived while I was having breakfast.

33

Notice the difference between:

a *I was standing at the bus stop when the accident happened.*
(I was already standing there at the moment when the accident happened.)

b *When the accident happened I ran to phone for an ambulance.*
(I ran to the phone the moment after the accident happened.)

2 To refer to two or more longer actions happening at the same time. *For example:*
While I was chatting on the phone, the dinner was burning.

3 To describe a scene or the background to a story. (The main events in the story are in the simple past.) *For example:*
The wind was increasing in strength and the sea was beginning to get rough. A few seagulls were circling overhead. Then the boat started to take in water.

4 To show that an action started before and continued after a particular time in the past. *For example:*
This time last month we were getting excited about our holiday and now it's all over.

5 To emphasise how long the action continued. The length of time is more important than the action itself.
Compare these two sentences:
He was talking to a policeman for two hours. I began to get worried.
He talked to a policeman at the door and then went into the building.

Note For a list of verbs that cannot be used in the continuous form, look back at Focus on grammar 1 (Unit 1) page 9.

EXERCISE 1 Complete the following sentences using a verb in either the simple past or the past continuous tense. Add any other necessary words. A suitable verb is suggested for the first five.

a While I was working hard my lucky sister .... (enjoy)
b I couldn't answer the phone when it rang because I .... (have a bath)
c When Jane's husband left her she .... (sell)
d I didn't hear a thing because I was watching television when the burglar .... (break in)
e The bus was late as usual so when I got to work everyone else .... (already/work)
f Before cars were invented people ....
g Just as I was parking my car another driver ....
h When I finally passed my driving test I ....
i Look at the rain! It's hard to believe that at this time last week we ....
j While David was waiting outside one cinema his girlfriend ....

EXERCISE 2 In the following passage put the verb in brackets into the most suitable tense (simple past or past continuous).

One of the most embarrassing incidents in my early career as a doctor .... (happen)[1] when I .... (work)[2] in the Accident Department of a large city hospital. I .... (usually, cycle)[3] to work when the weather was fine as I .... (try)[4] to lose weight. That particular morning it .... (just, begin)[5] to rain as I .... (leave)[6] the house but I .... (think)[7] I could reach the hospital before the rain .... (get)[8] too heavy. I .... (cycle)[9] down the hill, ... (turn)[10] into the main road and .... (head)[11] for the city centre when the bus in front of me .... (begin)[12] to slow down. As I .... (move)[13] out to overtake it, there was a loud bang and everything .... (go)⁽¹⁴⁾ black. When I .... (come)⁽¹⁵⁾ round, I .... (lie)⁽¹⁶⁾ on the pavement and a crowd of people .... (stand)⁽¹⁷⁾ around me. Then I .... (hear)⁽¹⁸⁾ an ambulance in the distance and my heart .... (sink)⁽¹⁹⁾. Five minutes later I .... (arrive)⁽²⁰⁾ at the hospital and was carried into the Accident Department on a stretcher.

Focus on listening 2 *A life at sea*

For questions 1–6, tick (✓) whether you think the statements are true or false.

		True	False
1	John didn't want to join the Merchant Navy at first.	☐	☐
2	He suddenly decided to leave his first ship just before it sailed.	☐	☐
3	His training course taught him how to serve at table.	☐	☐
4	The life at the training school was hard.	☐	☐
5	As a bellboy, he had to ring the ship's bells.	☐	☐
6	He often regretted joining the Merchant Navy.	☐	☐

For questions 7–10 put a tick next to the correct answer (A, B, C or D).

7   The total time John spent in the Merchant Navy was
   A two years.
   B four years.
   C six years.
   D ten years.

8   The worst thing about being a merchant seaman was
   A the low pay.
   B the accommodation.
   C the other seamen.
   D the time away from home.

9   On one occasion the ship was delayed outside Hong Kong because
   A it had lost important equipment in a storm.
   B there were too many ships already in the harbour.
   C it was impossible to enter the harbour.
   D conditions in the harbour were too dangerous.

10   He finally left the Merchant Navy because
   A he wanted to go and live in Australia.
   B he was tired of the life at sea.
   C he was persuaded by friends to leave.
   D he was offered the chance of a new career.

STUDY BOX 2 The use of articles I		
NO ARTICLE meals		**DEFINITE ARTICLE** meals
We had breakfast at 8 o'clock. lunch, tea, supper, dinner	but	*The* breakfast on the train was awful.
times of day		**times of day**
We left at sunrise. dawn, midday/noon, lunchtime, sunset, night, midnight.	but	in *the* morning/afternoon/evening
methods of travel		**methods of travel**
For example: by air. by sea/boat/train/coach/bus/car/bicycle, etc.	but	We came by *the* early train/*the* 140 bus/*the* express coach.

Focus on writing *Informal letters* WRITING BANK: PAGE 112

❶ Each country has its own conventions in letter writing. These concern the way that the sender's address is written, for example, and where different parts of the letter are placed on the page.

With a partner, decide where the following parts of a letter should be:

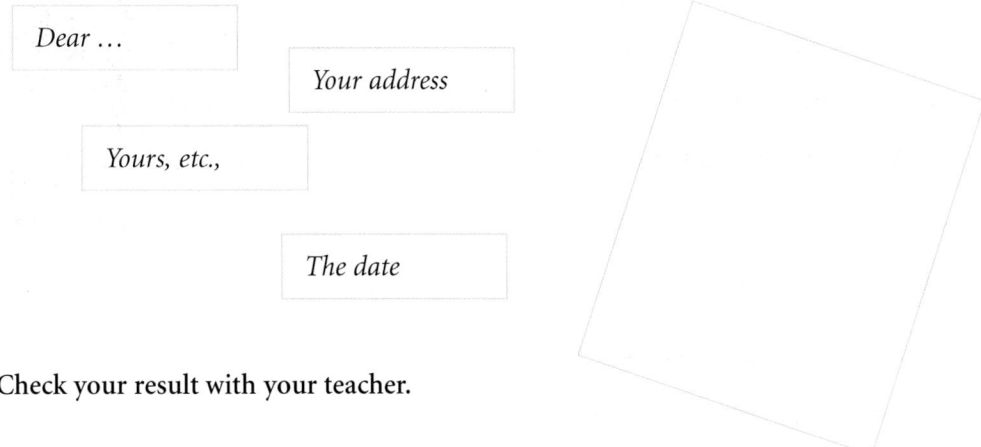

Dear …

Your address

Yours, etc.,

The date

Check your result with your teacher.

❷ Now copy these details on to the letter opposite so that you have a correct model.

Yours,

Flat 2,
9 Wood Road,
Barrington,
Somerset TE3 4LL,
England.

Dear Gill,

10th Sept. 19-

It's been ages since I've seen you and quite a lot has happened!

First of all, I've got a new job with an advertising company. It's much harder work but more interesting and better paid than my old job.

I've also moved to a new flat as you'll see from my address. It's quite a lot bigger and I've now got a spare bedroom for guests!

Why don't you come and stay for a weekend so we can catch up on each other's news? It would be lovely to see you.

Looking forward to hearing from you.

❸ Say whether you think the following are true or false.

		True	False
1	Write your name before your address.	☐	☐
2	Write the date in the form 4(th) Jan(uary) 19- (not 4/1/19—)	☐	☐
3	It's usual to begin *Dear Friend*.	☐	☐
4	Write the first line *(Dear …)* in the middle of the page.	☐	☐
5	Each paragraph of a handwritten letter should be indented, that is, it should begin about a centimetre after the margin.	☐	☐
6	Most letters have a brief sentence on a separate line before the end, e.g. *I look forward to/Looking forward to seeing you*.	☐	☐
7	Write the end of the letter, *Yours*, etc., on the left-hand side.	☐	☐
8	Begin the first word of the ending with a capital letter, the second word with a small letter: *Yours, Best wishes, Love from*.	☐	☐

Now check your answers by looking at the model in the Writing Bank on page 112, and correct the false statements.

❹ Look at the letter on page 37 again. How many paragraphs are there?
The first paragraph is an **introduction** or **beginning**. What headings could you give the other paragraphs?

WRITING
TASK

❺ Imagine you have received the letter on page 37 from an English friend. Write a reply either accepting the invitation and suggesting a date and time for your visit or turning it down (with reasons) and making an alternative suggestion.

NOTES
1 Remember to use separate paragraphs to:
   – thank your friend for the letter and invitation
   – say you can or can't come (and why)
   – comment on your friend's news
   – give some news about yourself
2 There are example informal letters on pages 37 and 112, and some useful language for beginning letters and for accepting and rejecting invitations on page 113.

STUDY BOX 3   Phrasal verb *put*

'Was there anything you found really hard to ***put up with***?'   (Listening 2)

put aside –	save (especially money/time). We've **put** some money **aside** for a holiday.	*put out* –	extinguish. Firemen managed to **put** the fire **out** after two hours.
put away –	store/tidy. Please **put** your toys **away** now, children.	*put through* –	connect. Could you **put** me **through** to the Manager, please?
put off –	postpone. They've **put** the wedding **off** for a month.		
put off –	discourage/distract. When I heard how difficult the exam was, it **put** me **off** entering for it.	*put up* –	provide accommodation. My sister will **put** me **up** while I'm in London.
put on –	get dressed. Why don't **you** put a thicker jumper **on**?	*put up with* –	tolerate. I will not **put up with** your rudeness!
put on –	increase (especially in weight). He eats like a horse but never **puts on** weight.		

Language review

Choose the word or phrase (A, B, C or D) which best completes each sentence.

1 He .... me gently on the shoulder and told me I was in the wrong seat.
   A stamped   **B** slapped   **C** punched   **D** tapped

2 My speech isn't ready yet but I'll have time to prepare it .... the journey, I hope.
   A for   **B** through   **C** in   **D** during

3 He enjoyed playing computer games at first, but after .... he got bored with them.
   A little time   **B** no time   **C** a while   **D** while

4   Mark was .... that he should apply for a university place.
    A suggested   **B** advised   **C** recommended   **D** explained

5   The school has .... rules about wearing jewellery.
    A strong   **B** stiff   **C** strict   **D** sharp

6   I'm afraid I didn't hear the doorbell when you rang. I .... in the garden at the time.
    A worked   **B** have worked   **C** was working   **D** have been working

7   He always .... paying the bills for as long as possible.
    A puts off   **B** puts away   **C** puts out   **D** puts aside

8   We had to move the furniture to .... room for the new piano.
    A make   **B** give   **C** set   **D** do

9   Each student must be .... for his or her own belongings.
    A interested   **B** responsible   **C** careful   **D** aware

10 I have two assistants in my department and we work together as a ....
    A crew   **B** team   **C** band   **D** gang

11 He soon realised that his girlfriend's only interest was .... his money.
    A for   **B** about   **C** with   **D** in

12 I wouldn't mind if he didn't .... me like a servant.
    A treat   **B** behave   **C** pretend   **D** speak

13 How much do you need to spend .... books for your course?
    A for   **B** with   **C** on   **D** in

14 The watch I bought is fine but the strap won't go round my ....
    A waist   **B** wrist   **C** ankle   **D** elbow

15 .... we do the same work, she earns more than I do.
    A Despite   **B** However   **C** In spite   **D** Although

Lead-in

Below are pictures of twenty different items connected with five different sports or hobbies. Write the name of each activity in the place provided below together with the four items connected with it.

Activity	....	....	....	....	....
Item 1	....	....	....	....	....
Item 2	....	....	....	....	....
Item 3	....	....	....	....	....
Item 4	....	....	....	....	....

Text 1 ❶

In this section, four well-known people describe an activity which they are enthusiastic about. The four activities are: windsurfing*,   running,   breeding budgerigars*,   tennis.

Below are the four people concerned, with clues about their hobby. Try to guess who has which hobby.

Sally Oppenheim
Member of Parliament
She has become more aggressive in her hobby since she entered politics.

Rosalind Plowright
International opera singer
Her hobby allows her to be completely alone with nature.

Bill Sirs
Trade unionist
His doctor disapproves of his hobby.

Geoff Capes
Shot put champion*
He describes his hobby as the absolute opposite of what he does in his sport in terms of aggressiveness.

---

* *windsurfing:* Windsurfers stand on a flat board and hold on to a bar on the sail to direct their course.
* *budgerigars* are small birds, usually blue or green. They are often kept as pets and breeders keep them in numbers in order to produce young ones, and sometimes to enter them in shows.
* *shot put:* a competition to throw a heavy metal ball the furthest distance.

❷ Now read through the four articles and write the correct names in the spaces (A–D).

From *The Sunday Times Magazine*

| **A** |

I think windsurfing is better than swimming. More exhilarating. You can really get away from it all. I love being alone with nature, and when you're out there on the water you can come around a headland and suddenly find that you're completely alone. Just me and the sea and the wind in my hair. Once, when I was working in San Diego, I suddenly felt I'd had enough of opera – studying the role and the claustrophobia of the rehearsal rooms – and found going out windsurfing a tremendous escape.

I think most of my singer colleagues are rather amused by the idea of me windsurfing. However, these days, at least 50 per cent of singers keep physically fit in some way – playing golf, or working out in gyms. A few years ago they tended to be a lot fatter, but now they are conscious of the need to keep fit.

| **B** |

I find the hobby gives me relaxation and peace of mind – it's the absolute opposite of what I do in my own sport in terms of aggressiveness. You can't be noisy and loud with budgerigars; but I'm as competitive when I'm showing my birds as when I'm competing with my iron. I say to the judge, 'Tell me why that bird has won and not mine.' That is the way to learn.

You should put in at least one and a half hour's work on your budgerigars a day if you want to be successful, especially in preparation for shows. You have to wash them in diluted washing up liquid and then rinse them. You blow-dry them with a hairdryer – not right up close, just a gentle blast of air. Or put them in front of the fire to dry naturally. But you get them more fluffy if you blow-dry. Those birds are better looked after than some human beings.

| **C** |

Apart from keeping you fit, the great thing about running is that it releases the tensions of work. You can't worry when you're running, and you can see all your problems from afar, making it easier to find solutions. During the 13-week steel strike in 1980 I ran a lot, thinking things out.

Recently, a senior hospital consultant looking at my knee shook his head and said, 'I don't really approve of all this running, you know. How long have you been doing it?' I told him 32 years, to which he replied, 'In that case, I give up.' With a bit of luck, I'll still be running in the next 15 years – unless, of course, I drop dead.

| **D** |

Social tennis is what I like best. Playing doubles with about eight regular friends for fun. It's generally a noisy, boisterous kind of game, with constant shouts of frustration.

We have long, loud arguments about line decisions, followed up by long arguments about the score. We're all pretty aggressive, and I think I make it worse, actually. I have noticed that since I entered politics my game has got a lot more aggressive, and I am very argumentative about the score.

The wonderful thing about tennis is that when you are playing it, you can't think of anything else. Your mind is totally absorbed in the game. And when you do that really good shot the elation is incredible. On the other hand, however, there is probably no frustration greater than the muffed shot at the net.

❸ Find a phrase or sentence in each passage which explains why each writer finds their hobby so important. Is there anything they all have in common?

❹ Choose from the four articles (A–D) to answer these questions and write the letters in the boxes provided. Some questions have two correct answers.

Who mentions the health aspect of their hobby?	1 ☐	2 ☐
Who doesn't always want their hobby to take their mind off their work?	3 ☐	
Who describes their hobby in the most detail?	4 ☐	
Who mentions other people's reactions to their hobby?	5 ☐	6 ☐
Who mentions an annoying moment experienced while enjoying their hobby?	7 ☐	
Who mentions the pleasure and excitement their hobby can give them?	8 ☐	9 ☐
Who seems to want to become more expert in their hobby?	10 ☐	
Who mentions the difficulties of their job?	11 ☐	12 ☐
Whose hobby involves an element of competition?	13 ☐	14 ☐

When you have finished, compare your answers with another student's and discuss any differences.

VOCABULARY ❺ The four writers use several words to describe emotions. Find words in the passages which mean the same as:

1 very exciting (adjective) ....

2 feeling of being enclosed in a small space (noun) ....

3 feelings of worry or anxiety (noun) ....

4 feeling ready for a quarrel or fight (noun) ....

5 feeling of annoyed disappointment when you are prevented from doing something (noun) ....

6 feeling of joy or pride (noun) ....

DISCUSSION POINTS ❻ Work with one or two other students to discuss the following:

1 Which of the four activities:

a would be the most expensive to do regularly?

b requires the most patience?

c would be the easiest to take up?

d requires the most skill?

e needs the most physical strength?

f is the most dangerous?

2 Which would appeal to you most and which least?

Focus on listening 1

You are going to hear information about three different leisure activities: judo, budgerigar breeding and windsurfing.

Before you start listening, study the table below and read through the sentences 1-5 carefully so that you know what specific information to listen for. As you listen, fill in the missing details.

Activity	First introduced	Made an Olympic event	Costs		
Judo		1964	Judo suit to buy	£............	
			Judo suit............	£5 a month	
Windsurfing	1969		....	£300	
			A racing board	£............	
Budgerigar Breeding		X	Price range for birds £.......... to £........		

1 The .... of the International Judo Federation is in Paris.

2 The season for windsurfing in Britain is ....

3 At other times you need to wear a ....

4 The telephone number of the Budgerigar Information Bureau is ....

5 The most highly prized colour would be ....

Focus on grammar 1   The present perfect simple

Look at these examples from Text 1:

Tell me why that bird has won and not mine.

I have noticed that since I entered politics my game has got a lot more aggressive.

The present perfect tense is used whenever there is a strong link between the past and the present. It gives information about the present as well as the past. Though the action happened before now, we are often more concerned with the present result or effect. *For example:*

I've mended the cooker. = You can use it now.

She's been to Japan. = She has some experience of the country.

We've already eaten. = We are not hungry.

Suggest the present result or effect in these examples:

My car has broken down.

I've spent all my money.

The bus drivers have gone on strike.

She's passed all her exams.

There has been an earthquake.

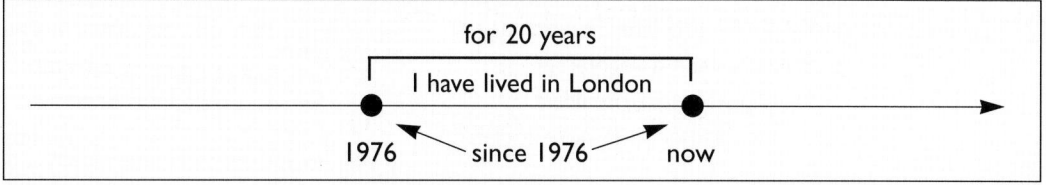

FORM   has
have + past participle

The present perfect is used:

USE 1

1 To refer to an action which began in the past and has continued until now. *For example:*

    He has worked hard all his life.

2 To refer to a number of individual actions which have happened up to the present (and may happen again). *For example:*

    She has changed her job three times in the last five years.

so far
recently
lately
up to now

Notice that the present perfect is often used with time expressions that refer to a period up to the present. The most common ones are shown in the box on the left. Underline the other examples used in (1) and (2) above.

In addition the present perfect is often used with **for** and **since**. *For example:*

I've lived in London for twenty years (and still do). (for + a period of time)

I've lived in London since 1976 (and still do). (since + a point of time)

In a diagram the two sentences can be represented like this:

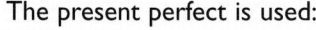

for 20 years

I have lived in London

1976   since 1976   now

43

EXERCISE 1   Add **for** or **since** to the following sentences.

a   He has been unemployed .... he left school.
b   I've known her .... six years.
c   The phone has been out of order ....
     a long time.

d   I haven't had a cold .... last
     November.
e   Where have you been 12
     o'clock?

USE 2   The other main use of the present perfect is to refer to an action which was completed in the
         past but where the time is not given. When the exact time is given, use the simple past.
         Compare: *I've found a new job!*
                     I found a new job last week.

EXERCISE 2   Look at these two pictures of David Sage and
              notice the changes that have taken place in recent years.
              Complete the sentences below with a suitable verb.

Since 1985 ...
a   he .... a lot of hair.
b   he .... a moustache.
c   his eyesight .... worse.

d   he .... weight.
e   he .... his style of dress.

Notice that the present perfect is used with these words
when they refer to an indefinite time in the past.

| just | already | before |

For example: *We've already done that exercise.*
                I think I've been to this restaurant before.
                She has just had a baby.

▶   Again, the **present** result is important.

EXERCISE 3   These words are also often used with the present perfect
              but in questions and negative sentences. In the following
              examples put the word in brackets in the correct place.

| ever | never | yet | still |

a   Have you been to the opera? (ever)
b   Have they arrived? (yet)
c   She has learned to drive. (never)

d   I haven't finished that book. (still)
e   Your father hasn't phoned. (yet)

EXERCISE 4   Match the two parts of these sentences so that every sentence is grammatically correct and
              makes sense.

1   I've had a headache
2   The cost of living increased by 10%
3   The television has gone wrong
4   Cars replaced horse-drawn vehicles
5   I haven't passed my driving test
6   I didn't sleep very well
7   You're too late! The film began
8   He's been a vegetarian
9   Did you have breakfast
10   He has become more sociable

a   for several years.
b   yet.
c   this morning?
d   last night.
e   in the last few weeks.
f   at least an hour ago.
g   nearly a hundred years ago.
h   last year.
i   since lunchtime.
j   several times in the last month.

Focus on writing 1 *Paragraphing*

Dividing a piece of writing into paragraphs is important because it makes the information much clearer and easier to read. Each new paragraph deals with a different aspect of the subject and begins on a new line.

1 1 Divide the following text into three paragraphs. Mark the places where you would begin a new paragraph with a line (|).

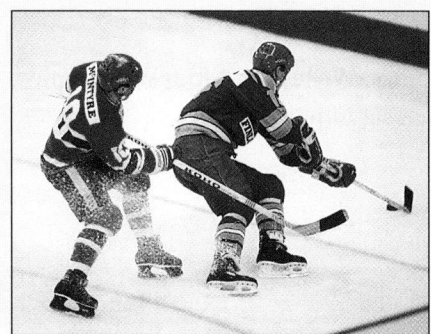

SKIING

The world's oldest ski was found in Sweden and is thought to be 4500 years old. The modern sport did not develop until 1843, however, with a competition in Tromsø, Norway. There are two main forms of skiing: Alpine, which is skiing downhill; and Nordic, which is either cross-country skiing or ski-jumping. Both forms are popular both as leisure activities and as competitive sports. The world's best skiers compete each winter for the World Cup titles in the Alpine and Nordic events. The other major skiing competitions include the World Ski Championships, held every two years, and the Winter Olympic Games, held every four years.

2 Choose a heading for each of the paragraphs from the list below. Two headings are not needed.

> **A** Skiing competitions **D** Skiing clothes
>
> **B** Skiing equipment **E** Types of skiing
>
> **C** Skiing history

2 1 The following paragraphs from an article about ice hockey are out of order. Number them 1–4 to show the correct order.

A	B	C	D
And if the hours weren't bad enough, the training sessions are very hard work. The Flames' coach obviously believes in keeping the team fit. After they've finished two hours of skating and hockey exercises, he sometimes makes them run up and down stairs!	The first thing we discovered was that the players have to be dedicated. The training session we went to started at ten o'clock and didn't finish until after midnight – and that was an early one! Some go on until 3 a.m.	So what is it about ice hockey that persuades the players to put so much effort into it? One of the players, Stephen King, explained, 'It's the fastest and most exciting team sport in the world. It's not as dangerous as everyone thinks, though – I've never been injured.'	Ice hockey is fast becoming one of Britain's most popular sports. There are now three times as many teams as there were ten years ago. So what's all the fuss about? We visited the Fife Flames, a junior team, to find out.

2 Paragraph D introduces the subject by telling us that ice hockey is very popular. What aspects of the subject do each of the other paragraphs deal with?

3 Each new paragraph has a logical link to the previous one. For example 'We visited ... to *find out*' in the first paragraph is followed by 'The first thing we *discovered*'. What links can you find between the other three paragraphs?

❸ Here is another topic and some paragraph headings. Put the paragraph headings in a suitable order 1–5.

Job Interviews

☐ a What to wear
☐ b Finding out about the organisation in advance
☐ c Lessons to learn from an unsuccessful interview
☐ d Preparing a good application
☐ e Answering questions effectively

❹ Imagine you had to write short articles on these two topics. Write about four paragraph headings for each one and decide the best order for each set of paragraphs.
 1 Camping holidays
 2 Organising a party

STUDY BOX I

ADJECTIVE/NOUN + PREPOSITION: OPPOSITE

the opposite (of) –	a person or thing which is completely different from another 'It's **the** absolute **opposite of** what I do in my own sport.' (Text I)
opposite (to) –	completely different from *My opinion is completely **opposite to** yours. The **opposite** sex.*
opposite (to) –	facing *The bank is **opposite (to)** the post office. The man sitting **opposite**.*

VERB + PREPOSITION

'I don't really *approve of* all this running.' (Text I)

*(dis)approve **of***	*listen **to***	*remind somebody **of/about** something*
*describe **as***	*pay **for***	*warn somebody **of/about** something*
*complain **about***	*rely **on***	
*concentrate **on***	*depend **on***	

Focus on grammar 2 The present perfect continuous

Look at this example from Listening I:

Windsurfing is very simple to describe, but, as I've been discovering, not so easy to do!

FORM

has have	+ been +	present participle

USE

The continuous form of the present perfect tense is used

 1 to suggest that a situation is temporary rather than permanent.

  Compare: *I've worked in this office for eight years.*
    I couldn't find a full-time job so I've been working part-time.

2 to show that an action is not finished.

Compare: *I've been waiting to see him since 10 o'clock.* (I'm still waiting.)

I've waited long enough! (I won't wait any longer.)

3 to emphasise that an action has only just finished, particularly when explaining results that can still be seen. *For example:*

Why are you covered in oil? – *I've been mending the car.*

Why is the floor so wet? – *The washing machine has been leaking again.*

EXERCISE 1   Now answer these questions in the same way:

a Why are Jane's eyes red?

b Why are you out of breath?

c Why does Guy's back ache so much?

d Why do you feel so tired?

Notes   1 Some verbs cannot be used in the continuous form. Look back at page 9 for a list of the most common examples.

2 The present perfect continuous cannot be used when a quantity is mentioned.

Compare: *I've been writing letters this evening.*

I've written five letters this evening.

EXERCISE 2   Complete the following sentences with the correct form of the verb in brackets. Use the simple past, present perfect or present perfect continuous. Where more than one tense is possible, decide which is more appropriate.

a I .... (share) a flat with two friends since I .... (come) back to England but I'd like a place of my own.

b After John .... (leave) the army, he .... (apply) for a job in a bank and .... (work) there ever since.

c I .... (see) the film a few weeks ago but I .... (never, read) the book.

d You look frozen! How long .... (you, stand) out here in the cold?

e Car workers .... (be) on strike since September when the company .... (reject) their claim for a 20% pay rise.

f .... (you, hear) the news? Simon Jones and Sally Drew .... (announce) their engagement. They .... (go out) together for ages but nobody .... (think) they would ever get married.

g What .... (you, do) lately? This is the first time I .... (see) you since we .... (meet) at the Smiths' party last May.

h There .... (be) heavy snowfalls in the West Country in the last twenty-four hours and the police .... (warn) drivers to take great care. Two serious accidents .... (already, occur) on the M5 motorway and the forecast is for more snow on the way.

i I still .... (not, hear) from Geraldine even though I .... (write) to her three times last month.

j Food prices .... (rise) steadily since Britain .... (join) the Common Market in 1973.

Communication activity *20 questions*

Work as a class or in groups.

INSTRUCTIONS

1 Think of three sports or hobbies and write them down. (Don't choose activities which are too obvious – for example, football – or ones that you know nothing about!)

2 Choose one student as 'Subject' to start. He or she picks one activity from their list. The rest of the class (or group) must ask the Subject questions about the activity in order to guess what it is.

RULES

1 You can ask each Subject a maximum of 20 questions.

2 The questions should be ones with Yes/No answers. For example:
Do you need special equipment? **not** *What special equipment do you need?*

3 All the questions should be in correct English! The Subject needn't answer questions which are incorrect.

NOTE   If you want to make this activity into a competition, allow the Subject to score 1 mark for every question asked. The highest score wins at the end of the activity.

PREPARATION

Here are some of the range of questions you could ask.

1 Is it expensive to do/play?
   dangerous

   ....

   ....

2 Can you do this indoors?

   ....

   .   ...

3 Do you need special equipment?

   ....

   ....

4 Would other people enjoy watching it?

   ....

5 Could you do it in this town?

   ....

   ....

6 Do you need to be very strong?
   Do you have to practise very often?

   ....

   ....

Imagine that the Subject's activity is football. What other questions would help lead you to the answer?

Text 2 *Keeping one jump ahead*

❶ **Read the following text through fairly quickly to answer these questions.**

1 What does Mike McCarthy do for a hobby?

2 What difficulties does he have with his hobby?

Any fool can jump off a 350-metre building – as long as he is wearing a parachute, that is. The really clever trick is to jump off a low one. And the new world record of 52 metres belongs to 27-year-old
5 parachutist Mike McCarthy, who took all of five seconds to travel that distance, from his exit point on the Leaning Tower of Pisa to the grass below. He hopes to beat his own record soon, by jumping maybe 48 metres. It is more or less all he thinks about.

10 Mike McCarthy cannot look at a bridge, a cliff or an ancient monument without wanting to jump off. As for jumping out of aeroplanes, he regards that as a hobby suitable only for **wimps.**

Mike would like to jump off all sorts of interesting
15 buildings, all over the world, but the authorities everywhere tend to be disapproving. They **busted** him in New York, for instance, for jumping from the Empire State Building, and they were quite unreasonable when he **took a flying leap** off the edge of the Grand Canyon. 'They
20 went through all the lawbooks until they came up with "powerless flight within the canyon area",' says Mike. 'They fined me $200.'

The judge in New York was kinder. She found him guilty of reckless endangerment after he brought the early
25 morning rush-hour traffic to a standstill by jumping off the Empire State Building and landing in Fifth Avenue, but she only fined him $86, which was a dollar a floor.

It is as well to **bear in mind** the view of the British Parachute Association that parachutes should be open, at
30 the very latest, by 762 metres. They have banned Mike from their club planes for three years. This is not something which particularly bothers him.

Mike has made some 3,000 jumps so far, without **mishap**. He says he has never had a girlfriend who
35 **objected to** his jumping enthusiasm, but girlfriends tend not to last very long because he is continually on the move.

'Jumping puts you in a good position to get to know the local culture,' he says. 'People **warm to you** more if you're doing something **loony**.' How loony is loony? Well,
40 Mike would not want to encourage anyone to follow his example without being hugely skilled and experienced.

One day he would like to see his enthusiasm accepted as an Olympic sport. Parachuting from a fixed object could work like high diving in a swimming pool. 'Jumping off
45 high buildings is more popular than you would imagine,' he says.

❷ **Eight words or phrases which you may not know are in bold in the text.**

1 Study them carefully and say what you think they could mean in the context.

2 Below are eight explanations for them but they are **not in the same order**. Match the explanation to the correct word or phrase.

a become more interested or friendly ....

b remember ....

c arrested (informal) ....

d accident ....

e ran forward and jumped ....

f crazy/mad (informal) ....

g weak or nervous person ....

h didn't accept ....

❸ **Choose the answer (A, B, C or D) which you think fits best.**

1 What is Mike McCarthy's main interest?
   A Finding a new building to jump from.
   B Jumping without wearing a parachute.
   C Jumping successfully from a lower height.
   D Becoming the world champion in his sport.

2 After Mike jumped down the Grand Canyon, the authorities
   A found that he'd broken several laws.
   B had to look hard to find a law he'd broken.
   C created a new law to deal with his case.
   D couldn't find any laws that he'd broken.

3 What happened when he jumped from the Empire State Building?
   A He caused an accident.
   B He injured himself.
   C He damaged the building.
   D He stopped the traffic.

4 How does Mike feel about being banned by the British Parachute Association?
   A He doesn't seem to care about it very much.
   B He doesn't understand the reason for it.
   C He's rather disappointed about it.
   D He's extremely angry about it.

5 He has difficulties with relationships because
   A he is a little bit mad.
   B he has such a dangerous hobby.
   C he travels so much.
   D he is often in trouble with the law.

6 What are Mike's hopes for the future?
   A He would like more people to try his hobby.
   B He would like his hobby to be in the Olympics.
   C He would like to win an Olympic medal.
   D He would like to become a champion high diver.

DISCUSSION POINTS ❹

1 What do you think Mike enjoys about jumping off high buildings?

2 Would you like to try it? Do you know anyone who would like to try it?

3 Do you think it will ever become an Olympic sport? Why/Why not?

Focus on listening 2

❶   You are going to hear a runner describe the route he took round the city of Bristol. Before you listen, study the map below and the four questions which follow.

❷   As you listen, mark the route which the runner took and then choose the correct answer (A, B or C) for questions 1–4.

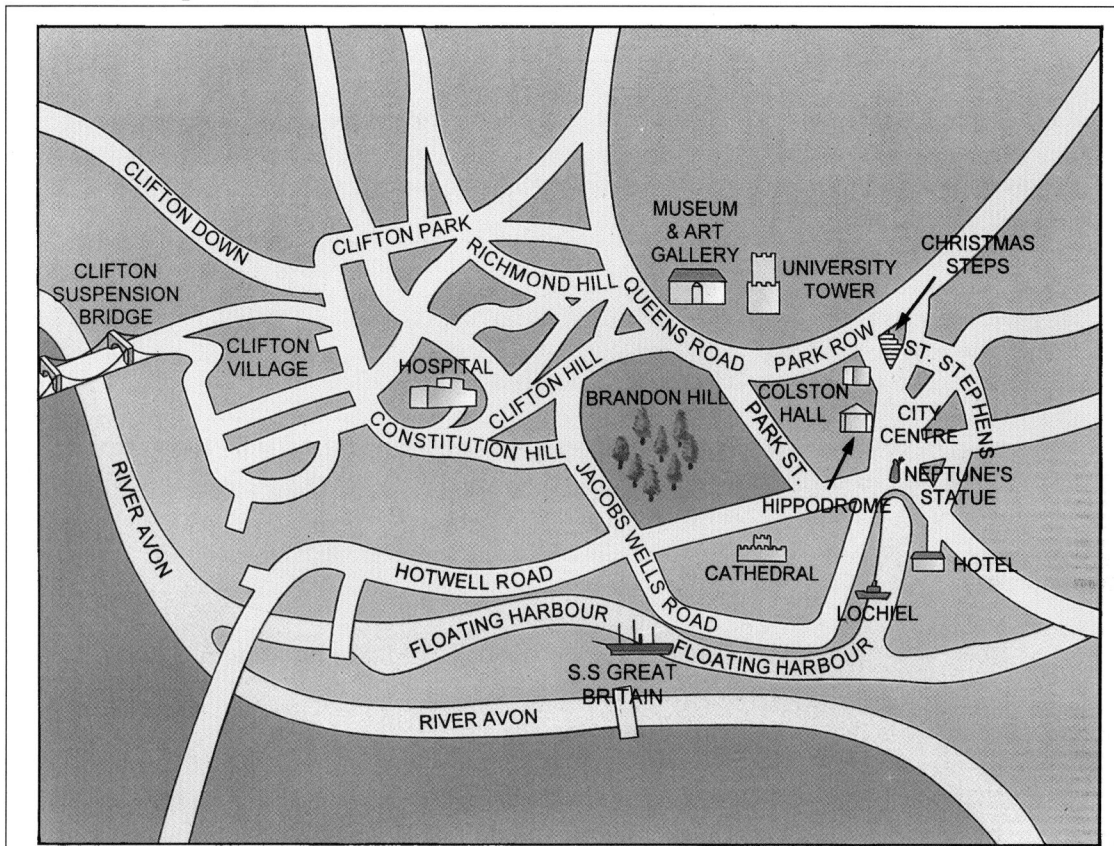

1   Ned didn't cross the Suspension Bridge because
   A he didn't want to waste time.
   B he couldn't pay the fee.
   C he thought it was too expensive.

2   The Hippodrome in the city centre was probably
   A a shop.
   B a theatre.
   C a race course.

3   The distance he ran was
   A the same as he had intended.
   B less than he had intended.
   C more than he had intended.

4   The only disadvantage of the Bristol run is
   A the difficulty of following the map.
   B the distance involved.
   C the number of hills.

STUDY BOX 2   **The order of adjectives**

'... those *little green* birds ...' (Listening 1)

Age Size Temperature Texture, etc.	Shape	Colour	Origin	Material	+ NOUN

A ***new white Chinese paper*** lampshade   A ***huge circular blue plastic swimming*** pool

Put the following adjectives in the correct order before each noun.

cat *black, fat, Persian*
package *paper, brown, thick*
jumper *old, woollen, blue*
jug *green, tiny, glass*
dining table *wooden, round, large*

Focus on grammar 3   Modal verbs 1: ability

Can, could **and** be able

USE

1   PRESENT. **can** is more commonly used than **be able** to express ability. *For example:*
    I can drive but I can't ride a bike.
    How many mistakes can you find?

2   PAST. In affirmative sentences there is an important difference in meaning between **could** and **was/were able to**. **Could** refers to general ability whereas **was/were able** to is used in cases of specific ability.

Consider the following situation.

Eric and Adam were both keen cyclists. At the weekend they often cycled from Bournemouth to Southampton, a distance of more than 20 miles. When they set off together last Sunday, the journey took Eric two hours. Adam's bike had a puncture just after he began the journey so he had to go back home.

    Both Eric and Adam could cycle 20 miles. (They were both fit enough to do it.)
    Last Sunday only Eric was able to cycle that far.

managed to can replace **was able to**.

Note

    In negative sentences **could** is normally used in both general and specific cases of ability. *For example:*
    The sea was so polluted that we couldn't swim.
    I couldn't walk until I was two and a half.

3 PERFECT AND FUTURE TENSES. These are formed with **be able to** because **can** has no infinitive or past participle. *For example:*

I'll be able to **visit you more next summer.**

He hasn't been able to **solve the problem yet.**

Similarly, **be able to** is the only possible infinitive. *For example:*

I'd like to be able to **offer you a job but there are no vacancies at the moment.**

4 **could have done. Could** + perfect infinitive is used to show that someone had the ability to do something but didn't do it. *For example:*

She could have been **a model but she became a nurse instead.**

He was so rude I could have hit **him.**

EXERCISE 1   Complete the following sentences using **can, could, could have** or a suitable form of **be able to.**

a   I .... play the piano much better when I was a child than I .... now.

b   The doctors say he .... (never) walk again.

c   Fortunately he .... swim quite well so he .... save the little girl from drowning.

d   He had a ticket so he .... come to the match but he was too busy.

e   .... (you) stand on your head?

f   I .... (not) write since I broke my arm.

g   Although she was not very tall, she .... reach the book she wanted by standing on a chair.

h   He was so confused that he .... (not) remember who he was.

i   I don't think that I .... mend it but I'll try.

j   He .... get out of the smoke-filled room by crawling on his hands and knees.

STUDY BOX 3   Adjectives with numbers

'... the *13-week* steel strike ...' (Text 1)
'... *27-year-old* parachutist Mike ...' (Text 2)

When a plural expression with a number is used as an adjective, before a noun it becomes singular.

a *5-mile* walk (a walk of 5 miles)   a *six-foot* man   a *5-litre* can
a *10-pound* cheque   a *4-storey* house

Now change the following in the same way:

a letter with 8 pages   a break of 20 minutes   a ticket which cost $20
a mountain which is 3,000 metres high   a baby of 3 months

NOTE: A hyphen is usually used, as in the examples.

Focus on writing 2 *Article* WRITING BANK: PAGE 124

You have been asked to write a short article for a students' magazine on a sports or leisure activity of your choice. It will be part of a series of articles called 'Time Off' in which writers describe an activity they enjoy and encourage others to take it up.
Write your **article** in **100–150** words.

❶ **Look through the instructions and underline or circle the parts which answer these questions:**
1 What form of writing do you have to produce?
2 Who are your readers going to be?
3 What is the purpose of writing?
4 How much do you have to write?

❷ **Think about the task a little more and discuss these questions with another student:**
1 How old do you imagine your readers will be?
2 What style would be suitable? Very formal? Formal? Fairly informal? Very informal?
3 What could you do to catch the readers' attention and make them want to read your article?
4 How can you keep them reading without getting bored?

❸ **Decide on an activity to write about. It could be something you're really keen on, or you could use your imagination to write about a more unusual subject. It might be fun to write enthusiastically about knitting, for example!**

Work with another student to plan both your articles.
1 Talk about your chosen activities and think of questions readers might have.
2 Make a paragraph plan for each article.
3 Think of a suitable headline for each article.

NOTE There are notes on writing articles in the Writing Bank (page 124)

Time Off

This week...

MOUNTAIN CLIMBING

Cristina Zamora tells us about her favourite sport.

Language review

Choose the word or phrase (A, B, C or D) which best completes each sentence.

1 I heard that the .... at the end of the match was 2–0.

   A account   **B** total   **C** score   **D** number

2 Most people .... to pay their bills by cheque nowadays.

   A tend   **B** used   **C** require   **D** practise

3 My company is very .... of the importance of advertising.

   A interested   **B** anxious   **C** keen   **D** conscious

4 When I first started learning to play golf it was just .... fun.

   A for   **B** as   **C** in   **D** by

5 All this running up and down stairs will keep me .... , if nothing else!

   A able   **B** fit   **C** sound   **D** fine

6 You must .... in mind that you're not as fit as you used to be.

   A take   **B** bear   **C** put   **D** think

7 He doesn't take much exercise, ... from walking the dog.

   A alone   **B** besides   **C** except   **D** apart

8 My new job is the complete opposite .... the one I had before.

   A for   **B** from   **C** of   **D** to

9 Will he be good enough to .... in the Junior Championships?

   A attempt   **B** enter   **C** compete   **D** go

10 I don't .... of smoking at all.

   A agree   **B** approve   **C** allow   **D** accept

11 Of course, it may rain and in that .... we'll organise indoor events.

   A case   **B** weather   **C** condition   **D** occasion

12 She's hoping to .... the world record of 2.09m in the high jump.

   A win   **B** lead   **C** pass   **D** beat

13 We must be at the airport by 5 o'clock at the ....

   A latest   **B** last   **C** least   **D** longest

14 It's a good plan and I hope no one will .... to it.

   A mind   **B** disapprove   **C** care   **D** object

15 I was so worried about the news that I couldn't concentrate .... my work.

   A to   **B** in   **C** about   **D** on

Lead-in ❶

Criminals are hard at work in the picture above. Work with a partner to see how many different crimes you can find. Then try to match them with the types of crime listed below:

vandalism	burglary	robbery	mugging
shoplifting	arson	stealing/theft	

DISCUSSION ❷ Now discuss with your partner:
Which of these crimes:
1 are the most serious? Why?
2 are the least serious? Why?
3 are the biggest problem where you live?

STUDY BOX 1 *steal vs. rob*

You **steal** things (**from** people, organisations or places).
*Thieves **stole** the radio **from** my car. My watch has been **stolen**.*

You **rob** people or institutions (**of** things).
*He tried to **rob** a bank once. Two men **robbed** her **of** her money.*

NOTE also: *The army **robbed** them **of** their youth. You have **robbed** me **of** my success.*

Text 1 ❶ Read the following article fairly quickly.

Seven banks a day are robbed in LA

John Barnes on a city's remarkable record

From The Sunday Times

OCTOBER 4, 1979, is a day of fond memory for FBI agents in Los Angeles. It's the last day that the city did not have a bank robbery.

5 Last year there were 1,844 bank robberies in the city and its suburbs, an average of about seven every business day, and a quarter of all the bank robberies committed in the United States.
10 The total haul was around four million dollars.

There are several reasons why Los Angeles heads the bank-robbery league – way ahead of San Francisco, second with
15 546, and New York, third with 443. The place has an awful lot of banks – 3,300 – and many stay open until 5 or 6 in the evening and at weekends. They are also very informal. 'You need a warm, inviting
20 place to do business,' says Stephen Ward of the British-owned Crocker Bank. Bank robbers are particularly appreciative.

The robberies are usually quite genteel, with none of the machine-gun
25 violence of the old movies. Usually, the robber passes a stick-up note to a teller, pockets the cash while the surveillance cameras click away, then makes a get-away via the nearest freeway. Tellers have
30 orders to hand over the money immediately. 'The banks believe, quite rightly, that you can replace money but you can't replace lives,' says one FBI man.
35 Most of the robbers are drug-addicts. But they also include 'pregnant women, one-legged men, husband-and-wife and father-and-son teams,' according to Joseph Chefalo, who heads the FBI's
40 bank-robbery squad.

The FBI is particularly keen to find the 'Yankee Bandit', who may have earned a place in the Guinness Book of Records with 65 bank holdups. Before making his
45 getaway, he always doffs his Yankee baseball cap, with a smile in the direction of the cameras. For a while, the FBI thought he had retired with his haul of 155,000 dollars. He was not seen over the
50 Christmas holidays. But when the first working day of the new year started off with 14 robberies, there he was, smiling for the cameras, Yankee cap in one hand, the cash in the other.

❷ **Now cover the article and see if you can answer these questions:**

1 How does Los Angeles compare with other American cities as regards bank robberies?

2 What was special about October 4th, 1979?

3 Are there any reasons why LA has so many bank robberies?

❸ **Find words or phrases in the article which mean the same as:**

Paragraphs 1–3
1 affectionate   ....
2 amount stolen   ....
3 is at the top of   ....
4 a list or class   ....
5 grateful   ....

Paragraphs 4 and 5
6 polite   ....
7 cashier in a bank   ....
8 takes (dishonestly)   ....
9 close watch   ....
10 escapes   ....
11 wide, high speed road   ....
12 is leader of   ....
13 group of people working as a team   ....

Paragraph 6
14 robber   ....
15 takes off   ....

❹ **Say whether the following statements are true or false, and why:** True False

1 Seven banks are robbed every day in Los Angeles. ☐ ☐

2 Bank robbers frequently injure bank staff or customers. ☐ ☐

3 Banks tell their staff not to try and resist robbers. ☐ ☐

4 The FBI disapproves of the banks' advice to staff. ☐ ☐

5 The FBI has no idea what the 'Yankee Bandit' looks like. ☐ ☐

6 There were no bank robberies in Los Angeles before 1979. ☐ ☐

7 Bank robbers don't usually need to speak to bank staff. ☐ ☐

8 Los Angeles banks have a more relaxed atmosphere than banks in other US cities. ☐ ☐

⑤ Now answer these questions in your own words:
1 What makes the 'Yankee Bandit' exceptional?
2 Why do most Los Angeles bank robbers rob banks?
3 How do most robbers escape?

⑥ Finally, discuss the following points:
1 Why is the FBI 'particularly keen' to find the 'Yankee Bandit'?
2 What would be written on a stick-up note?
3 What would you do if you were (a) a bank teller, (b) a customer during a bank raid?

Focus on grammar 1   Modal verbs 2: *obligation*

Read the following passage and underline any phrases that express an obligation.

Accommodation is always arranged with an English family. A single room costs between £60 and £70 a week and you have to pay a month's rent in advance. You should allow £15 a week for bus fares and other extras. Breakfast is provided and you don't usually have to pay extra for heating. You must complete and return the enclosed form as soon as possible but you needn't send any money until we find you a suitable family.

MUST and HAVE TO

In the present **must** is used when the obligation comes from the speaker. **Have to** is more common when the obligation comes from someone else, often a law or a rule. *For example:*

You have to pay a month's rent in advance. (This is a general rule.)
You must complete and return the enclosed form. (This is the agency's rule.)
In Britain, motorcyclists have to wear a crash helmet. (This is the law.)

In the future and the past **have to** is the only way of expressing obligation. *For example:*

There was a bus strike last week so I had to walk to work.
If they move to the country, they'll have to buy a car.

EXERCISE 1   Complete the following sentences by choosing the most suitable form of **have to** or **must**.
a My cough is terrible. I .... stop smoking.
b The bus .... turn back because there was so much snow.
c I .... take these tablets every day since I was a child.
d Everyone who works .... pay income tax.
e You .... work harder if you want a better job.
f In the army you .... obey orders.

MUSTN'T and NEEDN'T/DON'T HAVE TO

Mustn't expresses a negative obligation (= the action is forbidden).
Needn't and **don't have to** indicate that there is no obligation. Notice the difference between **needn't** and **don't have to**. *For example:*

You mustn't drink alcohol while taking these tablets.
You don't have to have a licence to own a cat. (No legal requirement)
You needn't wash up. I'll do it later. (No obligation)

EXERCISE 2 Complete these sentences by putting **mustn't, needn't,** or **doesn't/don't have to** in the spaces.

a You .... ask me when you want to use the telephone.

b This plant .... stand in direct sunlight or it will die.

c Students .... attend cookery classes if they don't want to.

d The doctor says I .... get overtired but I .... stay in bed.

e You .... park your car on double yellow lines.

SHOULD and OUGHT TO

Should and **ought to** are interchangeable and are used when the obligation is not so strong. Often they express advice or duty. *For example:*

You should write to your family more often.

I ought to stay in and work tonight.

NEED

In the present tense **need to** expresses a weaker obligation than **have to** and **must**. It is used mainly in questions and negative sentences. *For example:*

Need I really do it all again?

You needn't finish your lunch if you are not hungry.

In hot weather you need to water the grass every day.

NEEDN'T HAVE (DONE) and DIDN'T NEED TO

In the past **needn't have (done)** is used to show that an action was performed even though it wasn't necessary. *For example:*

We needn't have booked seats for the show because the theatre was half empty. Next time we won't bother.

Now suggest why the following actions were a waste of time:

You needn't have cooked all that food.

He needn't have taken his umbrella.

I needn't have bought two bottles of suntan lotion.

Didn't need to also refers to an action that wasn't necessary but, in this case, it wasn't performed. *For example:*

I didn't need to pay by cheque because I had plenty of cash.

Note **Didn't have to** is preferred when the obligation is imposed by someone else. *For example:*

I didn't have to go to work yesterday so I stayed in bed till lunchtime.

EXERCISE 3 Comment on each of these situations using the appropriate form of the word in brackets and **needn't have, didn't need to** or **didn't have to**.

a Patrick and Annie decided to go to France for a holiday. He went to evening classes to learn the language but she already spoke French well.

She .... (go) to evening classes.

b George was invited to a formal party but had nothing suitable to wear and no money to buy new clothes. Fortunately a friend lent him a suit.

He .... (buy) new clothes.

c It took Alan four hours to do his homework. The next day his teacher said his essay was rather long. She had asked for 200 – not 2000 – words.
He .... (write) so much.

d Sidney was ill. The doctor gave him some medicine to try but suggested that an operation was probably the only solution. The medicine worked and Sidney got better very quickly.
He .... (have) the operation.

e Judy looked through her bag several times but couldn't find her door key so finally she kicked the door down. Later she noticed the key lying on the path.
She .... (damage) the door.

EXERCISE 4 **Using a suitable expression of obligation write what you would say in the following situations.**

a There's a no-smoking sign in the room. Your friend takes his cigarettes out of his pocket.

b A friend is planning a holiday in the USA and he thinks he can get a visa when he arrives there.

c You invited some friends to dinner and spent all day preparing a wonderful meal. They telephone you at 8 p.m. to say they cannot come.

d You are looking after two children while their parents are out. It's 11 p.m. and the children are still watching television.

e Your parents have decided to go out for a meal. You recommend an excellent restaurant that never gets too crowded. They wonder whether they should reserve a table.

Focus on writing I *Report* WRITING BANK: PAGE 126

A report is a way of presenting information clearly for someone who needs it. Reports are divided into sections which deal with different aspects of the subject and usually end with suggestions or recommendations for making improvements. There is a main heading and also sub-headings (or numbers) for each section. There is an example report on page 126 of the Writing Bank.

You are staying in a student house which belongs to your college. The house has study-bedrooms for eight students and also a shared kitchen and TV room. There has recently been a burglary and you have been asked by the college's Accommodation Officer to write a short report giving details of what happened and suggesting what could be done to prevent another burglary. Write your **report** in about **120** words.

❶ Divide your report into five sections and begin with the following introduction:

Introduction	*The purpose of this report is to describe the burglary which took place on … (date) at … (place) and to suggest ways of improving security.*
Losses and damage	What was taken? Was any other damage caused? (Give full details.)
Method of entry	When and how did the burglar(s) get in? How do you know?
Action taken	Who discovered the burglary and what action did they take?
Conclusion	What could be done (by the students/by the college) to improve security?

❷ Before you begin writing:
1 Work in small groups to discuss ideas for each section.
2 Study the notes on writing reports in the Writing Bank on page 127.

Focus on listening 1 *Crime report*

You are going to hear part of a local radio programme which deals with crime in the area.

❶ As you listen for the first time, tick (✓) any of the objects below which have been stolen.

❷ As you listen for the second time, put a cross (✗) by any objects which have been found by the police.

Put your tick or cross in the small box in the bottom right hand corner of each picture (you may need a tick and a cross for some objects).

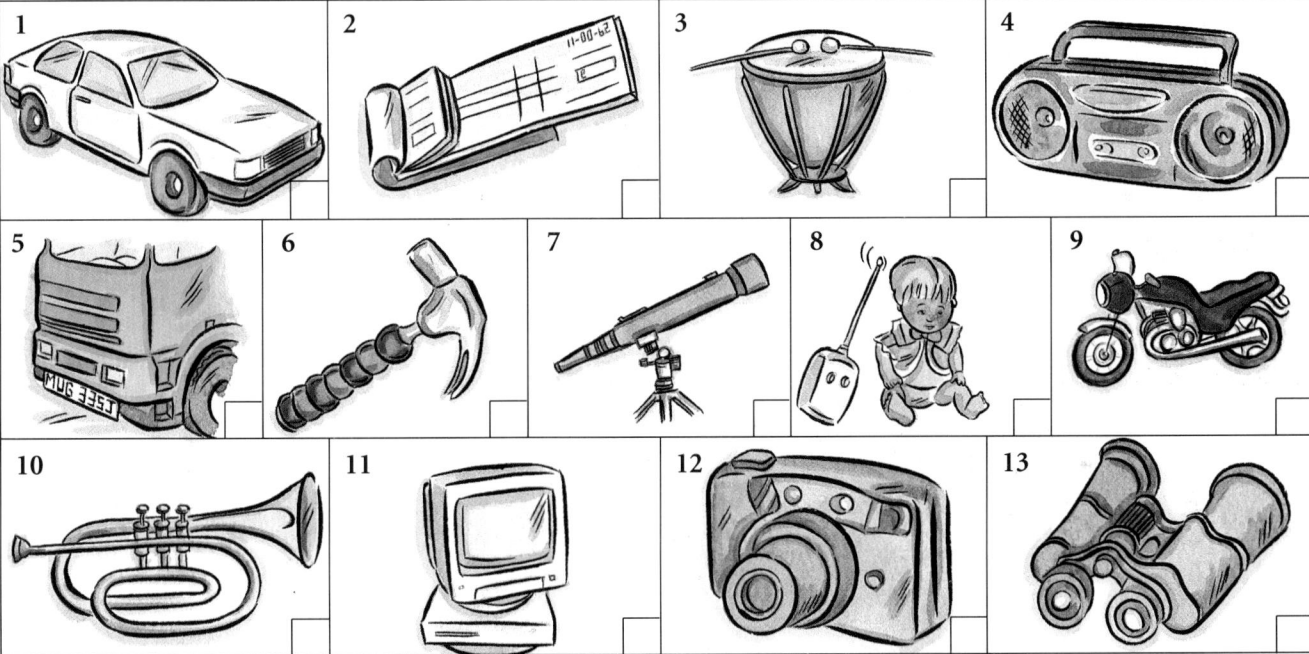

STUDY BOX 2   Phrasal verb *get* (1)

'The thieves **got *away*** in a stolen green van.' (Listening 1)

get across – communicate.	*Although I couldn't speak the language, I managed to **get** my meaning **across** when necessary.*
get (a)round – overcome or avoid a problem.	*I'm sure we'll find a way of **getting round** the difficulties.*
get (a)round – become known.	*The news of his arrest **got around** quickly.*
get at – reach.	*The cupboard is too high for me to **get at** easily.*
get at – suggest.	*What exactly are you **getting at**? Why don't you say what's on your mind?*
get away – leave/escape.	*I didn't **get away** from the meeting till late. (See example above.)*
get away with – escape with stolen goods.	*The burglar only **got away with** a few pounds.*
get away with – escape from punishment.	*He **got away with** his crime because of insufficient evidence.*
get back – regain possession.	*The police think there's a good chance we'll **get** our car **back**.*
get by – manage, survive.	*How will you **get by** on only a part-time salary?*
get down – cause depression.	*Don't let these problems **get you down**.*

Text 2

Read the following advertisement and then choose the best answer (A, B, C or D) to the questions which follow.

You're already well equipped to prevent crime.

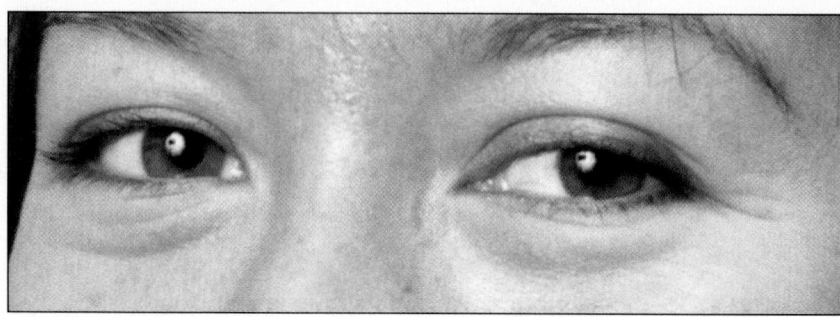

Everyone comes with their own built-in burglar alarm. It's called the sense of sight and sound.

Unfortunately, many of us go around with the alarm switched off.

We don't see the stranger loitering outside the house next door.

We overlook the kids trying the car doors.

We don't notice the sounds from the flat upstairs. (Weren't they supposed to be on holiday?)

The police can only do so much to prevent crime.

There never can be enough of them to guard every home in every town. So they need your help in combating the burglars, the vandals, the car thieves. Not, of course, by setting out to 'have a go' every time you see something suspicious. It'll always be the job of the police to arrest criminals.

But by acting as a line of communication between them and your community.

For instance, you probably know far more about your immediate neighbourhood than the police ever could.

A stranger in someone's garden would probably be far more obvious to you than it would to even the local bobby. Providing, of course, you were on the look-out.

And that's the whole idea behind the Neighbourhood Watch schemes now springing up around the country.

To create a spirit of watchfulness within a community, anything suspicious being reported to the police.

It's early days yet, but results so far are very encouraging. The crime figures are already dropping in many of the areas running a scheme.

And all due to people like you.

Don't let them get away with it.

From *The Central Office of Information*

1 The purpose of the advertisement is to

   A warn people about the increasing risk of crime.

   B encourage people to join the police force.

   C advise people how to protect their homes from crime.

   D explain how people can assist the police.

2 The advertisement points out that many people

   A are not very keen to co-operate with the police.

   B are not as observant as they could be.

   C don't control their children properly.

   D don't tell their neighbours about their holidays.

3 One of the ways we could help prevent crime is to

   A keep the alarm system in our home turned on.

   B try to stop criminals from escaping.

   C watch out for people behaving suspiciously.

   D inform the police if we hear noises upstairs.

4 One disadvantage the police have is that they

   A don't know local people personally.

   B are too busy arresting criminals.

   C know communities less well than residents do.

   D can't see what's happening in people's gardens.

5 Results of the Neighbourhood Watch schemes suggest that
   A they are already successful wherever they are run.
   B they are likely to be a success.
   C they are not successful in certain areas.
   D they are not popular with the police.

Communication activity *Witness*

① Look at these ways of describing clothes.

DESCRIBING
CLOTHES

Present
He's wearing a new pair of shoes.
I've got a thick sweater on.
We usually wear jeans at the weekend.

Past
She was wearing a flowery hat.
He had a scarf on.
I always wore a uniform.

Choose words from the following list to label the pictures below.

dress	apron	blouse	sleeve	skirt	overalls	boot	socks
belt	shoe	collar	overcoat	cap	slacks	trousers	
shirt	jacket	shorts	T shirt	raincoat	pullover	vest	

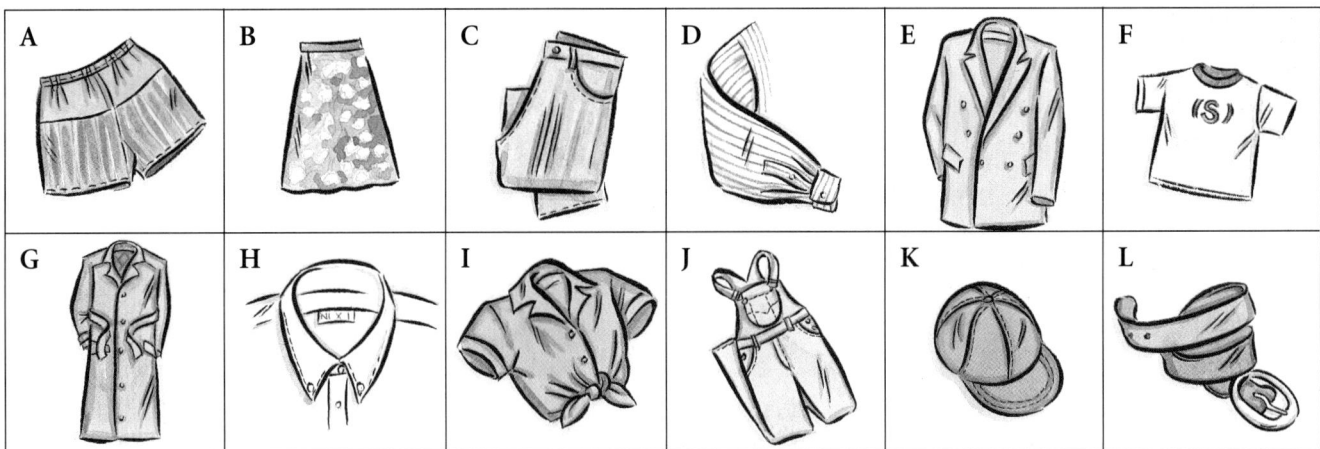

② Check your answers with another student. Make sure you know the meanings of all the words in the list!

③ In this activity you must work with a partner.

Student A will study a picture for 30 seconds. Meanwhile Student B will time Student A by counting 'one thousand and one, one thousand and two,' and so on (silently, of course!) until one thousand and thirty is reached.

After that, Student B will find out how much Student A remembers of the picture.

INSTRUCTIONS   Student A   Turn to page 71 and study the picture carefully.

Student B   1 Start counting!
            2 After 30 seconds, tell your partner to give you his/her book so that you can

now see the same picture. Hold it so that your partner can't see it.

3 Ask questions, using the past tense, about:
- what exactly the two people were doing at that moment.
- the two people's appearance – age, clothes, hair, expression.
- any other details of the surroundings.

4 When you have finished, ask Student A to look at the picture and point out any mistakes.

5 Make a note of any words you didn't know to ask the teacher.

Now change roles. The new Student A must look at the picture on page 67 and the new Student B must look at the instructions above.

❹ Who makes the best witness?

The two pictures on page 65 show how the scene in the first picture (page 71) was remembered by two different groups of people. The first were police officers and the second, members of the public. Both groups made mistakes but each group made a different kind of mistake.

Work with a partner again. Compare the two pictures with the real event on page 71 and discuss the mistakes each group made. For example:

The public said that the man had fair hair but in fact his hair was dark.

(You may find it useful to refer to the language for Describing People in the Functions Bank on page 111 before you start.)

When you've finished, decide what the main difference between the police officers' description of the scene and that of the public was.

Does the difference surprise you? Why/Why not?

STUDY BOX 3   Phrasal verb *break*

'Thieves ***broke into*** Bell's toyshop ...' (Listening 1)

break down – fail to work.	My car **broke down** on the way to work.
break down – collapse (in tears).	She **broke down** in tears when she heard the news.
break into – enter by force.	See example above.
break off – end suddenly.	He **broke off** in the middle of a sentence.
break out – escape.	Seven prisoners **broke out of** Leeds jail last night.
break through – force a way through.	The crowds managed to **break through** the barriers.
break up – separate.	She's **broken up** with her boyfriend.
break up – smash into pieces.	Can you help me **break up** this box to make firewood?

Focus on listening 2 *Bad start to a honeymoon*

For most of the questions below, you have to fill in the missing information by writing short answers. For question 2, tick (✓) the correct boxes. For questions 9 and 10, tick the correct answer A, B, C or D.

1 Where were Alan and Cheryl driving to when they stopped in Stratford-on-Avon?

....

2 Which of these things were stolen, according to Alan? Tick the correct boxes.

☐ tickets ☐ credit card
☐ passports ☐ cash
☐ traveller's cheques ☐ cheque book
☐ flight bag ☐ driving licence
☐ suitcases ☐ marriage licence

3 Who did Alan think had taken their things at first? ....

4 Where had Alan put the luggage in the car? ....

5 Why should Alan know what to do after a theft? ....

6 Were the police hopeful that they would get their belongings back? ....

7 What clothes did Alan have left? ....

8 What is Cheryl's job? ....

9 The travel agency helped them by
A giving them their money back.
B issuing new tickets for the original holiday.
C arranging a different holiday for them.
D making an insurance claim for them.

10 How do Alan and Cheryl feel now?
A cheerful   **B** nervous   **C** depressed   **D** angry

Police description   **Public description**

From *The Sunday Times*

Text 3

❶ Five paragraphs are missing from the following newspaper article.

How many of the following questions can you answer by reading the incomplete article?
Tick (✓) the ones you can answer and then discuss them with another student.

1 What weapon did the bank robber use? ☐
2 What kind of person was the bank robber? ☐
3 How did she begin her robbery? ☐
4 Why did she carry out the robbery? ☐
5 How was she caught? ☐
6 What punishment did she receive? ☐

Granny, 70, holds up a bank!

A GRANDMOTHER of 70 tried to hold up a bank by grabbing a hostage and pretending she had a gun.

1 ☐

Bespectacled widow Peggy Barlow tried her raid after watching a TV programme about robberies.

She suffered from arthritis and could not walk without a stick, so she got out her pensioner's pass and took a bus to the bank in Kensington, London.

Hostage

2 ☐

Then she pushed the perfume spray forward in her pocket to look like a gun, bundled her hostage into the manager's office and demanded:

'Keep your hands above the desk. Give me all the money in the bank.'

When the manager, David Ball, said he couldn't give her ALL the money, she asked for £85,000 – and eventually settled for the £50,000 he offered.

3 ☐

As Mrs Barlow was led away by police she apologised to the bank staff – and asked detectives if she could telephone some friends to cancel a bridge party.

She became desperate when her debts reached £70,000 after her husband – a bank manager – died in 1975, the Old Bailey* heard yesterday.

4 ☐

'If you behave from now on, you can forget this dreadful affair.'

Mrs Barlow said later: 'I can still hardly believe it was me. I'm normally very timid.'

5 ☐

* Old Bailey – the central criminal court of England.

From the *Daily Mirror*

❷ Now choose from paragraphs A–E below to fill gaps 1–5. Look for clues in the paragraphs before and after the gaps.

A But after Mr Ball left the office, Mrs Barlow was overpowered by her hostage, psychiatrist's wife, Mrs Julien Watkins, 48.

B But she was overpowered by the hostage – and the 'pistol' in her pocket turned out to be a perfume spray.

C She added: 'I read a lot of Agatha Christie but no one has written about a criminal as daft and unlikely as me.'

D First she grabbed a customer, warning her: 'Keep quiet and you won't get hurt.'

E Recorder, Sir James Miskin, sentenced her to nine months' jail, suspended for a year, after she admitted demanding money with menaces and assaulting Mrs Watkins. He told her:

❸ Now answer the questions you didn't tick in exercise 1.

❹ Say whether the facts below are true or false.

		True	False
1	Mrs Barlow bought a ticket on the bus to the bank.	☐	☐
2	She had difficulty in moving about easily.	☐	☐
3	She threatened a customer in the bank.	☐	☐
4	She owed a lot of money.	☐	☐
5	In court she denied that she had attacked a customer.	☐	☐
6	She told the judge that she was sorry.	☐	☐
7	She is not usually a brave woman.	☐	☐

Check your answers with another student.

❺ In what way(s) was this bank robbery different from those described in Text 1?

SEE
COMMUNICATION
ACTIVITY,
PAGE 63

Focus on grammar 2   Participles

The **present participle** consists of the **verb + -ing**. *For example:*
I've been listening.   *You're* lying.   *We'll be* waiting.

The **past participle** consists of the **verb + (e)d** or an irregular form. *For example:*
I was arrested.   *You're sure to be* promoted.   *They had already* left.

EXERCISE 1   Participles can be used like adjectives, before a noun. Underline the participles in these examples from texts in this unit:

a   You need a warm, inviting place to do business.
b   But when the first working day of the new year started off …
c   Everyone comes with their own built-in burglar alarm.
d   Bespectacled widow, Peggy Barlow, tried her raid …
e   She was able to sort out the problems about the stolen cheque book.

Note   1   Present participles usually have an active meaning. An **annoying** problem is a problem which annoys you.

2   Past participles usually have a passive meaning. An **annoyed** neighbour is a neighbour who has been annoyed by something.

EXERCISE 2   Use verbs from the following list to make present or past participles to be used as adjectives in the sentences below:

wear	*know*	*break*	*warn*	*frighten*	*tire*	*last*	*light*	*help*	*grind*

a   It's been an awfully .... day. I must sit down for a moment.
b   I prefer proper .... coffee to the instant sort.
c   This perfume is supposed to be very long- ....
d   Your jacket is rather .... on the elbows. You'll need a new one soon.
e   Haven't you heard of him? I thought he was quite well .... as an actor.
f   Don't tell the children a .... story or they'll never get to sleep.
g   Do you need a .... hand with the washing up?
h   She says she's got a .... heart but I'm sure she'll soon find another boyfriend.
i   The streets are very brightly .... at night.
j   I stopped speaking at once when I saw the .... look he gave me!

Participles can also be used in **participle clauses** to replace a subject and verb.

1   to give more information about a noun. *For example:*
That's the whole idea behind the Neighbourhood Watch schemes now springing up *around the country.* (Schemes which are springing up)
The two men arrested *for shoplifting were in their twenties.* (The two men who were arrested…)

2   to give more information about a verb. *For example:*
We all rushed out, thinking *there was a fire.* (We rushed out *because we thought* there was a fire.)

Driving home today, I got caught in the rush hour traffic. (I got caught in the traffic as/when I was driving home.)

Perfect participles are used to show that one action was complete before another started. *For example:*

Having spent five years in Portugal, I know the country quite well. (Because I spent five years …)
Having reached the station, they found their train had left. (When they reached the station …)

Negative participles are formed with *not*.

Not caring …   Not having seen …

EXERCISE 3   Complete the following sentences with suitable present or perfect participles. Add any other necessary words.

a .... the street yesterday, I nearly got knocked down by a bus.
b .... for ten years in a bank, she decided it was time to look for a more exciting job.
c .... the hotel window, I saw an amazing sight – a man with a bear on a lead!
d .... a bus the other day, I met a most interesting man.
e .... what present to buy you, I've decided to give you some money instead.
f .... all his money on clothes, he had nothing left to buy food with.
g .... the ambulance, I thought there had been an accident.
h .... unsuccessfully to phone you on several occasions, I thought I'd better write you a letter.

EXERCISE 4   Rewrite the following sentences, replacing the part in green with a suitable participle. *For example:*

He saw that I looked ill and told me to lie down.
Seeing that I looked ill, he told me to lie down.

a As we were unloading the car after the holiday, we realised that we had left our tent behind.
b She rushed to answer the phone because she knew that it might be her husband calling.
c The sergeant took my name and address and then asked me to make a statement.
d She didn't find anyone at home so she pushed a note through the letter box.
e As I had eaten a three-course meal already, I had to refuse their invitation to dinner.
f He tore open the letter and found a cheque for £100 in it.
g The shop assistant thought I had stolen the bag and called the police.
h As I wasn't used to the climate, I found it quite difficult to work at first.

STUDY BOX 4   Compound adjectives formed with participles

DESCRIBING PEOPLE

well-spoken*	well-brought-up
well-dressed	well-behaved*
kind-hearted	middle-aged
left-handed	short-sighted

DESCRIBING CLOTHES AND MATERIALS

hard-wearing	short/long-sleeved
long-lasting	tight/loose-fitting
well-cut	single/double-breasted

*NOTE: These participles are unusual because they are active in meaning.

Focus on writing 2 *Description* WRITING BANK: PAGE 117

Imagine that your car broke down miles from anywhere one evening and that you had to spend the night in it.

Meanwhile, friends who were expecting you back got worried and went to the police to report you missing. Your friends were asked to write a description of your physical appearance and of the clothes you were wearing when they saw you leave earlier in the day.

In two paragraphs, write the description which your friends might give.

NOTES
1 Study the language for Describing People in the Functions Bank (page 111) before you begin.
2 Use the clothes you are wearing now as the basis for your description.

PLAN
First paragraph:
Physical appearance: height, build, hair, complexion, eyes, any distinguishing features.

Second paragraph:
Clothes: colour, material, pattern, style, etc.

Language review

Choose the word or phrase (A, B, C or D) which best completes each sentence.

1 We started walking .... the direction of the town centre.
   A from   **B** to   **C** in   **D** by

2 My company .... a lot of business in the USA.
   A takes   **B** does   **C** makes   **D** runs

3 I'm sure I made a(n) .... lot of mistakes in the test.
   A horrible   **B** awful   **C** bad   **D** serious

4 French .... the list of the most popular foreign languages taught in this country.
   A leads   **B** wins   **C** beats   **D** heads

5 When the police arrived, they forced the robber to .... his gun.
   A hand out   **B** hand in   **C** hand on   **D** hand over

6 We tied all the old newspapers into a .... for the dustmen to collect.
   A packet   **B** bunch   **C** heap   **D** bundle

7 The hijackers took seven .... before releasing the rest of the passengers.
   A prisoners   **B** hostages   **C** witnesses   **D** slaves

8 When she got back to the hotel, she found she had been robbed .... all her money.
   A from   **B** for   **C** with   **D** of

9 I found I couldn't afford a new car so I had to .... for a secondhand one.
   A settle   **B** decide   **C** choose   **D** agree

10 The judge gave him a four-year prison .... for his crime.
   A time   **B** punishment   **C** sentence   **D** period

11 When I questioned him, he finally .... stealing my pen.

   A admitted   **B** accused   **C** accepted   **D** confessed

12 Although none of us wanted to go on the picnic, it .... to be quite enjoyable.

   A turned up   **B** turned out   **C** showed up   **D** showed off

13 Keep a(n) .... for the milkman. I don't want to miss him.

   A look-out   **B** outlook   **C** view   **D** sight

14 He's lost so much weight that if he doesn't wear a .... his trousers fall down!

   A strap   **B** band   **C** belt   **D** tie

15 I couldn't afford to buy any food but I managed to .... on some bread and cheese I had left.

   A get across   **B** get away   **C** get by   **D** get down

SEE COMMUNICATION ACTIVITY, PAGE 63

Lead-in

❶ **What are the names of these containers?**

Write the names against the numbers 1–8 in the list. Then choose two items which you can usually buy in that container from the words below. The first has been begun for you.

1 *bottle*   *perfume*
2 ....
3 ....
4 ....
5 ....
6 ....
7 ....
8 ....

matches	cigarettes	instant coffee	glue	honey	potatoes
chocolates	apples	cream	pineapple	toothpaste	orange juice
soup	vinegar	perfume	envelopes		

❷ **What is packaging for?**

Some packages have an important purpose. For example, the box that we buy matches in helps to keep the contents together. It also provides a way of using them, of course. Other packages are less important and may only be a way of attracting our attention.

Look at the examples of packages below and discuss with a partner what purpose they serve, if any.

1 a box of chocolates
2 a plastic container of salt
3 a plastic bag containing oranges
4 a packet containing one dose of medicine
5 a plastic packet containing a toothbrush
6 a bag containing a box containing a tube of expensive face cream

Text 1

❶ **Read through the text quickly, ignoring the gaps for the moment, and decide what it's about. Choose the best description from the list below.**

A How to save money when you go shopping

B How to get rid of your rubbish

C The problem about the rubbish we create

D The problem about the food we eat

A load of old rubbish?

'Waste not, want not,' my great-aunt used to say to me as she carefully snipped the string from parcels and folded brown paper away for re-use. If she received anything wrapped in fancy paper, she kept if for next year's presents.

Such economy seems strange in our throwaway society, where disposable means
5   convenient, and cupboards are filled with boxes and packets and cartons.
1 B The idea of a 'gift pack', where the gift wrapping is as important as the gift itself, would have been regarded as a cheat 30 years ago. Today it is acceptable for even a packet of biscuits to be enclosed in three layers of wrapping.

10   **2** It costs Britain £720 million a year to dispose of its rubbish (70 per cent of which is packaging). The average family uses up six trees' worth of paper a year and, if all the cans used in Britain in one year were placed end to end, they would reach to the moon and back twice!

Just how much rubbish does go into our bins? **3** As a young professional
15   couple working long hours, most of our shopping consists of convenience foods. We had expected to have a lot of rubbish, but even I was shocked to find that our final waste bag was 1 metre high and weighed over 6 kilos!

4 In one week alone we threw out 300 sheets of newspaper, 12 bits of junk mail, all unread, five old magazines and nine brightly coloured paper boxes
20   which had once been home to a pre-cooked meal, assorted pizzas and biscuits. The rest of our rubbish was a sad smelly assortment of baked bean and sweetcorn tins and burger cartons. 'Yuk,' said my husband, as we sorted through our bin bag.

5 According to Pippa Hyam of Friends of the Earth, our paper and the
25   metal in our cans are valuable materials which could easily have been re-processed and re-used. She was more worried about our use of plastic, which is difficult to dispose of and may last for hundreds of years. She would like to see people using less plastic. **6** Making plastic uses oil, which is running out. It should not be thought of as a cheap disposable product,' she says.

❷ **Six sentences have been removed from the text. Choose a sentence from the list (A–F) below to fill each of the gaps. Write the correct letter in the space. The first one has been done for you as an example.**

A I'm prepared to pay a little more for things that aren't packaged in plastic.

B Nowadays, packaging is not only used to protect goods but also as a positive selling feature.

C Our bin was bulging with paper.

D My husband and I offered to analyse the contents of our weekly household waste.

E 'Is this really what we eat?'

F But we pay a high price for our sophisticated packaging.

❸ Find words or phrases in the text which mean the same as the following. The paragraph numbers are given in brackets.

1 cut with scissors (1) ....

2 not plain or ordinary, with a lot of decoration (1) ....

3 saving of money (2) ....

4 intended to be thrown away (2) ....

5 a dishonest trick (3) ....

6 get rid of (4) ....

7 advertising material sent through the post (6) ....

8 collection of various things (7) ....

❹ Answer these questions.

1 Why does the writer mention her great-aunt?

2 Why is packaging a problem?

3 The writer's rubbish consisted of two main things. What were they?

4 Why is Pippa Hyam worried about the rubbish people throw away?

DISCUSSION POINTS **❺**

1 What do you think the saying 'Waste not, want not' means? Is there a similar saying in your language?

2 Is there anything you like to save (as the writer's great-aunt saved paper)?

3 Is there any system in your country to collect paper, bottles or cans from people's rubbish?

Focus on grammar 1   Conditional 1

ZERO CONDITIONAL

Look at these examples:

If you press *this button, an alarm* goes off.
You get *5p back* if you return *the bottle.*

These are things which always happen, and **when** could be used instead of **if**.

FORM

IF + Present form + Present form or Imperative

Note

Present forms include the present simple, present continuous, present perfect simple and present perfect continuous. *For example:*

Students only get *a certificate* if they have attended *the course regularly.*

EXERCISE 1

This kind of conditional is used to describe general truths, including scientific processes. Complete the following:

a If you lower the temperature of water, it eventually ....

b Wood floats if you ....

c If water is heated, it ....

d If you strike a match, it ....

e Plants die if you ....

f You put on weight if you ....

EXERCISE 2   This kind of conditional can also be used to give instructions. Match the **if-clauses** in Column A with the correct imperative from Column B, and revise your phrasal verbs!

	Column A		Column B
1	If you make a mistake,	a	tear it out.
2	If your car runs out of petrol,	b	cut it down.
3	If you're not ready for your driving test,	c	give it back.
4	If you see an interesting recipe in the magazine,	d	cut it up.
5	If you receive the application form,	e	rub it out.
6	If you've finished with his pen,	f	put it off.
7	If you can't remember the phone number,	g	tear it up.
8	If the meat's too big to go in the pan,	h	fill it up.
9	If you get another threatening letter,	i	fill it in.
10	If the tree's in danger of falling,	j	look it up.

▶ The **if-clause** may come first or second in a statement, as can be seen in the examples at the beginning of the section. When do you need to use a comma? Study some of the example sentences and say what the rule is.

CONDITIONAL 1

Look at these examples:

If you plan to go on a walking holiday, you will need strong shoes.
He will only get there in time if he leaves right now.

These are things which are possible and it's quite probable that they will happen.

FORM

If + Present form + Future form

Note   Future forms include the future simple, future continuous, future perfect simple and future perfect continuous. *For example:*

If he doesn't get the job, he will have done all this work for nothing.

EXERCISE 1   Change the verbs in the following sentences into the correct forms.

a   I (give) you a ring if I (need) any advice.
b   He (only/can) come if the meeting (take) place on a Friday.
c   If you (not/pass) the examination, you (take) it again?
d   She (just/must) take a taxi if she (miss) the train.
e   If you (go) to see him now, he (work).
f   We (lose) our way if we (not/keep) to the main road.
g   If the weather (be) sunny, we (bring) our umbrellas for nothing.
h   If you (not/speak) clearly, he (not can) understand.

EXERCISE 2   Write a conditional sentence for each of the following signs. *For example:*
If you buy 20 litres of petrol, you will receive a free wine glass.

A

SPECIAL OFFER
FREE WINE GLASS
with every 20 litres of petrol

LOST –
BLACK CAT
(answers to the name of 'Tibbles')
REWARD £25

B

NO PARKING
by order
FINE £50

C

ENTER
our
great photography
competition
FIRST PRIZE £1,000

D

NO ENTRY
without a
visitor's pass

E

Special Spring Dry Cleaning Offer
2 GARMENTS CLEANED FOR THE PRICE OF ONE

F

DANGER!
The contents of this
bottle are
POISONOUS

OTHER CONDITIONAL LINK WORDS

If is not the only link word used in conditional sentences.
The box shows other possible link words.

> Unless – if not
> As long as ⎤
> Provided (that) ⎦ = if and only if/ on condition that
> Suppose – Imagine

EXERCISE   Complete the following sentences:

a   I won't interrupt you .... I have an important message to give you.
b   .... you are stopped by the police, what will you do?
c   He'll let you borrow his camera .... you take good care of it.
d   The airship will make its first flight tomorrow provided ....
e   Suppose .... , will you have enough money to buy another?
f   My parents don't mind what time I come home as long as ....
g   I'll lend you the money you want provided that ....

Focus on listening 1 *The sweet, short life of products*

Listen to this talk on the lifespans of modern products. Answer questions 1–4. Then
complete the table.

1   Which product is mentioned as lasting a much shorter time in the home than it does in a
    factory? ....

2   What three changes can manufacturers make to persuade people to buy a new model?
    ....

3   Which two industries have been most successful in persuading people to keep buying new
    products? ....

4   Which item does the speaker say may soon be changed every year? ....

THE USEFUL LIFE OF PRODUCTS (IN YEARS)			
Products	Useful life of product (manufacturer's estimate)	Actual time in use in the USA	Actual time used in underdeveloped countries
Washing machines and irons	....	5	25
....	11	2.2	....
....	25	2	....
Construction equipment	....	8	100+
....	30	....	80+
Photographic equipment	35	....	50

Communication activity 1 *Pollution*

Work in pairs for this activity:

Student A: Look at the instructions below and the picture on page 87.
Student B: Look at the instructions below and the picture on page 227.

INSTRUCTIONS The picture on page 87 is the same as Student B's except that eight small changes have been made.

1 Try to find five of the differences by describing your pictures to each other. Do not let your partner see your picture!

Take it in turns to describe a section of the picture in detail. Be prepared to ask each other questions in order to be sure that what you see is exactly the same. When you discover a difference, make a note of it.

2 When you have found at least five differences, look at the two pictures together with your partner, and spot the ones you have missed.

'I can remember when all this was unspoilt countryside.'

Text 2 *Recycling*

Recycling means taking something that has already been used and treating it so that it can be used again. For example, old newspapers can be treated by removing the ink and mixing them with water under pressure so that they become pulp and can be made into paper again.

❶ Read the following information about recycling and then choose the best answer (A, B, C or D) to the questions which follow.

NOTE Compost is a mixture (usually made of vegetable matter) which gardeners use to make the soil richer.

1 The information tells us that a huge quantity of rubbish in Britain is
   A burnt.
   B recycled.
   C buried.
   D piled up.

2 The most difficult material to recycle is
   A paper.
   B glass.
   C aluminium.
   D plastic.

3 People in Oregon return more drinks containers than they used to because
   A they have been taught to be less wasteful.
   B they can't buy non-reusable bottles any more.
   C there is a law which says they have to.
   D there is a financial advantage in doing so.

4 Bottles collected from bottle banks are
   A cleaned and used again.
   B made into new bottles.
   C taken away and buried.
   D burnt to provide energy.

5 The problem with recycled paper is that sometimes
   A it is dearer than new paper.
   B it is less strong than new paper.
   C there isn't enough to satisfy demand.
   D there is too much imported from abroad.

6 The passage suggests that one thing the reader should do is to
   A mix rubbish with oil and burn it as fuel.
   B grind up rubbish and bury it in the garden.
   C find out where waste materials can be taken.
   D send all metal cans to Alcoa in Birmingham.

❷ **You may not know the exact meanings of the following four words which appear in the text. Look at the context again, and then choose the most likely meanings. The letters in brackets refer to the section of the text.**

7 *nourishes* (A)
   A supports
   B creates
   C provides

8 *fluctuates* (G)
   A rises
   B falls
   C moves up and down

9 *compressed* (H)
   A mixed together
   B bent into a shape
   C forced into less space

10 *ores* (J)
   A large factories which separate and melt metals
   B rocks from which metal can be obtained
   C mines where metals are found

PHRASAL VERB *WEAR*	**PREPOSITIONAL PHRASES**		
'Even the best products *wear out* in time.' (Listening 1)	*on* foot	*under* control	*out of* doors
wear off – pass away.　*The pain **wore off** gradually.*	*by* car/boat/bus	*out of* control	*by* oneself
wear out – become useless.　*My shoes are **worn out**.*	*in* sight	*in* reach	
	out of sight	*out of* reach	

Text 3

❶ Read the following short text about the Friends of the Earth organisation and then answer the questions which follow.

Friends of the Earth Trust is an educational charity set up to help people of all ages become aware of the threats to our environment.
5 Pollution is just one of these. The destruction of wildlife and wasting our natural resources are others.

In Britain, the countryside is disappearing or being destroyed –
10 modern farming, mining and quarrying, motorways and power stations are all adding to this destruction. By the year 2000 about half the world's animal and plant
15 species could be extinct.

Every year a forest the size of Wales is cut down to make paper for use in Britain. If more people used recycled paper, fewer trees would be
20 cut down, and there would be less waste to dispose of. Another important benefit would be the new jobs created in the collection of waste paper.
25 In Britain it is almost impossible to get away from noise. Even in remote

Friends of the Earth Trust Ltd.

26-28 Underwood St, London N1 7JQ

Telephone 0171-490 1555

by P Robey and C Frere Smith.
A registered charity, No. 2816811
Reg in London. Company No. 1533942

areas low-flying aircraft shatter the peace.

New jobs would also be created if
30 there was a large programme to save energy in buildings. It is cheaper to save energy than to produce electricity, but vast amounts of money are spent on nuclear power. From the
35 mining of uranium to the disposal of radioactive waste there are a number of threats to the environment. In addition there are close connections between nuclear power and nuclear
40 weapons. There are safer sources of energy.

Energy could also be saved if more short journeys were made by bicycle. This would reduce pollution and
45 traffic congestion. Cycleways should be built to make cycling safer.

The threats to our environment are all related. For instance building cycleways instead of unnecessary new
50 roads would save energy, reduce pollution and the destruction of our wildlife.

❷ Say whether according to the advertisement the following statements are true or false and why.

		True	False
1	The aim of Friends of the Earth is to warn about pollution.	☐	☐
2	The main danger to the British countryside is from road building.	☐	☐
3	Many types of animals are likely to have disappeared by the end of the century.	☐	☐
4	Large parts of Welsh forests are being destroyed to produce paper.	☐	☐
5	Recycling paper would increase unemployment.	☐	☐
6	More power is used in homes, shops and offices than necessary.	☐	☐
7	People should travel by bicycle instead of by car.	☐	☐
8	Special routes for cyclists are needed.	☐	☐

STUDY BOX 2   **Plural-form nouns**

A package can protect the **contents**.

The nouns below have no singular form.

Plural-form nouns which take the plural form of the verb:

clothes	contents	jeans	outskirts	shorts	surroundings
earnings	goods	pyjamas	scissors	trousers	

Plural-form nouns which take the singular form of the verb:

crossroads   maths   news   physics

Focus on grammar 2   Conditional 2

Look at this example from Text 3:

If more people used recycled paper, fewer trees would be cut down.

The **if** event here is possible but much less probable than in a conditional 1 sentence. The conditional 2 is also used for unreal events. *For example:*

If I had more time, I'd help you.

FORM

IF + Past simple or continuous + *would, could, might* + infinitive

Note

The correct form for the verb **to be** in the **if**-clause is **were** (For example: *If I were you, I'd complain*), but **was** is also possible and is often heard in conversation.

EXERCISE 1

Put the verbs in brackets into the correct form to make conditional 2 sentences.

a   Your uncle would really appreciate it if you (go) to see him.

b   If she (make) more effort to help herself, I (have) more sympathy with her.

c   Chris (not/take) a day off work unless he (be) really ill.

d   If you (know) her as well as I do, you (not/rely) on her at all!

e   We (must) reduce the price if we (want) to sell our house quickly.

f   If electric cars (not/have) such large batteries, they (be) faster to drive.

g   If you (call) the Fire Brigade, how long (it/take) them to arrive?

h   I (not/carry) your wallet around in your pocket if I (be) you!

EXERCISE 2

The picture on the right shows Martin ready for an interview for a job as a bank clerk. Although he's bought a new suit for the occasion, he's not likely to make a very good impression! Make sentences to explain what he could do to improve his chances at the interview. *For example:*

If he had his hair cut, he would/might make a better impression.

Communication activity 2 *Follow the country code*

Look at the pictures below and then do the exercise which follows.

Enjoy the countryside and respect its life and work.

Make no unnecessary noise.

❶ Match the instructions from the Country Code below to the pictures above. Do this by writing the correct letter in the box after the instruction.

Keep your dogs under control. ☐

Keep to public paths across farmland. ☐

Help to keep all water clean. ☐

Guard against all risk of fire. ☐

Take your litter home. ☐

Take special care on country roads. ☐

Fasten all gates. ☐

Protect wildlife, plants and trees. ☐

Leave livestock, crops and machinery alone. ☐

Use gates and stiles to cross fences, hedges and walls. ☐

❷ When you have finished, compare your answers with another student's and discuss any differences.

❸ Now say what **would**, **could**, **might** happen if you didn't follow these rules.
For example: *If you didn't keep your dog under control, it might frighten cattle.*
Write five similar sentences.

Focus on writing *Discussion*   WRITING BANK: PAGE 120

An international magazine is investigating the questions: *How does pollution affect our lives? What can be done about it?* Write a short **article** for the magazine. (**120–180** words)

PREPARATION **❶**   **Work with one or two other students.**

1   Look again at the picture on page 87 and make lists of the different examples of pollution that are shown under the headings: noise pollution; air pollution; litter.

2   Add any more examples you can think of to the groups on your list.

3   Compare your results with other students' and add any examples you hadn't thought of.

❷   1   Make notes about the **causes** – who or what is responsible for the different kinds of pollution on your list.

2   Practise talking about the causes you have written down using expressions from the table below.

Cause/result links

| Smoke from factory chimneys is | *due to*
caused by
the result of | modern industrial processes. |

| There is more rubbish these days | *as a result of*
because of | the amount of packaging used. |

The reason for the increase in rubbish is …

---

❸   1   Discuss with your partner(s) what effects pollution has on our daily lives and which types of pollution are the most serious. Use expressions from the table below.

Addition links

| Rubbish in the streets is | *not only*
both | unpleasant to look at | *but also*
and | unhygienic. |

| *Besides,*
What is more,
Furthermore, | it can be dangerous if it contains sharp metal or broken glass. |

---

2   Discuss how pollution could be reduced. *For example:*

a   A law could be introduced to make smoking illegal.

b   If bottles were reusable, there would be less rubbish.

3   Discuss what difficulties there might be, using expressions from the table below:

Concession links

Although lead-free petrol would be dearer, it would be less harmful.

Lead-free petrol would be dearer, *but* it would be less harmful.

| Lead-free petrol would be dearer. | *However,*
In spite of this,
Despite this, | it would be less harmful. |

PLAN   Headline:
Use 'Who cares about pollution?' or think of a better headline!

First paragraph:
Introduce the subject in an interesting way. *For example:*
– with a personal experience
– by asking the reader a question
– by commenting on the increase in pollution in recent years

Middle paragraphs:
Describe the main types of pollution – their causes and effects. Suggest ways of reducing this pollution.

Final paragraph:
Emphasise the importance of fighting pollution and finish with an overall comment or concluding remark.

Before you begin writing look at the notes on Articles and Discussions on pages 124 and 120 of the Writing Bank.

Focus on listening 2

You are going to hear a conversation in an information office. As you listen, answer the questions below.

❶ The first national parks in England were established in
A 1920
B 1949
C 1951
D 1957

❷ To answer questions 1–8 below, use the letters in red from five of the national parks on the map. The first one is done for you.
1 Which national park is suitable for rock climbing? ..*LD*..
2 Which has the highest mountain in England and Wales? ....
3 Which is divided into two sections? ....
4 Which has most people living in it? ....
5 Which receives most visitors each year? ....
6 Which has interesting Roman remains? ....
7 In which national park could you visit several castles? ....
8 Which is the most remote from towns and cities? ....

National Parks in England and Wales

NORTHUMBERLAND
LAKE DISTRICT
LD
NORTH YORK MOORS
YORKSHIRE DALES
PEAK DISTRICT
P D
S
SNOWDONIA
PEMBROKESHIRE COAST
BRECON BEACONS
PC
EXMOOR
DARTMOOR

❸ In this part, you must match the signs to the name of the correct national park.

Seven signs will be described. Write the number of the national park under the sign. Write X by those which are not described.

1 Brecon Beacons
2 Dartmoor
3 Exmoor
4 Lake District
5 Northumberland
6 Peak District
7 Yorkshire Dales

A ....

B ....

C ....

D ....

E ....

F ....

G ....

H ....

I ....

J ....

STUDY BOX 3 **Phrasal verb set**

'How were the national parks **set up**?' (Listening 2)

set down – write down on paper.	Could you **set down** your reasons in writing?
set in – start and seem likely to continue.	The rain's **set in** for the day, I'm afraid.
set off/out – begin a journey.	Don't **set off** without me!
set off – start.	This has **set off** a chain reaction.
set off – cause an explosion.	Don't **set** the fireworks **off** too near the house.
set out – begin a course of action.	He **set out** to beat the world record.
set up – establish.	The society was **set up** in 1906.

Focus on grammar 3 Modal verbs 3: permission

1 TALKING ABOUT PERMISSION: *CAN, MAY, COULD*

Can and **may** are both used to talk about what is and isn't permitted in the present.

Only **can** is used in questions. **Could** is used to express past permission. *For example:*
He said I could *borrow his car for the day.*

EXERCISE 1 Complete the following examples by referring to the Countryside Access Charter below.

a You may walk freely on .... but you may not ride a horse or bicycle on them.

b You can .... along a right of way but you can't ....

c Can you .... on commons? (Yes, you can sometimes.)

d Originally commons were areas of wild, uncultivated land where country people ....
take their animals to feed.

Now, with a partner, ask and answer four more questions about what you are allowed to do in the countryside.

YOUR RIGHTS OF WAY ARE
- Public footpaths – on foot only. *Sometimes waymarked in yellow*
- Bridleways – on foot, horseback and pedal cycle. *Sometimes waymarked in blue*
- Byways (usually old roads), most 'Roads Used as Public Paths' and, of course, public roads – all traffic. *Use maps, signs and waymarks. Ordnance Survey Pathfinder and Landranger maps show most public rights of way.*

ON RIGHTS OF WAY YOU CAN
- Take a pram, pushchair or wheelchair if practicable
- Take a dog (on a lead or under close control)
- Take a short route round an illegal obstruction or remove it sufficiently to get past.

YOU HAVE A RIGHT TO GO FOR RECREATION TO
- Public parks and open spaces – on foot
- Most commons near older towns and cities – on foot and sometimes on horseback
- Private land where the owner has a formal agreement with the local authority.

IN ADDITION you can *use* by local or established *custom or consent*, but ask for advice if you're unsure:
- Many areas of open country like moorland, fell and coastal areas, especially those of the National Trust, and some commons
- Some woods and forests, especially those owned by the Forestry Commission
- Country Parks and picnic sites
- Most beaches
- Canal towpaths
- Some private paths and tracks.

Consent sometimes extends to riding horses and pedal cycles.

2 ASKING FOR AND GIVING PERMISSION

Informal	Can I May I Could I Might I	(possibly) ...
Extremely formal	I wonder if I could I wonder if I might	

Yes, (of course) you can/may.

No, (I'm afraid) you can't/may not.

Can is the least formal. **May** and **could** are more formal and **might** is extremely formal.

The addition of **possibly** or the use of the form **I wonder if I ...** make the request more polite.

Only **can** and **may** are used in replies. Some replies may use neither. *For example:*

Can I ask a question?   Yes, of course. Go ahead.

Could I go early today? No, I'm afraid not. There's a lot of work to do.

EXERCISE 1   What would you say in the following situations? Choose suitable forms to ask for permission and give suitable replies – with reasons where appropriate! See Functions Bank, page 107.

a   You need to borrow your friend's ruler. (Answer: **No, because …**)

b   You want to speak to your boss. You open the door … (**Yes**)

c   Your car has broken down and you'd like to telephone the garage. You're outside a very grand house. (**Yes**)

d   You're trying to find your way to the station and you see a man looking at a map … (**Yes**)

e   There's a short cut from your camp site to the river across a field. You are just going to take it when you see the farmer ! (**No!...**)

f   Your friend has a fantastic new sports car. You'd love to drive it. (**No...**)

g   Some colleagues of yours are having an important meeting. You need to interrupt in order to give one of them a message. (**Yes**)

h   You urgently need to borrow £100 (but only for 2 days). Ask a friend. (**No...**)

SEE COMMUNICATION ACTIVITY 1, PAGE 77

Language review

Choose the word or phrase (A, B, C or D) which best completes each sentence.

1 If you can't keep your dog .... control, you shouldn't bring him to the park.
   A on   **B** under   **C** in   **D** with

2 Leave that machine .... ! You might get hurt if you touch it.
   A apart   **B** along   **C** aside   **D** alone

3 As long as we .... to the footpath, we won't get lost.
   A keep   **B** stay   **C** follow   **D** remain

4 He's been trying to persuade his father .... him a bicycle.
   A buy   **B** buying   **C** to buy   **D** for buying

5 My old riding boots served me well for eleven years before they finally ....
   A wore off   **B** wore out   **C** broke down   **D** broke up

6 How much water does that tank .... ?
   A include   **B** keep   **C** consist   **D** contain

7 It was my grandfather who first .... the company in 1926.
   A set down   **B** set off   **C** set up   **D** set out

8 The island has many natural .... , including oil and copper.
   A resources   **B** sources   **C** fuels   **D** materials

9 This information pack is designed to make children more .... of the things they can see in the countryside.
   A interested   **B** aware   **C** curious   **D** awake

10 I think you're .... your energy by sweeping up those leaves. The wind will only blow more down.
   A spending   **B** spoiling   **C** losing   **D** wasting

11 She made a delicious pudding consisting .... apricots and cream.
   A from   **B** with   **C** of   **D** in

12 '............. you ride a horse along a public footpath?' 'No, it's forbidden.'
   A May   **B** Can   **C** Might   **D** Must

13 I don't know what I can have spent all my money .... !
   A on   **B** for   **C** at   **D** in

14 It's a great shame all those old oak trees are going to be ....
   A cut up   **B** cut off   **C** cut down   **D** cut out

15 Unfortunately, he is .... as a rather lazy man.
   A thought   **B** supposed   **C** believed   **D** regarded

Lead-in

❶ The photographs below show a number of inventions designed by amateur inventors. Describe what you can see in the pictures and try to guess what each invention is.

❷ Look quickly at sections A–E in the text on page 91 to match the pictures to the inventions. Did you guess any correctly?

Text 1 *What's the big idea?*

❶ **Read the first part of the text and answer these questions.**

1 Why did Zillah Loewe stop on the country road?
   A She had a problem with her car.
   B She saw someone signalling her to stop.
   C She realised that there had been an accident.
   D She needed to ask for directions.

2 What results has Ms Loewe had with her invention?
   A It has been an expensive failure.
   B It has made her ill with worry.
   C It's too early to say if it will be popular.
   D It has been a commercial success.

Zillah Loewe, a restaurant manager from Cambridge, was driving home alone from work one night along a winding country lane, when she came across some figures in the road waving her to a halt. 'I was rather frightened. After all, I was a lone woman in the middle of nowhere and I suddenly wished I had a companion with me.'

The hold-up turned out to have been only a minor accident but by the time she got safely home, Ms Loewe had conceived an idea – the inflatable passenger. This week, if all goes to plan, she will give birth to Auto-mate, her handy, go-anywhere fellow traveller. He has been five years in the making, has cost her around £8,000 in development and patent fees and, like most babies, has driven her almost out of her mind with frustration on occasion.

Auto-mate is due to make his public debut at the first Great British Innovations and Inventions Fair in Birmingham this week, when he will be among more than 200 great ideas likely to make the rest of us ask: 'Why didn't we think of that?'

❷ **Now read about the five inventions in the second part of the text. For questions 1–12, choose from the inventions A–E and write the correct letter in the box. (You will need to use some information from the first part of the text for question 5.)**

Which inventor(s)

has developed several other inventions? `1` `  `

has been less successful than they had hoped? `2` `  `

invented equipment for an enthusiasm of theirs? `3` `  `

developed their invention after a warning? `4` `  `

had their idea after a frightening experience? `5` `  ` `6` `  `

Which invention(s)

can be used in various different ways? `7` `  `

has cost the most money to develop? `8` `  `

has been well received by different customers? `9` `  `

has a very large number of potential users? `10` `  `

have been shown to the public already? `11` `  ` `12` `  `

SUPERGROOM ALL-IN-ONE DOG AND HORSE GROOMING BRUSH   A

• **Inventor:** *Jim Griffiths, 50, who runs a soft furnishings shop in Wales.*

Necessity was the mother of invention when Mr Griffiths was warned against shampooing his dog, Nell, in a local river by anti-pollution officers. He went home and designed a grooming brush with built-in shampoo dispenser which would fit on to a garden hose or shower pipe. Perfecting the design has taken two years and cost £25,000 – raised mostly from remortgaging his home. 'I have never invented anything else in my life before. But I know this will work. All I need is a proper marketing strategy,' he says.

MULTI-PURPOSE SHELTER AND SURVIVAL BAG   B

• **Inventor:** *William Courtney, 48, a science teacher from Cheshire.*

'I got the idea a few years ago when I was stuck on a Swiss mountain for 18 hours after an avalanche. I spent the time reviewing my climbing equipment and dreaming about improving it.' Through an ingenious arrangement of webbing handles and openings the SAS bag can be used as an emergency tent, a weatherproof walking coat, a snow-hole cover, stretcher, hammock, water carrier, and survival bag. William has been inventing products for four years, and has spent a total of about £6,000, mostly on patent applications.

AUTO-MATE CAR PASSENGER   C

• **Inventor:** *Zillah Loewe, 31, a restaurant manager from Cambridge.*

'It's a dummy which inflates and deflates in seconds via a compressor powered through a car's cigarette lighter. It is a serious attempt to give people travelling in cars alone – especially women – the reassurance of having a passenger. Auto-mate looks realistic enough to deceive other motorists, even in daylight. When you pull into a petrol station or get into a city centre you just have to press the button and he disappears. There are 25 million motorists in the UK. It has to work.' Cost so far: £8,000.

COSY ROLL DRAUGHT EXCLUDER   D

• **Inventor:** *Deirdre Carney ,50, a farmer's wife from Oxfordshire.*

'It is a dead simple idea: just two 'sausages' which sit either side of the door linked together by a piece of webbing. When you open the door the Cosy Roll moves with it. But it is difficult to get established. I have had lots of disappointments and I am still not in profit.' An unsuccessful promotion in a national magazine left her with 10,000 metres of unused fireproofed cotton material. 'What keeps me going is the encouragement from satisfied customers.'

THE IT'S-A-GOAL   E

• **Inventor:** *John Wilson, 44, engineer and designer from Sheffield.*

'I am a keen footballer and I knew there was a market for a portable football pitch which would fit inside a single bag and include everything from goal posts to corner flags. After two years' hard work we are just coming out of the research and development stage. The potential is immense, but the costs are tremendous: I have remortgaged my house and borrowed over £160,000. It's been adapted by the FA for mini-football and was demonstrated yesterday at the Wembley Cup Final.'

❸ Find the word or phrase which means the same as:

Main text			
	1	met unexpectedly (Para 1)	....
	2	nearly made her mad (Para 2)	....
	3	first public appearance (Para 3)	....
A	4	a detailed plan for advertising and selling something	....
B	5	very cleverly designed	....
C	6	a model that looks like a human being	....
D	7	a current of cold air in a room	....
	8	extremely (informal)	....
E	9	possible to carry	....

DISCUSSION POINTS

❹ 1 Which of the inventions do you think is – the cleverest?
 – the most useful?
 – the most likely to be successful?

2 Which of the inventions could you imagine using yourself?

3 Have you ever had any ideas for new inventions?

Focus on grammar 1   Talking about the future 1

Look at the examples below and underline the verb forms used to talk about the future:

a   We're having a party next Saturday. Can you come?

b   Be careful! I think that car is going to pull out in front of you.

c   What time does our flight leave?

1   The **present continuous** (a) and the **going to future** (b) are both used to talk about future actions or events which have already been planned.

Very often either form can be used. The **going to** future, however, tends to suggest a more personal intention and can also express determination. *For example:*

I know you don't want me to come but I'm going to, all the same.

Note   The **going to** future is not usually used with the verb **to go**.

EXERCISE 1   Fill the spaces in the following sentences with a suitable verb in the **present continuous** or with **going to**.

a   Which dress .... for the party tonight?

b   I'm afraid I can't give you a lift tomorrow because I .... my car repaired.

c   I feel nervous already and I .... my driving test till tomorrow!

d   We .... dinner at 8 o'clock. Is that all right?

e   .... anything special tonight, or would you like to call round and see us?

f   Why .... to work tomorrow? Is it a holiday?

g   A friend of mine .... the guitar in a concert tonight.

h   When .... your homework? It's almost 9 o'clock already!

2   The **going to** future is also used to talk about things which we feel sure are going to happen, because of the evidence that we can see, hear, feel or sense. *For example:*

Look at the sky! I'm afraid it's going to rain at any minute.

If she continues working like this, I'm afraid she's going to be ill.

EXERCISE 2   Complete the following sentences, using the **going to** future.

a   Listen to that thunder ! It sounds as if there ....

b   You'd better buy another suitcase. The handle on that one .... before long.

c   That dog doesn't sound very friendly. I hope it ....

d   Cars come round this bend much too fast. One of these days there ....

e   Look at the petrol gauge. I think we .... petrol any minute.

f   Have you got a paper handkerchief? I think I ....

g   No goals and only five minutes of the match left. I'm afraid the result ....

h   The government is refusing to give the teachers any more money. I hope there ....

3   The **present simple** is used to talk about future events or actions which are part of a fixed programme or timetable.

What examples of such a programme can you think of? *For example:*

The train gets in at 7.30 tomorrow evening.

EXERCISE 3   Work with a partner. Imagine that you are going on holiday together, and you have received the following details about the programme. Take it in turns to ask and answer questions. *For example:*

A *What time do we leave London?*   **B** *We leave at 8.30 in the morning.*

a   How .... Dover?
b   Which French port .... ?
c   What time .... Paris?
d   What .... the first evening?
e   What .... Monday?
f   Where .... Tuesday?

g   What .... the afternoon?
h   When .... Epernay?
i   What else .... there?
j   What time .... London?
k   Where .... during the trip?
l   Are there any extras that .... ?

---

5 Day Luxury Coach Tour of France

SUNDAY
8.30 a.m. *Departure from Victoria Coach Station for Dover. Travel by midday ferry to Calais, and then by train to Paris (arrival late afternoon). Evening free.*

MONDAY
a.m. *Sightseeing tour of Paris.*
p.m. *Boat trip up the River Seine.*

TUESDAY
a.m. *Departure for Orléans, a large city on the River Loire.*
p.m. *Visit to cathedral and famous rose gardens.*

WEDNESDAY
a.m. *Early start for the drive to Epernay, in the heart of the champagne country.*
Evening tour of the cellars.

THURSDAY:
Return drive to Calais, stopping off at Rheims to look at the magnificent cathedral. Stop for lunch en route.
Arrival in London: 21.00 hours.

Accommodation throughout this tour is in comfortable 2 and 3 star hotels. Our luxury coach has reclining seats, WC, refrigerator and tea and coffee making facilities.
Price does not include: Lunches, entry fees to rose garden.

Focus on listening 1 *Word processor mishaps*

❶   Fill in the missing words in the short text below. Then answer the questions which follow.

Word Processing

A word processor is a computer designed to make .... quick and easy to produce a perfect text. It .... a little time to learn to use a word processor but here are the main steps: first you .... the **keyboard** to type in the words, and these appear .... a screen (or '**monitor**'). .... you can **edit** your text, to get rid .... mistakes and make changes. With an ordinary typewriter this .... probably mean a lot of re-typing, ... with a word processor you can do it electronically, before printing. .... example, a word or phrase can .... removed, and the word processor will automatically close up the space left. Finally, when you are satisfied .... your work, you print out the finished text using a separate **printer**. You can also store your text on a **disk** .... future use.

1   What is the advantage of using a word processor rather than a typewriter?
2   How is the equipment for word processing different from a typewriter?

❷ You are going to hear four people describing things that went wrong while they were using word processors. Answer questions 1–5 below.

	A	B	C	D
1 **Profession**	*Cookery writer*			
2 **Make of machine**	*X*	*Astra*		*X*
3 **What was lost**			*2 Chapters*	*Script for a documentary*

4 **The cause.** Tick (✓) the correct box.

	A	B	C	D
A fault of the machine				
The speaker's mistake				
Someone else's mistake				
Another reason (say what it is)				

5 Which speaker stopped using a word processor as a result of this experience? Write the correct letter …

Focus on writing 1 *Instructions*

The picture below shows you how to unpack part of a home computer and assemble the equipment correctly.

The equipment consists of a **monitor** (the part with the screen), a **systems box** (the computer and disk drives) and a **keyboard** (which has keys like a typewriter). When the equipment is assembled, the monitor can be moved to the left or right, it can turn, and it can tilt forwards (picture 8) so that the user can choose a suitable position.

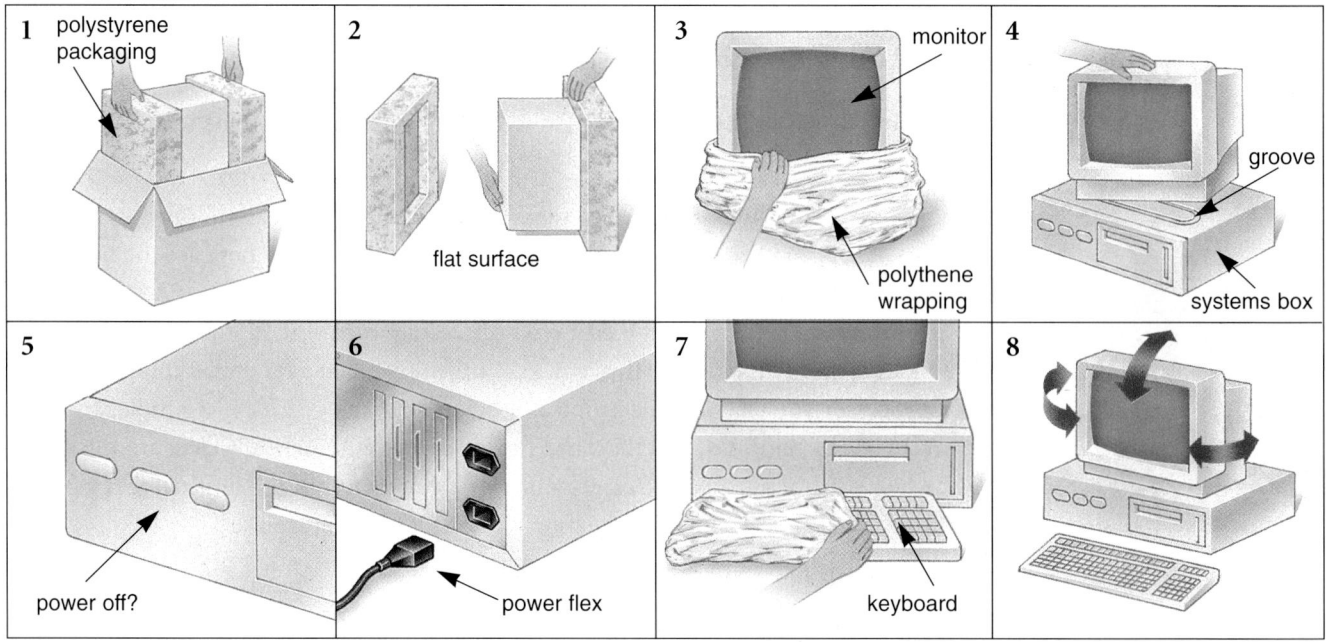

1 polystyrene packaging
2 flat surface
3 monitor / polythene wrapping
4 groove / systems box
5 power off?
6 power flex
7 keyboard
8

Write a paragraph of instructions to replace the pictures. (Remember that the equipment is expensive, so care is needed!) Begin:

Congratulations! You are the owner of a new Tangerine. Your computer has been carefully packed to protect it during delivery. Please follow the instructions below for unpacking and assembling your computer …

Useful language
1 **First**
2 **Next, After That**
▲ **When**
  Once } you have (done that)
▼
5 **Before** | (doing)
          | you (do)
6 **Finally**

remove	plug in
take off	connect
switch on	place
switch off	adjust

Focus on grammar 2   Sudden decisions, offers, suggestions, threats

Look at this example:
  Have we run out of coffee? I'll go *out and buy some.*

The future simple is used here to express a sudden decision (taken at the moment of speaking), and is often an offer to do something.

Remember how the **going to** future is used and note the difference between the following sentences:
a *There's no need to walk.* John's going to give *us a lift.*
b *There's no need to walk.* I'll give *you a lift.*

a This is a plan I have already made, and probably arranged.
b This is a decision I have just made.

The future simple is also used to express:
1 Offers   *Shall I post that letter for you?/I'll pay, if you like, etc.*
2 Suggestions   *Shall we go to Scotland this summer?*
3 Promises   *(I promise) I'll never do it again.*
4 Threats   *Don't tell that joke again or I'll scream!*

EXERCISE 1   Complete the following sentences with a suitable verb in the future simple. In each case say whether it is a sudden decision, an offer, a suggestion, a promise or a threat.
a It's very hot in here, isn't it? … ?
b Doesn't anybody know what this word means? I know, I …
c For the last time, turn that TV down! If you don't, … !
d The dog's looking very thirsty. … ?
e Oh, I've spilt coffee on your jacket! Don't worry, I …
f I think there's someone knocking at the door. … ?
g The children have made a terrible mess in your living room. Never mind, I …
h I'm sure I can see smoke coming from the window of the house opposite. … ?
i £5 for a 5-minute taxi ride! If you don't tell me the correct fare, I … !
j Are you going to drive back tonight, or … hotel for you?

STUDY BOX 1	Phrasal verb *let*

'When your computer *lets* you *down*, it can be just as bad as a broken love affair.' (Listening 1)

let down – lower.	*He escaped by **letting down** a rope ladder from the window.*
let down – disappoint.	*See example above.*
let in – allow to enter.	*They won't **let** you **in** without a ticket.*
let off – allow to explode.	*Don't **let** any fireworks **off** too near the house.*
let off – excuse from punishment.	*The judge **let** him **off** with a warning.*
let out – release.	*Be careful not to **let** the cat **out** when you leave.*

Focus on listening 2 *Life in the future*

You are going to hear the views of two groups of people on what life will be like in the future.

❶ As you listen the first time, put a tick (✓) in the boxes below to show the subjects that each group mentions.

	First group	Second group		First group	Second group
space travel			test tube babies		
robots			unemployment		
computers			future places for people to live		
nuclear weapons			future forms of energy		
overpopulation			future forms of communication		

❷ As you listen the second time, look at questions 1–4 and choose the correct answer: (A, B, C or D).

1   The people interviewed were probably
   A   children at primary school.
   B   pupils at secondary school.
   C   students at university.
   D   workers of mixed ages.

2   The first speaker thinks that by the year 2000
   A   robots may have disappeared.
   B   computers may be in control of the world.
   C   civilisation may have been destroyed.
   D   people will be living on the moon.

3   The first speaker in the second group is fairly hopeful about the future because she thinks
   A   computers will prevent nuclear weapons from being fired.
   B   nuclear weapons could never be fired by accident.
   C   nobody would want to start a nuclear war.
   D   nuclear weapons will disappear from the world.

4   The presenter of the programme is surprised at the end because the two groups
   A   had such strange ideas.
   B   knew so much about technology.
   C   had such different opinions.
   D   mentioned such similar subjects.

Focus on grammar 3   Talking about the future 2

I   Look at these examples from Focus on listening 2 and underline the verb forms used to talk about the future.

  a   In the year 2000, I think I'll probably be in a spaceship …
  b   I may be in charge of a robot court.
  c   There just won't be enough jobs to go around.
  d   Perhaps we'll be able to convert brain waves into radio waves.

We use the **future simple** to express:

1	future fact:	*She will be nine years old tomorrow.*
2	prediction:	*That man will be a millionaire one of these days.*
3	opinion about the future:	*I expect we'll be tired after the journey.*
	(especially after verbs like *think,*	*I suppose you'll have to change trains.*
	expect, suppose, and *doubt if,*	*I doubt if he'll have time to speak to you.*
	and also after *probably* and *perhaps.*	

FORM

> will   + infinitive (without 'to')
> won't

Note   The future of **can** is **will be able to** and the future of **must** is **will have to**. If we are less sure about an event in the future, we can use **may, might** or **could**. *For example:*

> *It could rain. If it does we'll hold the party indoors.*

EXERCISE 1   Work with a partner to talk about the future. Take it in turns to ask each other's opinion about the developments below. Give answers too! *For example:*

A: *Do you think there will be giant televisions in every home by the year 2020?*
B: *Yes, I think there will/could/may/might (be) and I hope so because …/but I hope not because …*
or *No, I don't think there will (be)/could be because …*

  a   Video telephones (where you see as well as hear each other)
  b   Robots that think
  c   Personal flying machines
  d   Day trips to the moon
  e   People living on other planets
  f   One world language

EXERCISE 2   Now make predictions of your own about the subjects below. *For example:*

  Education: *(As far as education is concerned,) I think computers will replace teachers in the future. There probably won't be any schools by 2020.*

  a   Transport
  b   Entertainment
  c   The Third World
  d   Nuclear power
  e   Working hours
  f   The weather
  g   Population

2   Look at this further example from Focus on listening 2:

The population will have gone up so much that everyone will be living in big plastic domes ...

We use the **future continuous** to express:

1 an action which will be going on at a future time. *For example:*
   At this time tomorrow, our plane will just be taking off.

2 an action in the future when the process is a continuous one. *For example:*
   The buffet will be closing in about five minutes.
   We'll be moving to London in a few months.

Note   The **future continuous** is also used to ask a polite question about a person's plans. *For example:*
When will you be checking out, sir?
Will you be going to the party tonight?

FORM

will be / won't be	+ verb + -*ing*

EXERCISE 3   Work with a partner to try and arrange a meeting.
Imagine that you each have one of the diaries shown. *For example:*

A: *When shall I call round? How about Monday morning?*
    What if I drop in on ...

B: *No, don't call round then because I'll be ...*
    No, Monday morning's no good because ...

> **Useful Language**
> call in
> call around
> come around
> pop in
> drop by
> drop in

A

	MORNING	AFTERNOON	EVENING
SUN			Homework
MON			Opera on radio
TUES		Preparation for dinner party	Dinner party
WED	Spring clean kitchen	Plumber (to install washing machine)	

B

	MORNING	AFTERNOON	EVENING
SUN	Guitar lesson	Wallpaper sitting room	
MON	Repair roof	Lunch with mother	
TUES	Accountant		
WED			Football on TV

3   The **future perfect** is used to express:

1 an action or event which will be complete by a future point of time. *For example:*
   The population will have gone up so much that everyone will be living in big plastic domes ...
   The course will have finished by 22nd July.

2   the length of time that an action or an event will have lasted, at a future point of time
(also future perfect continuous). *For example:*

*I'll have lived **here for six years by next autumn.** (or been living)*
*He'll have been working **here for a year by 1st September.***

FORM

will have	+	Past participle (done)
won't have		been + verb +-ing (been doing)

EXERCISE 4   Work in pairs. Using the information given, take it in turns to ask questions and give answers.
For example:

FILM TONIGHT   Starts at 7.30 pm

A   *Let's meet outside the cinema at 7.45.*
B   *It's no use meeting then because the film will have (already) started.*

a   **SALE**   Monday–Friday

A   Shall we look for a carpet in the sale on Saturday?

b   **Bank Opening Hours**   9.30–3.30

A   I'll call at the bank when I finish work at 4 o'clock.

c   **Last Train:** 10.30 pm

A   We can leave the party about midnight, can't we?

d   **ARRIVALS** from London: 12.30 pm

A   I'll be at the station to meet you at midday. (Careful!)

e   **Cambridge First Certificate**   Papers 1–3: 17th June

A   I'll phone you on 15th June to see how you got on in your exam.

Useful Language
It's no use … -ing
It's no good … -ing
There's no point in … -ing

EXERCISE 5
REVIEW

Change the verbs in brackets into the correct form of the present continuous, **going to**
future, future simple, future continuous or future perfect. Make any other changes necessary.

a   Give me a ring on Thursday. I (hear) the results by then.
b   This wind is so strong that it (probably/cause) some damage before long.
c   I can't believe it! This time next week I (swim) in the Indian Ocean.
d   Don't try to move that table all by yourself. Wait and I (give) you a hand.
e   On 1st March we (be) married for a whole year!
f   What do you think (happen) to their dog if they go abroad?
g   Don't phone them now. It's only 7 o'clock in New York and they (just/get) up.
h   I'm sorry to hear that you've lost your job. What (you/do) now?
i   The builders (finish) work on the house by the weekend?
j   I doubt if you (get) home before midnight.

Communication activity 1 *Role play*

Work in pairs. Student A should look at the notes below. Student B should turn to page 104.

ROLE A   You are a salesman/saleswoman for a small office equipment company. Your sales this month have been very good and you are sure that your boss will be pleased with you. You want him/her to agree to install a car phone in your company car. You think it would be useful and that it would also help the company's (and your!) image.

Your boss tends to be very cautious about new ideas but you've arranged to see him/her and you're hoping to produce a convincing argument.

Remember to introduce the subject gently – don't mention the car phone too soon! Let your boss start the conversation.

Text 2

❶ Discuss these questions with another student:
1 Can you name the parts of these watches?
2 Is there anything special about the watch you're wearing (maybe the person who bought it, or when it was bought)? If so, tell your partner.
3 What style of watch do you prefer? What features do you find useful?

analogue watch

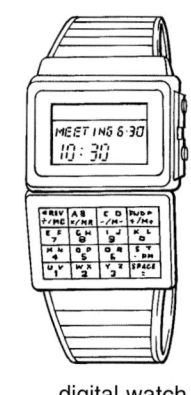

digital watch

❷ You are going to read some information about watches. For questions 1–8 choose from the watches A–G. Some of the watches may be chosen more than once. There is an example at the beginning (0).

Which watch or watches would be useful for someone who:

wants to know when someone is trying to contact them?	0	F
needs to make calculations?	1	
enjoys deep-sea diving?	2	
wants to keep a check on their health?	3	
needs to remember both phone numbers and appointments?	4	5
doesn't want to take too much exercise?	6	
may need to know the time in another country?	7	
sometimes needs to use their watch to dial telephone numbers?	8	

❸ For question 9 choose the answer (A, B, C or D) which you think fits best according to the text.
9 The purpose of this text is to
   A describe some new developments in watches.
   B warn the reader about cheap, unreliable watches.
   C explain how watches work.
   D advise the reader about the best watch to buy.

Super-watches

Telling the time is the very least the latest generation of watches can do. From monitoring your health and the weather to making phone calls, it's all in a day's work for the super-watch.

An office on your wrist

Wristwatch personal organisers like these will tell you the time on the other side of the world, remind you to make a call at a certain hour, find you the number and do a few calculations, all at the flick of a switch – or a touch of the screen. They can store up to 100 telephone numbers. The touch-screen Casio VDB is even programmed to give the day of the week until the year 2089.

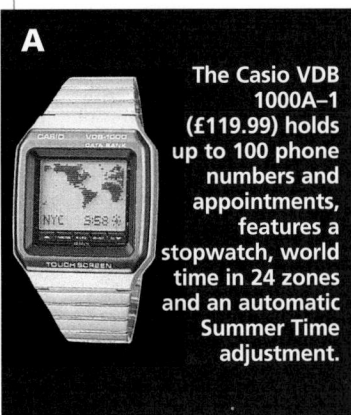

A

The Casio VDB 1000A–1 (£119.99) holds up to 100 phone numbers and appointments, features a stopwatch, world time in 24 zones and an automatic Summer Time adjustment.

B

The DBC-62 (£39.99) has a keypad for entering messages, phone numbers, appointments, or for using as a calculator.

The super-watch as an aid to fitness and health

The watchmakers are also competing to develop watches with new functions for the health and fitness markets. As a result, you can now strap on a 'personal fitness data manager' before exercising – and afterwards check you didn't overdo it.

C

The Casio AW60 (£59.99) calculates the number of calories burned while performing a specific exercise, and an alarm sounds when the target is reached so that you can stop the activity before it damages you. Simply enter details, such as age, sex and build, along with the activity you're performing.

D

Along with traditional timekeeping functions, Casio's BP-100 (£113.99) measures your pulse rate and blood pressure. Just place the first and second fingers of the right hand onto the sensors and results are displayed in graphical form at the top of the screen.

In place of a pager

Some watches with personal communications functions can dial telephone numbers. Others act as pagers by making a noise when someone wants to telephone you.

E Casio's DBA-800A Phone-Dialler (£45.99) automatically dials telephone numbers when your phone is on the hook and can store up to 50 numbers.

F

The Swatch Peipser is a pager that can recognise four preset numbers and make a distinct audible tone for each (so far unavailable in UK).

Deep and still meaningful

G

The Rolex Sea-Dweller 4000 (£1,945) can be used underwater at depths of up to 1,219 metres. The steel casing has a tiny valve allowing air to escape and so preventing explosive decompression during ascent.

Communication activity 2 *Describe and draw*

Work in pairs for this activity. You will each describe a picture of a house (one contemporary, one futuristic) so that your partner can draw it.

Before you start, look at the Functions Bank on page 109 (Describing Location and Describing Objects). Study the language briefly and then mark the place in your book for future reference.

INSTRUCTIONS

1 Turn your chairs so that you are facing each other. (You must not be able to see each other's drawings!)
2 Remember to describe your picture clearly, and in a way which is easy for your partner to follow. Begin with the size (how many floors, etc.), shape and other general details.
3 The person who is drawing should ask questions to check if anything is unclear.
   For example: *How big is the window (in relation to the door)?*
                  Is the door in the middle? etc.

Student A should now turn to page 104 and look at the house. Start describing it as soon as you are ready.

Student B should take a clean sheet of paper and be ready to draw what A describes. When you have finished, compare the two drawings and note any differences. Discuss how the description could have been improved.

After that, **Student B** should turn to page 229 and begin describing the house on that page.

Focus on writing 2 *Description/discussion*

An English-language magazine wants to find out what its readers think life will be like in the year 2050. The magazine has invited readers to send in their ideas in the form of a short composition. Write your **description/discussion** in **120–180** words.

PLAN

First paragraph / introduction:
Here you can make general comments about likely developments, based on what is happening now. For example: advances in technology, population growth, etc.

Middle paragraphs:
Choose 3–5 topics that you would find interesting to discuss in detail, and deal with them in separate paragraphs. For example:
   transport (public, private)
   communications (telephone, TV, satellite, computers, etc.)
   employment (working hours, skills needed, retirement age, etc.)
   domestic life (family size, house design, entertainment, equipment, etc.)
   .... (Add your own ideas)

Final paragraph / conclusion:
Finish off with a general comment on the developments you've described. You might express your own feelings about them (excitement, anxiety, etc.) or you could mention dangers you foresee, or you could explain why you feel your predictions may not be correct at all!

STUDY BOX 2   Phrasal verb *cut*

'The cleaning lady took out the plug. This **cut off** the electricity.' (Listening 2)

cut across – take a short cut.	*We'll* **cut across** *the park to save time.*
cut down – bring down by cutting.	*Several trees had to be* **cut down**.
cut down (on) – reduce.	*You ought to* **cut down (on)** *your smoking.*
cut in – push in suddenly.	*That red car* **cut in** *so suddenly in front of me that there was nearly an accident.*
cut off – stop flow.	See example above.
cut up – divide into small pieces.	*They* **cut** *the old sheet* **up** *to make cleaning rags.*

Language review

Choose the word or phrase which best completes each sentence.

1   I'm relying on you and I hope you won't let me ....
    A off   **B** out   **C** in   **D** down

2   Don't forget that .... to our new office by the time you get back from holiday.
    A I'm moving   **B** I'll move   **C** I'll have moved   **D** I'll be moving

3   I think something's gone wrong .... the television. I can't get a picture at all.
    A to   **B** with   **C** about   **D** on

4   You can do whatever you like as .... as I'm concerned.
    A much   **B** long   **C** well   **D** far

5   If you don't pay your bill, they'll .... your electricity.
    A cut off   **B** cut down   **C** cut in   **D** cut out

6   Oh dear, I don't feel well. I think ....
    A I'll faint   **B** I'm fainting   **C** I'm going to faint   **D** I've fainted

7   It's hard to find a .... that's narrow enough to fit my watch.
    A band   **B** belt   **C** strap   **D** cord

8   I was driving .... a country lane when I saw some rabbits in a field.
    A by   **B** through   **C** over   **D** along

9   Do .... by if you're ever in the neighbourhood.
    A drop   **B** pop   **C** look   **D** stay

10 You can have your money back if you're not satisfied .... our work.
    A of   **B** with   **C** at   **D** from

11 The reason it won't work is that no one has .... it in.
    A plugged   **B** connected   **C** switched   **D** adjusted

12 I don't know if I'll be able to help you but I'll .... my best.
    A make   **B** give   **C** work   **D** do

13 I don't enjoy going to the theatre .... myself. I'd rather have company.
    A on   **B** by   **C** with   **D** for

14   I bought a large Chinese .... lampshade to put in my bedroom.
     A round   **B** paper   **C** white   **D** old

15   It doesn't say on the box what the contents ....
     A is   **B** are   **C** has   **D** have

COMMUNICATION ACTIVITY 1 PAGE 100 ROLE B

You are the director of a small office equipment company. Unfortunately things are not going too well at the moment – sales are down and you owe the bank quite a lot of money. You are even thinking of sacking some of your staff and selling their company cars in order to raise money.

One of your salesmen/saleswomen, A, has asked to speak to you but you don't know what it's about. A's sales have been very poor until this month (when he/she managed to sell equipment to three members of his/her family). He/she also managed to damage a company car two months ago while parking. You begin the conversation.

SEE COMMUNICATION ACTIVITY 2, PAGE 102

FUNCTIONS BANK

EXPRESSING LIKES, DISLIKES AND PREFERENCES

LIKES

I (really) | like / enjoy / love | noun / …ing

I'm (very) (really) | fond of / interested in / keen on | noun / …ing

I find …ing (really) | interesting / enjoyable / relaxing / fascinating / exciting, etc.

DISLIKES

I don't (really) like | noun / …ing

I (really) (absolutely) | hate / detest / can't bear / can't stand | noun / …ing

I'm not (very) (really) | fond of / interested in / keen on | noun / …ing

I find …ing (a bit) (rather) | boring / dull / tiring, etc.

PREFERENCES

I prefer | tennis / playing tennis | to | badminton. / playing badminton.

I'd (I would) rather dance than jog.

ASKING FOR AND EXPRESSING OPINIONS

What do you think of … (the weather/the new Prime Minister/my hat)?
How do you feel about … (this suggestion/the idea of moving/going out for dinner)?
What's your opinion of … (yesterday's match/the news/the strike)?

I think … / I believe … + STATEMENT

In my opinion, … / In my view, … + STATEMENT

It seems to me that … / From my point of view, I think / As far as I'm concerned, … / If you ask me, … (informal) + STATEMENT

AGREEING

STRONGLY

Yes, you're | quite / absolutely | right.

Yes, that's | quite / absolutely | right/true.

Yes, I | quite / absolutely | agree with you.

Yes, I couldn't agree with you more!

RELUCTANTLY

Well, perhaps.   Well, I suppose you may/could be right.

DISAGREEING

GENTLY

Do you really think so?

I'm not sure you're right (about that).

Are you sure | that's right?
| about that?

I agree up to a point, but don't you think …?

MORE STRONGLY

But surely | that can't be right!
| you don't really think …

No, I'm | sorry but
| afraid

I disagree with you
I think you're wrong | (there).
I can't agree with you | (about that).

VERY FORCEFULLY

But that's | absolute
| complete | nonsense!
| total | rubbish!

You can't be serious!
You must be joking!

INTERRUPTING

Sorry to interrupt (you) but …

I'd like to make a point …
Hold on a moment!

May I | interrupt (you)
Can I | break in | for a second …

ASKING FOR ADVICE

I've got a small problem …
I'm not sure what to do …
I don't know much about …
You know a lot about …
You know more than me about …
You're the expert!

Could you | give me some advice?
Can you | offer me some advice?
I was wondering if you could | advise me?

I'd like
I'd appreciate | your advice,
I'd welcome | some advice, | if you don't mind.

What would you do | in my place/position?
| if you were me?

GIVING ADVICE AND RECOMMENDATIONS, AND PERSUADING

Why don't you …
You could …

How about …
What about … | + noun or
Have you thought of … | …ing

You (really) ought to …
should …

I should … if I were you.
If I were you, I'd …

MORE FORMAL

I'd recommend you to …
My advice to you is to …

STRONGER

The best thing you can do is to …

What you really | ought to do is …
           | need is …

I strongly advise you to …

Take my advice. You won't regret it!

ACCEPTING AND REJECTING ADVICE

Yes, | what | a good idea.
    | that's |

Thank you | for the | advice,
Thanks | | recommendation,

Yes, I think I'll | take | your advice.
           | follow |

but (I think) I'd | rather … | (all the same).
           | better … |
           | prefer to … |

MAKING AND RESPONDING TO SUGGESTIONS

Let's
Shall we | + infinitive?
Why don't we

How about | + …ing?
What about

I think that | we should | + infinitive
         | it would be a good idea to |

I suggest that we + infinitive

We'd better (not) | + infinitive
We could |

RESPONDING POSITIVELY

That's a (very) good idea.
What a good idea!
That sounds (like) a (very) good idea (to me).
I think that's a very good suggestion (myself).

RESPONDING NEGATIVELY

I don't think that's a very good idea (myself).
That doesn't sound (like) a very good idea (to me).

ASKING FOR AND GIVING PERMISSION

Can | I (possibly)
Could | he | come in?
May | she, etc.

Is it alright if I
Would it be possible for me to | come in?

Do you | | come in?
Would | mind if I | came in?

Yes, (of course) you | can | (come in).
            | may |

Yes, of course.
No, (I'm afraid) you can't.

No, | not at all.
   | not in the least.

Yes, (I'm afraid) | I do.
          | I would.

MAKING A REQUEST

Please shut the door.

Do you think you could shut the door?

Could
Would | you shut the door please?

I wonder | if you'd mind shutting the door?
| if you could shut the door?

Would you mind shutting the door (please)?

EXPRESSING NEED AND USE

I'll need a camera | because …
| to …

I'll | need | to | have | a | camera with me | because…
| have | | take | | | to…

I can't | do | without a camera because…
I couldn't | manage |

A camera | is | (absolutely) | essential | for + …ing
Scissors | are | (very) | useful |
| will be | (really) | handy |
| would be | (extremely) |

If I | have | a camera | I can … | A camera | will | enable | me to…
take		I'll be able to …		would	allow
had		I could …
took		I'd be able to …

ASKING FOR AND GIVING DIRECTIONS

Excuse me, could you | tell me the way | to the station, please?
| direct me |
| tell me where the station is, please?

No, I'm afraid I'm a stranger here myself!

Yes, of course …

 It's straight ahead.

 It's on the left/right.

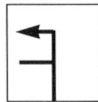 Go straight ahead | until you | get to …
Carry on | | come to …
Keep going | | see …

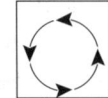 Go past the park.

Turn (sharp) left/right
(at the junction/crossroads).

Go across the
crossroads.

Take the first/second, etc., turning
on your left/right.

Go round the
roundabout.

 Fork | left/right.
Branch |

Go to the | end | of this | road.
| top | | hill.
| bottom |

You can't miss it!

DESCRIBING LOCATION

IN 2 DIMENSIONS

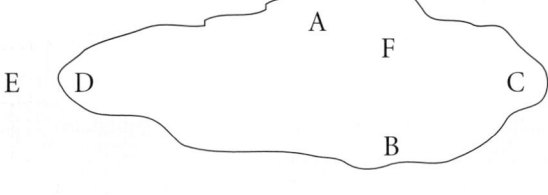

X is in the middle (of the page).
A is at the top.
B is at the bottom.
C is on the left.
D is on the right.
X is between C and D.
C and D are on either side of X.
E is above X.
X is below E.
F is in the top left-hand corner.
G is in the bottom right-hand corner.

A is in the north (of the island).
B is in the south.
C is in the east.
D is in the west.
E is to the west of the island.
F is to the north of B.

IN 3 DIMENSIONS

There is a garden in front of the house.
There is a tree behind the house.
There is a windmill beyond the house.
There is a pond next to/beside the house.
There are ducks on the pond.
There is a cloud above the house (higher than).
The house is below the cloud (lower than).
There is a bird over the tree (directly above).
The tree is under the bird (directly below).

DESCRIBING OBJECTS

2 DIMENSIONAL SHAPES

Noun		Adjective		Compound Adjectives
A square	■	It's square in shape.	∪	It's U-shaped.
A rectangle	▬	It's rectangular in shape.	★	It's star-shaped.
A circle	●	It's circular in shape.	◆	It's diamond-shaped.
A triangle	▲	It's triangular in shape.	♥	It's heart-shaped.
An oval	●	It's oval in shape.		
A semi-circle	◗	It's semi-circular in shape.		

3 DIMENSIONAL SHAPES

A cube		It's cubic in shape.		It's dome-shaped.
A cylinder		It's cylindrical in shape.		It's wedge-shaped.
A cone		It's conical in shape.		It's pear-shaped.
A sphere		It's spherical in shape.		

109

OTHER ADJECTIVES DESCRIBING SHAPE

straight	parallel	rounded
curved	horizontal	pointed
diagonal	vertical	sloping (of a path, garden, roof, etc.)

COLOUR

It's	a	pretty	pale	green	colour.
They're		lovely	bright	yellow	
		horrible	dark		

| It's | pinkish | in colour. |
| | reddish-brown | |

DESCRIBING SENSORY PERCEPTION

LOOK, SEEM, APPEAR + ADJECTIVE

She	looks	tired.
	seems	
	appears	

Look + like + noun (resemble)
He looks like a detective.

TASTE, SMELL + ADJECTIVE

| This soup | tastes | absolutely delicious. |
| | smells | |

It tastes	deliciously	sweet.
	slightly	creamy.
	rather	salty.
	very	bitter.
	extremely	
	too	
	horribly	

Taste, smell + of (have a particular taste)
This cake tastes of honey.
My hands smell of petrol.

Taste, smell + like (remind one of …)
This wine tastes like vinegar!
It smells like cocoa. What is it?

FEEL, SOUND + ADJECTIVE

This material feels beautifully smooth.
Your music sounds rather loud.

Feel, sound + like + noun
This material feels like silk.
It sounds like Japanese music. Is it?

DESCRIBING PEOPLE

HAIR

A  B  C

| He
She | 's got | short
shoulder-length
long | straight (A)
curly (B)
wavy (C) | blonde
fair
red
brown
dark
black | hair. |

He's bald.

FIGURE

| He's
She's | fairly
quite
very
extremely | thin.
slim.
plump.
fat.
well-built. | | He's
She's | tall.
short.
medium height. |

COMPLEXION

| He's
She's | got a | pale
fair
dark | complexion. |

DISTINGUISHING FEATURES

A  B  C  D  E

| He's
She's | got | a fringe. (A)
freckles. (B)
a scar. (C) |

| He's got | a beard. (D)
a moustache. (E) |

Letters: Informal/Formal

INFORMAL LETTERS

WRITE YOUR ADDRESS (BUT **NOT** YOUR NAME) ON SEPARATE LINES IN THE TOP RIGHT-HAND CORNER.

WRITE THE DATE BELOW YOUR ADDRESS.

WRITE THE FIRST LINE NEXT TO THE MARGIN, FOLLOWED BY A COMMA. ALWAYS USE A NAME. NEVER BEGIN *Dear Friend.*

USE SEPARATE PARAGRAPHS TO:
- BEGIN YOUR LETTER
- DEAL WITH DIFFERENT TOPICS
- CLOSE YOUR LETTER.

END YOUR LETTER WITH AN INFORMAL GREETING (e.g. *Yours, Best wishes,* OR *Love*) WRITTEN NEAR THE MIDDLE OF THE PAGE.

> 23 Oxford Rd
> Cheltenham
> Glos. GL50 4QZ
> 4th August 19–
>
> Dear Gill,
>
> Thank you for your postcard from New York. I really envy you going to all those exciting places! There's no chance of a holiday for me this year, I'm afraid. I'm saving up to buy a car. The driving lessons are going well and my test is booked for next month. Wish me luck!
>
> I haven't seen you for ages and I'd love to hear all your news. Why don't you come down and stay one weekend? Let me know if/when you'll be free.
>
> Looking forward to hearing from you.
>
> Love
> Hazel

Important note: In the First Certificate exam, you do not have to include your address in the letter.

Notes and useful language

BEGINNINGS

It is usual to begin by referring to a letter you've received, or by making some other polite introductory comment:

- *Thank you for/Many thanks for* your (recent) letter/postcard.
- *It was good/nice to hear from you recently.*
- *I'm sorry I haven't* written/been in touch for such a long time.
- *It's ages since* I've heard from you. *I hope* you're well/you and your family are well.

ENDINGS

It is usual to end with a polite remark, written on a separate line:

- *I look forward to/Looking forward to hearing from/seeing you.*
- *See you soon./Write soon./Hope to hear from you soon.*
- *Once again, thank you for all your help.*
- *Give my regards/love to …*

APOLOGIES

Say what you are apologising for and give reasons to explain your behaviour. Try to suggest a way of putting things right, if possible.

- *I'm writing to apologise for* missing your party last week *but I'm afraid* I was in bed with flu.
- *I'm really sorry that I* forgot to send you a birthday card *but* I was so busy with my new job.
- *If you let me know* where you bought it/how much it cost, *I'll gladly* pay for it/replace it.
- *Please let me know* how much the bill is *and I'll gladly pay it.*

INVITATIONS – ACCEPTING/REJECTING

Say what the event is and give clear details of the date, time and place. It may be helpful to give other information such as how to get there, who else is coming and what (if anything) to bring. It is usual, too, to ask for confirmation:

- *I'm/We're having a party on* Friday 19th and *I/we hope you'll be able to come.*
- *Would you like to* come/go to see 'Room With a View' with me at the weekend?
- *I was wondering if you'd like to go* to the theatre/come on holiday with us?
- *Could you let me/us know if* you can come/you'd like to join us?
- *Thank you very much for your invitation. I'd love to come.*

- *Thank you for asking me/inviting me to … but I'm afraid I won't be able to come/join you because …*

REQUESTS

In some cases, you may want to introduce your request immediately. In others, you may prefer to begin your letter with some brief news before going on to make the request. Either way, explain exactly what the request is, with reasons, and emphasise how grateful you would be for the help you are asking for:

- *I'm writing to ask for your help/you (if you could do me) a favour.*
- *I wonder if/I was wondering if you could help me/do me a favour.*
- *I hope you don't mind me asking but could you (possibly) …?*
- *I'd be very/really/terribly grateful if you could …*

THANK YOU/ CONGRATULATIONS/GOOD LUCK

When thanking someone for something, it is usual to say as much as possible about how useful/enjoyable/helpful it was. When offering congratulations for some success, you usually mention how well deserved it is. When wishing someone good luck, try to reassure them or offer some friendly advice:

- *I'm writing to thank you for* your hospitality/the wonderful present.
- *It was so kind of you to* invite me to stay with you.
- *I really appreciated* all your help/advice.

- *Congratulations on* passing your exams/your excellent exam results!
- *You really deserved to succeed* after all your hard work!

- *I wish you good luck/Good luck in/with* your exams/your driving test/your interview.
- *Don't worry, I'm sure you'll* do well/pass.
- *Do be on time, won't you, and don't forget to …*

NEWS/INFORMATION

- *I thought you might be interested to hear about/know that …*
- *This is just to let you know that …*
- *By the way, have you heard about/did you know that …?*

FORMAL LETTERS

THE WISE OWL BOOKSHOP
Part-time sales assistant required.
Please apply in writing to:
The Manager,
The Wise Owl Bookshop,
Market Street,
Malvern, WR12 2PO

23 Oxford Road
Cheltenham
Gloucestershire
GL50 4QZ

4th August 19-

> WRITE YOUR ADDRESS ON SEPARATE LINES IN THE TOP RIGHT-HAND CORNER. DO NOT WRITE YOUR NAME.

> WRITE THE DATE BELOW YOUR ADDRESS.

> WRITE THE NAME AND ADDRESS OF THE PERSON OR COMPANY YOU ARE WRITING TO ON THE LEFT-HAND SIDE, BELOW THE DATE.

The Manager
The Wise Owl Bookshop
Market Street
Malvern
WR12 2PO

> WRITE *Dear ...* NEXT TO THE LEFT-HAND MARGIN, FOLLOWED BY A COMMA.

Dear Sir or Madam,

I was interested in your advertisement in today's edition of the 'Evening Mail' and I would like to apply for the position of part-time sales assistant.

I am 19 years of age and have recently returned from six months' travelling in the United States. I have 'A' levels in French and Art History and I have gained some work experience since leaving school, both as a waitress and as an assistant in a newsagent's shop.

My reason for applying for this position is that I hope to go to university next year and I would like to combine part-time work with studying for a further 'A' level. I feel that the work would be very interesting and that I would enjoy the opportunity to meet people and help them with their enquiries.

I would be free to attend for interview on any day after 11 a.m.

> USE SEPARATE PARAGRAPHS TO:
> – SAY WHY YOU ARE WRITING
> – GIVE DETAILS OR EXTRA INFORMATION
> – CONCLUDE YOUR LETTER.

> END YOUR LETTER *Yours faithfully,* OR *Yours sincerely,* FOLLOWED BY A COMMA. (FOR THE DIFFERENCE, SEE PAGE 115).

Yours faithfully,

HAZEL SMITH (Ms)

> WRITE YOUR NAME CLEARLY AFTER YOUR SIGNATURE.

Important note: In the First Certificate exam, you do not have to include the addresses in the letter.

Notes and useful language

BEGINNING/ORGANISATION

Write *Dear* + the person's name, if you know it (*Dear Mr Smith*). If not, begin *Dear Sir* (for a man), *Dear Madam* (for a woman), or *Dear Sir or Madam* (if it could be either). Don't use a title like *Dear Manager*.

In the first paragraph, clearly state your reason for writing. Use the middle paragraphs to explain the details, beginning a new paragraph for each main point. In the final paragraph, sum up and/or say what action you want to be taken.

ENDINGS

Don't forget! If you began with a person's name, e.g. *Dear Mrs Blake*, you must end with *Yours sincerely*, **not** *Yours faithfully*. These endings are followed by a comma.

JOB APPLICATIONS

First make it clear which job you are applying for, and mention where you saw the advertisement, and when. Give all the necessary information about yourself (including age, qualifications, past employment and other experience). Say why you are particularly interested in the job, and what you have to offer. Use a new paragraph for each main topic. It may also be useful to mention when you would be available for an interview:

- *I was interested in the advertisement in* (newspaper/ magazine) *on* (date) *and I would like to apply for the post/position of* (job title).
- *I am 21 years of age and I have a* Diploma in Business Administration.
- *My reason for applying is that* I am interested in tourism and I would like to be able to use my foreign languages.
- *I would be happy/able to attend an interview* at any time which is convenient to you.

APOLOGIES

Explain why you are apologising and what the reasons were for your behaviour. If possible, offer to make up in some way (e.g. by paying for the damage) and/or promise that the problem won't happen again:

- *I am writing to apologise for* the things I said at our last meeting/losing my temper.
- *I would like to say how sorry I am* about the trouble I have caused/that you were disturbed.
- *The reason I missed the meeting was that* my car broke down.
- *Please let me know how much it cost and I will gladly replace it.*

- *I assure you that this will never happen again.*

COMPLAINTS

State the subject of your complaint clearly in the first paragraph. Use the following paragraphs to give all the necessary details (including dates and times, the people involved, the inconvenience you've been caused, etc.). Try to be clear and factual rather than emotional. Use the final paragraph to say what action you want to be taken now:

- *I am writing to complain about* a holiday I booked with your company.
- *I am writing to say that I am not satisfied with* the standard of service at your restaurant.
- *I must insist that you* refund the cost of the bill.
- *I must ask you to …*

ENQUIRIES

In the first paragraph, explain what information you need. If you are responding to an advertisement, mention where you saw this. Use extra paragraphs to mention any specific questions you would like answers to:

- *I am writing to enquire about …*
- *I was interested in your advertisement in* 'The Daily News' *and I would like to have further information about …*
- *I would be grateful if you could send me full details of …*
- *Could you send me* your brochure/catalogue?
- *I look forward to hearing from you/receiving* the information.

OPINIONS

Introduce the topic and give details of any letter, article, book or TV programme you are responding to. Develop your argument in separate paragraphs and sum up in the final one:

- *I strongly disagree with/I completely* agree with Mr Smith's letter, which appeared yesterday.
- *I was interested to read the article* on immigration in Monday's **edition of your newspaper but** I don't think it gave all the facts.
- *I was interested/fascinated/amused/delighted to see/hear/read …*
- *I was horrified/shocked/disgusted to …*
- *In my opinion* there is far too much violence in television dramas these days.
- *In conclusion I feel/I believe …*

Practice

INFORMAL LETTERS

1 An English friend of yours is planning to spend a week touring your country and has asked for your advice on what to see and do. Write a letter giving your friend practical information which you think will be helpful.

2 You recently stayed with an English penfriend and his or her family. Write a letter thanking them for their hospitality.

3 An English friend of yours is going to take an important examination soon. Write a letter wishing your friend good luck and offering any advice you can.

4 You are going away for a week and you are hoping a friend of yours will be willing to call round to feed your pet(s) and water your plants. Write a letter to your friend explaining the problem and asking for his/her help.

5 You promised to visit an English friend while on a visit to the town where he/she lives, but you were unable to do so. Write a letter apologising and explaining the reasons.

FORMAL LETTERS

1 You recently had a party at your house and your next-door neighbour rang up in the middle to complain about the noise. Write a letter of apology.

2 You have seen an advertisement for a company which specialises in bicycling holidays. Write a letter requesting more information and asking for some answers to specific questions.

3 You belong to a film club which shows a lot of English and American films but you are not happy with the type of film that has been shown recently. Write a letter to the Club Secretary explaining your views and making a few suggestions for the future.

4 You had a very bad meal at a restaurant recently. Write a letter complaining about the food and the service.

5 An English travel company is advertising for host families for English students on study visits to your country. Write a letter of application, describing your family and home.

Descriptions

PERSON

An English penfriend has asked to hear more about your family.
Write a description of a favourite member of your family

INTRODUCTION
sets the scene

My cousin, Christopher, is the son of my father's brother. He's three years younger than me and we didn't know each other very well as children because he and his family lived on the other side of the country at that time. Since then, he's married and moved closer so we meet quite often and I've got to know him much better.

different tenses to fill in the background

appearance/
clothes

There's nothing very remarkable about Chris's appearance. He's of average height and medium build, and he's got curly, mousy hair and a fair complexion. As he's quite short-sighted like me, he wears glasses. The clothes he likes are mostly casual: jeans or shorts and a tee-shirt. I don't think I've ever seen him in a suit!

character

He's a very active person who loves the outdoor life. He's extremely practical and he can build or repair almost anything, no matter how complicated it is. Another characteristic he has is that he's very outgoing. If you go to a show with him and members of the audience are invited onto the stage, Chris will be the first to volunteer. The thing I appreciate most about him, however, is his sense of humour. If I'm depressed, he can always cheer me up with a joke or a funny story.

vary the sentence structure

CONCLUSION
sums up your
feelings

They say you can choose your friends but not your relations. In Chris's case, I feel I'm very lucky because he's not only my cousin but also one of my best friends.

PLACE

A young people's travel magazine has asked readers to write about a town or city anywhere in the world that they particularly like. The best description will win a holiday! Write a description that you can send to the magazine.

INTRODUCTION sets the scene	I've visited many interesting cities in my life but I think my favourite must be Sydney in Australia. I've been lucky enough to go there several times and it's certainly a place I would be happy to live in.
location	Sydney's biggest advantage is its superb setting on one of the most beautiful harbours in the world. The views of the harbour bridge and the Opera House are magnificent and you find that you are never very far from water wherever you go.
special attractions	Then, a short drive away you have beaches like the famous Bondi beach and national parks where you can walk for miles without meeting anyone except, perhaps, the odd kangaroo!
atmosphere	It's a very relaxed and cosmopolitan city and there's plenty to see and do. Even if you can't afford the price of an opera ticket, you can visit some of the museums and art galleries or wander round Darling Harbour or Paddington Market completely free.
amenities	And when you're hungry, there are hundreds of restaurants, at all prices, serving every possible type of cuisine from Australian to my favourite, Mongolian!
CONCLUSION people summing up	So, with its wonderful setting and all its other attractions, Sydney takes a lot of beating, in my view. But in the end, it's the people who make a city and Sydney-siders (as they're called) are some of the friendliest and most welcoming people I know.

Notes and useful language

STRUCTURE

Descriptions need to be structured, like other types of writing, so that they have an introduction, a middle and an end. In the introduction, you should briefly set the scene, perhaps by saying why you have chosen the person or place you're going to describe. After that you should deal with the different main aspects of the subject in separate paragraphs. Use the final paragraph to sum up your feelings about the subject, if possible in a humorous or memorable way.

PERSONALISATION

Some topics give you more opportunity for personal comment than others. In general, though, including your reactions and feelings and an occasional touch of humour will make your description more interesting and enjoyable for the reader.

TENSES

You may be asked to write a description in the present, in the past or to make a comparison between the past and the present. Think carefully about the tenses you use: *He rides a bicycle* (present habit), *He's learning to play the violin* (happening now), *We've been friends for years* (links past and present), *It was raining* (sets the scene), *She frowned when she saw me* (past action).

SENTENCE STRUCTURE

One problem which arises with this kind of writing is that you can find yourself beginning all your sentences in the same way: *He looks …, He's got …, He wears …*. This makes the description rather boring to read, so try to vary the sentence structure: *His eyes are …, The first thing you notice is …, Another characteristic is …*.

VOCABULARY

Descriptions give you a golden opportunity to show off your vocabulary. Don't waste it! Avoid using a narrow range of adjectives like *big/small, good, nice* – think about better, more precise ones.

DESCRIBING PEOPLE

Possible aspects: your relationship with the person/how you met, their appearance and style of clothing, their character, and your personal feelings about them.

Appearance   (SEE FUNCTIONS BANK, PAGE 111):
- *She/he looks/seems/appears …*
- *She/he's got short, curly hair and a fringe.*
- *She/he's short with a pale complexion.*

Clothes   (SEE PAGE 63):
She/he usually wears jeans.

Order of adjectives   (SEE STUDY BOX, PAGE 52):
a brand-new white woollen sweater

DESCRIBING PLACES/EVENTS

Possible aspects: your interest in the place/event, your impressions when you first went there, main characteristics, location, atmosphere, sights, sounds, people, summing up/comparison with later visit.

Location   (SEE FUNCTIONS BANK, PAGE 109):
- *in the middle, at the top/bottom, on the left/right*
- *in the north, to the north of …*
- *in front of, behind, beyond, above, over, below, under*

DESCRIBING OBJECTS

Possible aspects: structure, shape, colour, material, use.

Shape   (SEE FUNCTIONS BANK, PAGE 109-110):
- *It is shaped like a circle./It's circular in shape/It's star-shaped.*
- *straight, curved, horizontal, diagonal, vertical, pointed, sloping*

Sensory perception   (SEE FUNCTIONS BANK, PAGE 110):
- *It looks/seems/appears … + adjective*
- *It tastes/smells/feels/sounds … + adjective*
- *It feels/sounds like … + noun*
- *It's a pretty pale pink colour.*

DESCRIBING PROCESSES/INSTRUCTIONS

Sequence markers:
- *First …, Next/After that … /Finally …*
- *When/Once you have (done) that …*
- *Before/After doing/you (do) …*

Purpose clauses (see Study Box, page 188):
- *for + -ing*
- *to/in order to/so as to + infinitive*
- *so that + clause*

Practice

1 Describe your ideal house and its location, giving reasons for your choices.

2 Write a description of a person who has had an important influence on your life.

3 Describe a party you've attended recently.

4 Describe a favourite meal or dish. What ingredients are needed and how is it prepared?

5 Write a description of your bedroom, its furniture and contents.

Important note: In the First Certificate exam you must write between 120 and 180 words. The models given on pages 117-118 are longer, in order to illustrate the various useful points.

Discussions

Your class has been asked to write a composition discussing the topic:
There's no need to write letters any more. Telephoning is a better way of communicating with people. Write a discussion composition.

OPENING
introducing topic and argument

It's certainly quicker to telephone than to write a letter but it may not always be the best way to communicate. The right form of communication to use depends, like so many other things in life, on the circumstances.

qualifying the statement

points in favour of telephoning

Telephoning is ideal if you want immediate action. You wouldn't want to write to the plumber if you had water pouring through your ceiling, for example! It's also the obvious choice if you need a quick answer to a question like 'What time is the next train to Oxford?' or 'Did I leave my wallet in your shop?' Many problems can be solved more easily and decisions taken more quickly if you can discuss them with someone on the phone rather than wait for a reply to a letter. Finally, few people would disagree that telephoning is a pleasant way to keep in touch with friends and family.

giving specific examples

introduce opposite point of view

On the other hand, there can be a number of disadvantages to telephoning. In the first place, some problems are too complicated to explain on the phone, especially if they involve facts and figures, and it may be clearer if you set them out in a letter. Secondly, it might be important to have a record of what you say, especially if it's a booking or a complaint. Last but not least, telephoning, especially long-distance, can be terribly expensive.

points against telephoning/in favour of writing

listing reasons

further support for letter writing

The nice thing about receiving letters is that you can keep them and re-read them. Who wouldn't rather have a six-page letter full of news from a friend abroad than a two-minute telephone call on a bad line?

CONCLUSION
expressing personal view and summing up

To sum up, letter writing is far from dead, in my view. Each form of communication has its advantages and disadvantages: the important thing to recognise is which is more appropriate for what you want to say, and to whom.

balancing the argument

Notes and useful language

TOPICS

Typical discussion topics include statements which you are asked to agree or disagree with (e.g. *There's too much violence on television.*) and invitations to discuss aspects of a subject (e.g. *What are the advantages and disadvantages of air travel?*)

APPROACH

Generally, the important thing is to consider the various aspects of the topic before giving a balanced opinion. Occasionally, you may be asked directly for a personal opinion (e.g. *What's the best way to bring up children?*); but even here you would need to consider some different views so that you can contrast them with your own.

STRUCTURE

The structure of a discursive composition should be clear and logical. In the first paragraph, introduce the topic and your argument. In the next, deal with one aspect of the topic. Give supporting evidence in following paragraphs if necessary. After that, consider the opposite point of view. In the final paragraph, sum up your argument and give a balanced personal opinion.

INTRODUCING THE TOPIC

- *Many people believe/feel that …*
- *It is said …*
- *People's opinions on … differ widely.*

SUPPORTING YOUR ARGUMENT

- *One of the main advantages of … is that …*
- *In the first place,/Firstly,/To begin with,/Secondly,/ Thirdly,/Finally, /Last, but not least, …*

ADDING FURTHER REASONS

- *both … and/not only …   but also …*
- *In addition,/What is more, /Furthermore, …* (see Addition Links, page 83)

EXPRESSING AN OPPOSITE POINT OF VIEW

- *On the other hand, there are (also) a number of disadvantages.*

LINKING SENTENCES

- *Although …,/However,/In spite of this,/Despite …* (see Concession links, page 83)
- *Some people … while/whereas others …*
- *On the one hand … on the other hand …*

EXPRESSING OPINIONS

- *In my view/opinion,/It seems to me that …*
- *I think/feel that …* (see Functions Bank, page 105)

SUMMING UP

In conclusion,/To sum up,/On balance,

Practice

1 What do you think the advantages and disadvantages of living in the country may be?

2 What, in your opinion, is the best way to learn a language?

3 It has been said that childhood is the happiest time of one's life. Do you agree?

4 What do you think of the idea, expressed in some countries, that women should be paid a wage for the work they do in the home?

5 'The most important quality in a partner is a sense of humour.' Do you agree?

Important note: In the First Certificate exam you must write between 120 and 180 words. The model given on page 120 is longer, in order to illustrate the various useful points.

Narratives

Write a short story for your school/college magazine about a journey where everything went wrong.

OPENING
to catch the reader's attention

You don't necessarily expect everything to go smoothly when you're travelling. There's always likely to be the odd delay or small problem to deal with. Just occasionally, though, it seems that everything that can go wrong does go wrong, and then you begin to wish you'd stayed at home.

past continuous to set the scene

background

perfect participle for events before the main events

I had spent a week staying with friends in Eastern Europe and I was now beginning my journey home. Having got to the station in good time to catch the train, I went to the ticket office to buy a ticket. Imagine my dismay when the ticket clerk explained that the train had been cancelled and that there wasn't another one that day. Luckily there was a bus I could catch, but it didn't leave for two hours so I spent the intervening time walking the streets of the town, getting hotter and stickier by the minute. When I finally boarded the bus, all the seats had been taken, so I had to stand for the first hour of the journey.

events in clear sequence

sequence link

By the time we arrived, I was exhausted and longing for a shower, so I looked for a taxi and showed the driver the name of the hotel my friends had recommended. You've guessed it! He didn't recognise the hotel and wasn't interested in finding out where it was. Instead, I took a tram but, believe it or not, the tram broke down before we reached my stop. Fortunately, I had a map so I walked the last kilometre before practically collapsing in the hotel.

new paragraph for each main stage

Things seemed to go better after that. I was relaxing in my room when an American girl I'd met at Reception knocked on my door and said, 'Hi, I've got a lot of food left over from my journey and I can't possibly eat it all. I was wondering if you'd like to come and share it?' She was very friendly and we had great fun picnicking and chatting about our adventures. My flight was leaving the next morning so, after an hour or so, I said goodbye to her and returned to my room to pack my bags and look out my travel documents. It was only then that I discovered I had lost the return half of my airline ticket!

past perfect for events before the main events

direct speech for variety and interest

ENDING
to explain the final result or to surprise or amuse the reader

Notes and useful language

BEGINNINGS AND ENDINGS

A narrative needs an interesting beginning to catch the reader's attention and encourage him or her to read on, and a clear ending to round the story off satisfactorily. A weak beginning or ending can spoil the effect of the story, so it's worth spending time working out how to start and finish.

THE STORY

It's usually easiest to write a story which is based on your own experience, but don't be afraid to change the details slightly or invent new parts if this helps to make the story more interesting or entertaining.

It's usual to describe events in the order in which they happened and to use a new paragraph for each main stage of the story. The sequence of events is also shown by verb tenses and time links.

VERB TENSES

We use:
- the **simple past** to describe the main events (see Focus on grammar, page 28):
  I **ran** to answer the phone but it **stopped** ringing as **I picked up** the receiver.
- the **past continuous** to set the scene (see Focus on grammar, page 33):
  It **was raining** heavily as we set off.
- the **past perfect** to describe events which happened before the main events (see Focus on grammar, page 139):
  When I got on the bus all the seats **had been taken**.
- **present participles** to show two actions which are linked (see Focus on grammar, page 68):
  Noticing that she looked lost, I asked if I could help.
- **perfect participles** to show that one action was complete before another started (see Focus on grammar, page 69):
  Having reported my stolen passport to the police, I returned sadly to the hotel.

TIME LINKS (SEE FOCUS ON GRAMMAR, PAGE 182):

before …	then …
at first,	next …
while …	later …
during …	after that …
meanwhile,	afterwards …
when …	finally,
as soon as …	eventually,
immediately …	in the end,
once …	

Make a point of knowing the difference between:
first(ly)/at first, lastly/at last, after/afterwards,

while/during/meanwhile

ADDING VARIETY AND INTEREST

There are various ways of making your story more lively and interesting. These include:
- using **direct speech** occasionally, for dramatic effect (remember to use inverted commas correctly):
  'No,' he yelled, 'don't touch that switch!'
- using **a range of reporting verbs** for reporting speech (see Focus on grammar, page 156):
  e.g. accuse, admit, advise, argue, ask, complain, deny, encourage, explain, invite, promise, recommend, remind, suggest, warn.
- using **a range of adjectives and adverbs** to describe actions and feelings as precisely and vividly as possible:
  I was **absolutely horrified** when I saw the bill.
  He shook his arm **threateningly** at us.

Practice

1 'And I've never been on another camping holiday from that day to this.' Write a story ending with these words.

2 You had put your briefcase on the chair next to you but when you turned round it had gone. Describe what happened next.

3 Describe an event or day which changed your life.

4 You suddenly realised you were completely lost. Describe what you did and how you managed to get out of trouble.

5 'It's all a big mistake. You've got the wrong person!' Write a story which begins with these words.

Important note: In the First Certificate exam you must write between 120 and 180 words. The model given on page 122 is longer in order to illustrate the various useful points.

Articles and Reports

Articles and reports both discuss a particular topic, but because they have different purposes and are aimed at different readers, the approach is a little different in each case. An article is written for a newspaper, magazine or newsletter and is designed to make a topic interesting for the general reader. A report is usually more formal and detailed because it is written for a particular person (or group of people) with a particular interest in a subject.

ARTICLE

> You have been asked to write an article describing your experience of an unusual type of holiday for a students' magazine.

HEADING

FANCY A DOWN-TO-EARTH HOLIDAY?

OPENING
INTRODUCE the topic in an interesting way

Are you fed up with lazing on the beach? Do you want to do something a little different this year? Well, there are now quite a number of educational holidays available and I decided to try one of these out.

addressing the reader directly

I'd always been interested in history so when I saw an advertisement for a week's break which included training in archaeology, it seemed ideal.

There were eight of us in the group, including a retired school teacher, two American college students and an out-of-work actor. Accommodation was simple but comfortable and the food was all home-cooked and delicious.

giving specific examples

USE separate paragraphs for different aspects of the subject

After some basic training, we were allowed to take part in a dig at a nearby archaeological site. It was a fascinating process and the high spot for me was finding a tiny piece of pottery which was later identified as Roman – 'Beginner's luck', according to the teacher!

quoting

ENDING
overall comment + concluding remark

I can thoroughly recommend an educational holiday. As far as I'm concerned, learning a new skill beats lying on the beach any day, and I still came home with a sun tan!

Notes and useful language

CONTENT

An article is usually based on a discussion, a description or a narrative (or it may involve a combination of more than one of these). See the relevant sections in the Writing Bank for more information about these types of writing.

APPROACH

An article should catch the reader's attention and make him or her want to read on. Think about the age group you are writing for and ask yourself how much they might know about the subject and how you can make it interesting for them. With a light-hearted topic, humour is often helpful. You can also make your article more lively and readable by:

- addressing your readers directly (*Did you know …? What would you do if …?*)
- using a personal approach (*Personally, I can't imagine anything worse!*)
- giving specific examples and quotations (*As Mrs X explained, '……'*)

GENERAL STRUCTURE

- Give your article a heading or headline which makes the subject clear and also catches the reader's attention.
- Divide the article into paragraphs to help the reader follow the argument.
- Begin with an interesting introduction – an example, perhaps, or a question.
- End with an overall comment or concluding remark.

HEADINGS

Use your imagination to make the headline catch the reader's attention. Here are some of the ways writers do this in this book:

- a dramatic word or phrase: *Freezing!*
- a summary of the story: *My Lone Walk to the North Pole; Rescue from the rapids*
- a question: *What's the big idea? Just a normal day?*
- a surprising fact: *Seven banks a day are robbed in LA; You're already well equipped to prevent crime.*

See the sections on Descriptions, Discussions and Narratives for detailed information about structure and useful language.

Practice

1 You have been asked to write an article which will appear in a guide to your town or city for English-speaking visitors. Write about the sports and leisure activities which are available.

2 Your school or college wants to publish an article giving advice and encouragement to new students in its English language newsletter. Write the article.

REPORTS

The Student Services Manager at your school or college has asked you to write a report on the library facilities and to suggest any improvements that could be made.

HEADING

INTRODUCTION

SUBHEADINGS
(or number each point)

quoting

summary and recommendation

alternative heading

saying how you have gathered the information

mentioning a negative point

reporting an impression

generalising

Report on College Library Facilities

In order to prepare this report, I visited the college library on several occasions and interviewed the librarians and a number of students.

General

The library has a welcoming atmosphere and most people said that it was easy to find your way around. It is well decorated and well-lit and the only problem is that there are not quite enough tables and chairs for everyone at busy times.

Books

There is a very good selection of books for all subjects but according to the librarians there is sometimes a waiting list when a particular book has been recommended by a teacher. The catalogue system is rather complicated and surprisingly it doesn't appear to have been updated recently.

Newspapers and magazines

The range of newspapers and magazines is excellent and these seem to be well used.

Conclusion

The library facilities are very good, on the whole, but I would recommend providing additional copies of popular books, supplying a small number of extra chairs, and improving and updating the catalogue system.

From:	A Student
To:	The Student Services Manager
Subject:	College Library Facilities

Notes and useful language

APPROACH

A report should be practical and business-like. It should present the necessary information as clearly as possible so that the reader can follow it easily, and it should express an overall opinion at the end. You can simply begin with a heading or you can write the report in the form of a memo to a particular person or group if you wish.

STRUCTURE

- Give your report a clear, factual heading.
- Divide the report into paragraphs or sections to deal with separate aspects of a subject and use numbers, letters or subheadings to make this clear.
- Start by saying what the report is about and/or how you gathered the information.
- End with a conclusion which gives a summary of the situation (and a recommendation if necessary).

INTRODUCTION

The aim/purpose of this report is to …,
This report looks at …
In order to prepare this report, I visited/interviewed/ studied …

REPORTING IMPRESSIONS AND FINDINGS

It seems/appears that …
Most people/The majority of people seem to/tend to …
It is interesting/surprising/strange that …
Interestingly, Surprisingly, Strangely,…

QUOTING

According to X, Y said/felt/mentioned that … +
reported speech

GENERALISING

In general, On the whole,

SUMMING UP

In conclusion, To sum up, On balance,

MAKING A RECOMMENDATION

In my opinion/view,
I would recommend (+ -ing)

Practice

1 Your English penfriend is doing a project on the subject of television and has asked you for information about the different TV channels and the most popular programmes in your country. Write a report.

2 You belong to an English students' club which has a meeting room and a small library of books, videos and tapes. The club has recently received a small grant. You have been asked to write a short report on the club's facilities and to suggest the best way in which to spend the money.

Lead-in

A

B

C

D

❶

1 Describe what you can see in each of pictures A, B and C.
2 Describe the appearance of the people in each picture.
3 In picture A, what do you think is the reason for the flag?
4 What does the man seem to be doing in picture A? What might he be saying?
5 In picture C the men have cycle panniers on each side of the front wheels of their bicycles. What might they contain?
6 In picture D what kind of boat do you think this is?

❷ Opposite are headlines from articles about the journeys which were made by the people in the pictures. There are also lists of the stores they took with them. Work with a partner to match the headlines and lists to the pictures and fill in the first three lines of the table which follows.

	Picture A	Picture B	Picture C	Picture D
Method of travel				
Destination				
Stores list				
Extract				

Headlines:

**My Lone Walk
to the North Pole**

*Slow Boats
to China*

**HARD TRACK
TO AFRICA**

Australia!
– by pedal power

Stores lists:

a clothes / camping equipment / 5 gallon jerrycan of petrol / 1 week's food and water / tools

b tent / boots / gloves / balaclava / goggles / sleeping bag / radio / satellite relay kit / compass / 200 kilos food / camping stove / pencils and notebooks / rifle

c notebooks and ballpoint pens / several novels / 2 Pentax cameras / Polaroid camera / metal suitcase with combination lock / money belt / zip-fastened bag / medicines (septrin, mexaform and aspirin) / thick-soled shoes

d tent / sleeping bags / clothes / first aid kit / tools / cycle spares / food / £1000 in travellers' cheques

❸ Which item/s from each list helped you to decide on your answers?

❹ Look at the lists again and discuss:
1 the meanings of any unknown words. For example, *balaclava* and *goggles,* which can both be worn.
2 why the various items were necessary. For example, why is there a Polaroid camera as well as two ordinary cameras in List c.
3 how the lists differ from each other and why.
4 whether there are any items which seem to be missing from the lists.

STUDY BOX I   The use of articles 2

DEFINITE ARTICLE

oceans, seas, waterways and rivers	mountain ranges	plural countries	roads
the Pacific Ocean, *the* Sulu Sea *the* Suez Canal, *the* Channel *the* Mississippi	*the* Himalayas *the* Alps	*the* United States *the* Philippines	*the* London Road

NO ARTICLE

cities	mountains	countries	streets, squares, circuses
New York Hong Kong	Mount Everest Ben Nevis	France Argentina	Oxford Street Leicester Square Piccadilly Circus

❺ Now look at these short extracts from descriptions of the four journeys. Match the extracts to the journeys and fill in the last line of the table on page 129.

i)

—·—·—·—·—·—·—·—·—·—·—·—·—·—·—

From Dubai, they travelled to Pakistan and India. There, while cycling through a small village on the road from Hyderabad to Khairpur, they met a young man who invited them back to his village 10 miles off the main road.

It was to be a memorable experience.

When they arrived at Talpur, Rick and David found themselves surrounded by the entire population of the village – more than 300 people.

ii)

We cruised gently through France, Switzerland, Italy, Yugoslavia and Greece, getting the 'feel' of the bikes. With clothes, camping equipment, spares and enough tools to do practically a complete rebuild, we were loaded up fairly heavily, but we found that with good weight distribution the bikes still handled excellently. Did they have enough in reserve, we wondered, to cope with the additional load of five gallons of petrol and a week's food and water, and with the extra strains of off-road riding?

iii)

WHERE SHOULD I START? I went back to the lists again, but the decision was soon made. Not Rotterdam or Southampton; the Channel and the west Mediterranean were well-known and well travelled. I would start in Europe, but as close to Asia as possible: Athens. Friends had told me of a steamer that shuttled passengers from Piraeus to the Greek island of Patmos, near Izmir in Turkey. From there I could find my way slowly to the Suez Canal, a first and formidable major hurdle.

iv)

Now I was cold, tired and confused, the visibility on the frozen sea water was less than 10 yards in freezing fog. I could not contact my small back-up team in Resolute by radio, atmospheric conditions near the magnetic North Pole preventing that.

My compass was swinging steadily back and forth from north to south. It was cold, about minus 15°C, but the wind in the fog lowered this to nearer minus 45°C.

But why was I there?

Because no one man had walked the place alone before. It was my Mount Everest and I was almost there, a miserable windswept icy hell somewhere where no one had ever stood alone.

❻ Now work with a partner to answer these questions:

1 In extract i), why did the two cyclists receive such a welcome from the villagers?
2 What does the writer mean by *getting the 'feel' of the bikes* in extract ii)?
3 What *spares* could the two motorcyclists have been carrying in extract ii)?
4 How did they manage to handle their bikes with such heavy loads on them?
5 Explain in your own words why the writer in extract iii) began his journey in Athens.
6 What kind of boat did he plan to take first?
7 Did he think it would be difficult or easy to pass through the Suez Canal? Which words give you the answer?
8 In extract iv), what problems was the writer facing?
9 What reasons does he give for making his journey? Is his reason understandable?
10 If you had to choose, which of these journeys would you go on?

Text 1

❶ Here is another extract from the story of the two cyclists' journey to Australia. There are six gaps where a short section is missing. Read the incomplete text fairly quickly to answer these questions:

1 What problem did the two cyclists face in North Africa?
2 What happened to Rick?
3 What happened to save him?

FREEZING!

From Morocco, the two cycled into Algeria – and it was there that their adventures almost turned to disaster.

For neither cyclist was prepared for the freezing temperatures in the hills of North Africa.

0 F

'We lay there wearing every article of clothing we had with us and wrapped up in our sleeping bags, but it was no good. We just couldn't get warm.

'Since our tent had no groundsheet, we were lying on the frozen ground and it just seemed to get colder and colder.'

1

'All I could feel was a terrible burning sensation in my fingers,' said Rick.

They decided to warm up by cycling on. But it only lasted for a few minutes. A mile down the road Rick, who was in front, came to a halt … and keeled over to lie motionless in the snow.

2

Desperately he worked to bring his companion round. For a while there was no response.

Eventually Rick opened his eyes … but he was clearly in danger. His face was blue and he was shivering violently. And they were miles from any town or village at 6 a.m.

3

David was aware of something approaching. And before he had a chance to say anything, a huge figure was next to them. It was a man on a horse.

'He was wearing a brown cloak and

hood,' said David. 'He was Algerian and couldn't speak a word of English, but he took control of the situation immediately.'

4

David said, 'It was rather frightening. I had absolutely no idea where he was taking him and the man made no effort to explain.'

5

'I am convinced that Rick could have died if it had not been for that man,' said David. 'It took Rick three hours to thaw out properly in front of the fire and all the time the Algerian fed us with milky coffee and biscuits.

'By about 10 a.m. we were back on the road after thanking the man profusely for everything he had done.'

2 Now choose one of the sections A–G to fit each gap. There is one extra sentence which you do not need to use. The first answer has been given as an example.

A With David wheeling the two bikes behind, the horseman rode for over a mile before stopping at a large camp in the mountains.

B Then something happened which they will never forget.

C By the early hours of the next morning, with their hands and feet completely numb, they could take it no longer.

D Horrified, David jumped off his bike and ran to the rescue.

E Terrified, the two realised they were surrounded by men with guns.

F The nights became colder and colder until one night they found it impossible to sleep.

G The Algerian heaved Rick up on to his horse and began to ride off down the road.

3 Now say whether the following statements are true or false without looking back at the text.

		True	False
1	The two cyclists had no shelter from the cold during the night.	☐	☐
2	They had put on all the clothes they were carrying.	☐	☐
3	Rick was too weak to continue cycling.	☐	☐
4	David didn't know what to do to help him.	☐	☐
5	When Rick opened his eyes, David knew he was going to be alright.	☐	☐
6	A stranger appeared very suddenly.	☐	☐
7	David hadn't heard the stranger coming up to them.	☐	☐
8	David is sure the stranger saved Rick's life.	☐	☐

4 Now look at the text again to check your answers. Find the word or phrase which gives you the correct answer.

131

Focus on listening 1 *Overland to Australia*

Listen to the interview on tape and answer these questions. For questions 2–6 below you must tick one or more of the boxes.

1 The part of Francesca's journey which will take the longest time is by
A car. ☐   **B** coach. ☐   **C** plane. ☐   **D** bus. ☐

2 Which countries will she pass through more than once?
A Italy ☐   **B** Greece ☐   **C** Turkey ☐   **D** Syria ☐   **E** Jordan ☐
F Iran ☐

3 Which countries did she have to obtain a visa for?
A Turkey ☐   **B** Syria ☐   **C** Jordan ☐   **D** Iran ☐   **E** Pakistan ☐
F India ☐   **G** Nepal ☐   **H** Burma ☐   **I** Australia ☐

4 Where will she sleep?
A In a tent ☐   **B** In the bus ☐   **C** In the bus and in hotels ☐
D In the bus and in a tent ☐

5 The information Francesca received told her about
A visas. ☐   **B** work permits. ☐   **C** clothes. ☐   **D** luggage. ☐
E injections. ☐   **F** insurance. ☐

6 The price includes
A hotel accommodation only. ☐   **B** all accommodation. ☐   **C** food. ☐
D transport. ☐   **E** spending money. ☐   **F** the cost of visas. ☐

7 The whole journey takes
A 10 weeks. ☐   **B** 12 weeks. ☐   **C** 4 months. ☐   **D** 6 months. ☐

8 One reason Francesca gives for wanting to make the journey now is that
A she can't find work in Britain. ☐
B she hasn't got anywhere to live in Britain. ☐
C she'll be too old for the company's age limit soon. ☐
D she hasn't any responsibilities to prevent her from going. ☐

Text 2 ❶

Here is another extract from the story of the motorcycle journey to Africa which Trisha Greenhalgh and her companion, Mat, made.

Read the text through once and find the answers to these questions:
1 What difficulty did the two meet?
2 How did they each react to it?
3 What happened in the end?

TRISHA GREENHALGH *tested her delight in danger on a motor-bike ride from England to the Sudan*

One morning, when we had been riding in the blazing sun and stifling humidity for five hours, we came to a narrow, rickety bridge
5 where the railway crossed a stagnant pond. For 30 feet there was nothing but the widely-spaced wooden sleepers under our wheels, and nothing to stop us falling into
10 the steaming bog below if we overbalanced. Right under the bridge lay the body of a dead cow. I watched Mat as he approached the bridge and rode straight over,
15 bump-bump-bump, without even slowing down. I stopped.

'What's up?' he yelled, from the other side.
'I'm not riding over that thing.
20 If I slip, I'll be in there with that cow!'
'There's nothing to it. I just did it, didn't I?'
'You're stronger, and taller. My
25 feet don't touch the ground. You do it for me!'
Mat said strength didn't come into it and rode off, leaving me staring down into the sickly brown
30 soup. He would be waiting for me around the next corner, but I knew he would give me at least an hour

before coming to help. The sun burned my face; sweat ran off my
35 forehead into my eyes and stuck my shirt to my body; big black tse tse flies stung me through my clothes and mosquitoes flew into my mouth when I breathed. To
40 remain stationary in this place was suicide; anyway, to sit around waiting for Mat to help was more than my feminist pride could take. I rode back along the track a few
45 hundred yards to get a good run-up, and over I went; bump-bump-bump. Mat was right: all the obstacles were in the mind.

From *'Hard Track to Africa'* by Trisha Greenhalgh in The Observer

❷ **Now study the following five questions and then read the text again to find the answers.**

1 The bridge looked dangerous to Trisha because
   A there was a 30-foot drop to the water below.
   B it had no barriers at the sides.
   C there were pieces of wood all over the road.
   D there was a railway line below.

2 Trisha stopped because
   A she was exhausted.
   B she suddenly saw the dead cow below.
   C she wanted to let Mat go first.
   D she was afraid of losing her balance.

3 Mat argued that
   A the bridge was not at all difficult to cross.
   B she had no other choice but to cross the bridge.
   C the cow was harmless because it was dead.
   D there was no difference between them in strength.

4 Mat rode away leaving Trisha because
   A he didn't know what he could do to help.
   B he felt she should overcome her fear by herself.
   C he didn't believe she was really afraid.
   D he couldn't wait any longer for her.

5 Trisha finally decided to ride across the bridge because
   A she realised that it was easier than it looked.
   B she was tired of waiting for Mat to come and help her.
   C she knew she couldn't stay where she was any longer.
   D she was afraid that Mat would go and leave her behind.

VOCABULARY ❸   Find the words in the passage which match the following definitions:
MATCHING
1   burning brightly ....
2   making it difficult to breathe ....
3   not strongly built, likely to break ....
4   not flowing or moving, often bad-smelling ....
5   heavy pieces of wood supporting a railway track ....
6   an area of soft, wet ground ....
7   shouted loudly ....
8   causing a sick feeling ....
9   standing still, not moving ....
10   things which stand in the way of progress ....

Focus on grammar 1   The gerund

The gerund, or **-ing** form, is a verbal noun. Gerunds can:
1   stand on their own as nouns: *Camping's fine for a couple of weeks.* (Listening 1)
2   follow certain verbs: *I enjoy camping very much.*
3   follow prepositions: *I like the idea of camping.*

1   GERUNDS AFTER PREPOSITIONS

EXERCISE 1   There have been several examples of gerunds following prepositions in the texts so far. Choose the correct preposition from the list below to complete the sentences.

of   after   before   without   by

a   They decided to warm up .... cycling on.
b   The horseman rode for over a mile .... stopping at a large camp in the mountains.
c   By about 10 a.m. we were back on the road .... thanking the man for everything he had done.
d   David was aware .... something approaching.
e   Mat rode straight over .... even slowing down.

▶   In fact the gerund may be used after **all** prepositions. Here is another example:
It's just a case of changing the money as you get into the new country. (Listening 1)

EXERCISE 2   Complete the following sentences by adding the correct prepositions and the gerund form of a suitable verb. (There is a list of the missing prepositions below, if you need help.)
a   I left home as soon as I was capable .... enough money to live on.
b   I would never use your telephone .... your permission first.
c   He explained that the machine was used .... bread into thin slices.
d   I'm afraid I'm awfully bad .... names. What's yours again?
e   She insisted .... her share of the bill.
f   He gave up his job because he was fed up .... such long hours.
g   My parents did nothing to prevent me .... a pop music group.
h   I had some difficulty .... a taxi at the station.

at   for   from   in   of   on   with   without

▶ The gerund also follows **to** when it is used as a preposition. The phrases below are the most common examples of this use and are all worth remembering!

look forward to   object to   prefer … to …   be used to

EXERCISE 3   Finish the sentences below with a suitable gerund form:

a   There's a small entrance fee and so far no one has objected to ....

b   Although he's a champion jockey, he actually prefers breeding dogs to ....

c   Now I've got a really good camera, I'm looking forward to ....

d   Don't worry about leaving me in charge of the children; I'm quite used to ....

2   GERUNDS AFTER VERBS

▶ The gerund is also used after certain verbs. *For example:*

Couldn't you delay sending the letter for a day or two?

The other common verbs which are followed by a gerund are listed below:

admit	delay	finish	involve	miss	resist
appreciate	deny	give up	keep	postpone	risk
avoid	dislike	can't help	mention	practise	can't stand
consider	enjoy	imagine	mind	put off	suggest

EXERCISE 1   Match the two halves of the sentences below so that they make sense:

a   He had been considering

b   The smell of the soup put me off

c   In court she strongly denied

d   He looked so funny that I couldn't help

e   If you don't take a map, you risk

f   Before our holiday we practised

g   As everyone was away we postponed

h   It's so hot, would you mind

1   meeting again till September.

2   getting completely lost.

3   starting his own company.

4   being anywhere near the scene of the crime.

5   wanting to taste it.

6   opening the window.

7   laughing out loud.

8   saying a few phrases in Greek.

EXERCISE 2   Complete the following sentences with suitable gerunds:

a   If you seriously want to save money, you'd better give up ....

b   I don't mind most housework but I can't stand ....

c   The puppies looked so sweet that I couldn't resist ....

d   If you want to learn to ride a horse, you won't be able to avoid ....

e   Must you keep .... ? It's really annoying!

f   I'd hate to be a miner. Can you imagine .... ?

g   Can I have the newspaper if you've finished .... ?

h   The man the police caught finally admitted ....

i   When he said he'd forgotten the phone number, I suggested ....

j   My job as Tourist Officer for Birmingham involves ....

3   GERUNDS AFTER OTHER EXPRESSIONS

Gerunds are also always used after the expressions in the following examples:

*It's no use **crying**.*

*It's no good **complaining to me**!*

The exam isn't worth worrying about.

135

4 GERUNDS AFTER POSSESSIVES

▶ Gerunds can be used after possessive adjectives and **'s**, as in the following examples:
I appreciated his meeting me at the station.
She mentioned Mike's telephoning last night.

▶ It is also correct in informal spoken and written English to use the alternative forms:
I appreciated him meeting me at the station.
She mentioned Mike telephoning last night.

Note

Some verbs like *begin* and *continue* can be used with either gerund or infinitive with no change of meaning. Others like *stop* and *remember* can be used with either but there is an important change of meaning. This second group will be dealt with in Unit 11.

STUDY BOX 2   Phrasal verb *bring*

'... he worked to **bring** his companion **round**.' (Text 1)

bring about – cause to happen.	*Disagreements between the two countries finally **brought about** a war.*
bring in – introduce.	*The government is **bringing in** a new law.*
bring off – to succeed in something difficult.	*I didn't think he'd win the race but he **brought** it **off** magnificently.*
bring out – make clear.	*The way he read the poem really **brought out** its meaning.*
bring round – help back to consciousness.	See example above.
bring up – raise a child.	*I was **brought up** in the country.*

Communication activity *Quiz*

John Ridgeway took his wife, Marie, on a 30,000-mile round-the-world yacht race. There were 12 other members of the crew, each chosen carefully by John, after a week-long selection process.

❶ Do you have the qualities needed to undertake such a long and difficult journey?

Do the special quiz (set by John) and find out.

How do you rate as a round-the-world rover?

1 **How old are you?**
   a 18–25
   b 25–35
   c over 35 or under 18

2 **Are you**
   a married and a parent?
   b single with a regular girlfriend or boyfriend?
   c single and unattached?

3 **Do you prefer to spend your lunch hours**
   a alone?
   b with one other person?
   c with a crowd in the canteen?

4 **You are just arriving at a bus stop as a bus is leaving. Do you**
   a run for the bus?
   b wait for the next one?
   c walk?

5 **You discover that a borrowed book on your shelves belongs to a friend who has left the district. Do you**
   a post it to him immediately?
   b write to him and ask if he wants it returned?
   c keep it as a souvenir?

6 **You wake at 10 a.m., and were due at work at 9 a.m. Do you**
   a risk getting into trouble by telephoning to say why you'll be late?
   b go in, and blame everything on public transport?
   c go the next day and say you were too ill to phone?

7 **The zip in your skirt/trousers breaks before an important interview. Do you**
   a tell the interviewer what happened?
   b buy a new skirt/pair of trousers?
   c buy a packet of safety pins?

8 **Which of the following habits do you have?**
   a smoking
   b playing a musical instrument
   c reading books

9 **There has been an argument in your office. Do you**
   a keep well out of it?
   b sympathise with both sides separately?
   c suggest to each side that the other might just be in the right?

10 **Are you doing your present job (or would you choose a job)**
   a because it pays well?
   b because there was nothing better around?
   c because it fits your career plan?

11 **You are staying in a youth hostel with friends. Returning to your dormitory after a hard day, you find you have an 'apple-pie' bed (as a joke, someone has made your bed in such a way that you can't get into it!). Do you**
   a switch on the lights and demand to know who made it?
   b wait until morning to find out?
   c wait until next morning and make 'apple-pie' beds all round?

12 **The company with which you have worked for ten years is in serious financial difficulty. Do you**
   a ask your union to fight for the highest possible redundancy pay?
   b leave immediately?
   c offer to give up your next pay rise to help keep down the company's costs?

13 **What is the longest period of full-time training you have undergone since leaving school?**

14 **How many days have you had off work or study because of illness during the past year?**

❷ Now compare your answers with those of another student. Discuss your reasons for choosing them.

❸ One answer in each question will earn the highest mark. This will be the answer which shows the qualities or attitudes needed by someone who is going on a long and difficult journey, as a member of a team. Work through the questions again, with your partner, and choose the answers which you think will earn the top mark. Be prepared to say why you have chosen them!

❹ When you have chosen your answers together, check the answers on page 228. Would you make a round-the-world traveller? How many correct answers did you and your partner choose? Did you choose them for the right reasons?

Text 3 *The call of the wild*

Christina Dodwell has travelled extensively for many years and during her time in Papua New Guinea, Central America and South East Asia she's learnt something about how to survive in distant places. Here are a few of her tips.

❶ Read through the text fairly quickly and then choose suitable headings from the list below (A–I) for each section. There is one extra heading which you do not need.

A Out for the night	**D** Eat like a native	**G** Keep well
B On the move	**E** Welcome to my home	**H** Make the right impression
C What to pack	**F** In deep water	**I** Watch out for the wildlife

0 D

First make a fire – modern travellers can use a camera lens to do this. Now choose your menu.

Lion meat can taste like beef if it is slowly pot-roasted, and monkey meat is much improved by marinating it beforehand. Crocodile tail is a delicacy, a white fish meat which tastes similar to lobster. Ostrich eggs are very rich and creamy and are excellent scrambled.

Big leaves will serve as extra plates; a small twig, peeled and sharpened, is a fork.

1 G

To prevent painful blisters on feet, put soap on the inside of your socks before setting out. Plants have been used in healing wounds from the earliest days. Yarrow used to be carried into battle to stop bleeding. It also has antiseptic qualities and can be chewed to relieve toothache. Crushed strawberries help to soothe sunburn.

2 I

Most insects are harmless but don't rely on this. I was once bitten by a hunting spider. Within a short time my body had become paralysed and my heart was hammering as though I'd run up a mountain. I was freezing cold, but at the same time sweat poured off me, and the pain was excruciating.

It was two weeks before I recovered enough to walk.

The bites of poisonous creatures like scorpions and snakes are very seldom fatal and you can take avoiding action. Always knock shoes or boots before putting them on, for instance.

3 C

Sand is lovely to sleep in. Wriggle until it fits your shape. To be warmest in your sleeping bag, you should take off your clothes so that your body heat circulates properly. Old newspaper provides excellent insulation so screw some up loosely inside your sleeping bag.

4 B

Travelling with pack animals can be a maddeningly slow business. Donkeys walk at about 4 km an hour for 12 hours; a sturdy camel carries 250 kg with ease, walks at about 5 km an hour and covers about 27 km a day. But its speed and distance are better if it marches by night and rests by day. To obtain a camel, look in desert headquarters for retired army animals. Nomads often do not want to sell because their animals represent wealth.

5 H

Shabby, scruffy clothes will affect people's attitude to you; if you look respectable, you will usually be treated with respect.

6 A

If you are walking in hostile territory, it is better to stay overnight in a village. The same people who would rob you in the bush are honour-bound to protect you if you stay in their village.

7 C

Photographs of your home and family; remote people love to see pictures of where you come from. Photos of snow get interesting reactions in the tropics. The most successful trade goods are tobacco, lighters, pens and T-shirts. Don't forget a supply of pencils – a pencil will work on damp paper.

❷ Find words or phrases in the text which mean the same as the following. The number of the section is given in brackets:

1 something rare which is considered good to eat (0) *delicacy Crocodile*
2 a very small thin branch of a tree (0) *a small twig*
3 not able to move (2) *paralysed*
4 beating strongly (2) *Hammering*
5 extremely bad (of pain) (2) *exeruciating*
6 twist and turn your body (3) ....
7 something which stops heat from escaping (3) ....
8 strong (4) ....
9 members of a tribe which moves from place to place (4) ....
10 unfriendly (6) ....

Focus on grammar 2   The past perfect

EXERCISE 1 Look at these extracts from the texts in this unit. Underline all the examples of the past perfect tense in them.

a Within a short time my body had become paralysed ... (Text 3)
b ... my heart was hammering as though I'd run up a mountain. (Text 3)
c By about 10 a.m. we were back on the road after thanking the man profusely for everything he had done. (Text 1)
d One morning when we had been riding in the blazing sun and stifling humidity for five hours, we came to a narrow, rickety bridge ... (Text 2)

FORM Now complete the tables below to show how the tense is formed:

Past perfect simple

Had   +
Hadn't

Past perfect continuous

Had   +
Hadn't

MEANING In extracts b, c and d above there are at least **two** actions in the past. The past perfect is used to show which one happened first.

Here is another example. The numbers show which action happened first and which happened later:

2   1
When the police arrived, the thieves had left the building.

a Did the police make any arrests? Why not?
b How would the meaning change if we used the past simple for both actions?
c Would the numbers change if we used the past simple for both actions?

Write the numbers 1 or 2 above the main verbs in extracts c and d above to show which action(s) happened first, before the other action(s).

Notes

1   The past perfect simple is used when one action has finished before another one starts and there is usually a time gap between the two actions. If one happens very quickly after another, or is the immediate result of the other, the past simple is used for both. *For example:*

> When I *heard* his car arrive, I *rushed* out to meet him.

2   If the order of events is clear anyway, it's not necessary to use the past perfect. *For example:*

> I *went* to the doctor's surgery and then *called* at the chemist's.

3   The past perfect continuous is used when the first action continued for some time or was unfinished. *For example:*

> I knew by the look on their faces that they *had been talking* about me.

EXERCISE 2   Complete the following story by putting the verbs in brackets into the correct tense, past simple, past perfect simple or past perfect continuous:

I (just/finish) [1] writing a letter when the door bell (ring) [2]. I (go) [3] immediately to answer it because a neighbour of mine (tell) [4] me she was going to call round. When I (open) [5] the door, I (see) [6] that there was no one there although I was sure I (hear) [7] the bell. After I (look) [8] up and down the street for a few minutes, I (shut) [9] the door again and (begin) [10] to wonder if I (dream) [11]. I (decide) [12] finally that I (mistake) [13] a car horn for the sound of the door bell. Just as I was turning round, I (notice) [14] something white on the door mat. I (examine) [15] it more closely and (realise) [16] that someone (push) [17] a note under the door. As I (never/see) [18] the handwriting before, I (begin) [19] to feel slightly alarmed.

EXERCISE 3   The past perfect tense is often used in **reported speech** where both the past simple and present perfect in the original words are changed to the past perfect.

Change the following into reported speech:

a   I hope you have read the instructions carefully.
The examiner said he hoped that we ....

b   I'm not sure I've found the answer to your question though I've spent a week thinking about it.
She explained that she wasn't sure that she ....

c   I can't shake hands with you because my hands are oily. I've been working on the car, you see.
He said he couldn't shake hands with me because his hands were oily and explained that

....

"Because it was you who forgot the flag, that's why."

Focus on listening 2

You are going to hear part of an interview with David Hempleman-Adams, who walked alone to the North Pole. For questions 1–10 tick (✓) whether you think the statements are true or false.

		True	False
1	David spent two years planning the first expedition.	☐	☐
2	On that expedition he succeeded in reaching the geographical North Pole.	☐	☐
3	Many people thought he wouldn't survive the cold.	☐	☐
4	He enjoyed making the expedition.	☐	☐
5	He missed the sense of danger after he returned to England.	☐	☐
6	He had air support [1] on both his expeditions.	☐	☐
7	He hadn't expected to be attacked by a polar bear.	☐	☐
8	The bear ate the Mars bar [2] before attacking him.	☐	☐
9	He immediately tried to kill the animal.	☐	☐
10	He regretted having had to kill it.	☐	☐

---

[1] regular supplies of food dropped by plane
[2] a type of chocolate bar

STUDY BOX 3   **Verbs of perception**

see   *watch*   *hear*   *notice*   *feel*   *observe*

These verbs are followed by an object + *-ing* when they refer to part of an action.
   I **heard** him singing. (I didn't hear the whole song.)
   We **watched** the man mending the road. (We didn't wait until the job was done.)
   I **felt** something crawling up my arm. (I didn't wait for it to reach the top!)

They are followed by an object + infinitive (without *to*) when they refer to a complete action.
   Did you **see** that woman steal a watch? (take it and put it in her bag)
   I **noticed** an old lady cross the road. (from one side to the other)

Focus on writing *Formal letter 1*   WRITING BANK: PAGE 114

LAYOUT   **❶**   Working in pairs, put the following information in the correct places on the letter below.

1 **Your address:**

   22 Green Lane, Bath, Avon

2 **The name and address of the person you are writing to:**

   The Project Director, Amazon Expedition, 8 Bell St., London WC3 5YA

3 **The date:**

4 **The beginning:**

   Dear Sir,

5 **The ending:**

   Yours faithfully,

I was very interested in your advertisement in today's edition of The Evening Post and I should like to apply to be a member of the Amazon Expedition team.

I am twenty-three years old and have an honours degree in Botany from Bath University. Since leaving university I have been working in a research laboratory but my contract comes to an end in six weeks. I would particularly like to join the expedition for the opportunity it would give me to study the plant life of the area.

I enjoy several outdoor activities including rowing and rock climbing and I consider myself to be both fit and healthy enough to undertake such an expedition.

If you would like me to attend an interview, I would be able to come at any time convenient to you, as my employers have agreed to give me time off for the purpose.

I look forward to hearing from you.

❷   Do you think this applicant is suitable? What questions would you ask him?

STYLE **3** This letter was sent in response to the same advertisement but it didn't create a very good impression! Read it through to see why not.

4 Work with a partner to underline all the features of style which are unsuitable in this kind of letter. What else in the letter makes you think that David Morecambe would not be a very suitable member of the team? When you have finished, check your result with that of another pair.

NOTE
A formal letter does not need to be written in very formal language these days. You should aim to express yourself clearly and concisely and to avoid slang, idiomatic expressions and abbreviations.

> Dear Sir,
> I noticed an ad. in the paper today which said you were looking for people to join your expedition team. It sounded as if it might be fun so I'm writing to say I'd like to come along.
> About myself: I left school at 16 because I couldn't stand the teachers and I wanted to earn a bit of money.
> After that I got a few part-time jobs as a waiter, etc., but I didn't stick any of them for long.
> Recently I've been doing a bit of hitch-hiking round Europe so I've had some experience of travelling the hard way which should come in handy on the expedition you're planning.
> By the way, I'm a great guitarist so I can keep you all amused round the campfire at night.
> Let me know when I can call in for a chat about dates and other details, etc.
> Yours
> David Morecambe

WRITING
TASK
PART 1
FORMAL LETTER

5 In Part 1 of the Writing Paper in the First Certificate examination, you have to write a letter based on information that you are given. It is important to read the instructions and information very carefully so that you include all the important points.

You are interested in joining the short expedition advertised below. Read carefully the advertisement and the notes which you have made beneath it. Then write your letter to the group leader, covering the points in your notes and adding any relevant information about yourself. Write your **letter** in **120–180** words (excluding the addresses).

when?

how long for?

Do something different
this spring!

how many?

(Small group) expedition to the Atlas Mountains in Morocco aiming to observe the everyday life of local people, with opportunities for trekking, bird-watching, etc. You should be reasonably fit and prefer mountain huts to grand hotels. We need people with useful skills, e.g. cooking, first aid, or photography. French/Arabic speakers also welcome.

If you want to apply to join us or if you would like more information, write to: *Rob Nales, 23 The Shrubbery, Downend, Clevedon.*

cost?

Is any special equipment needed?

Remember to mention:
* why you are writing
* your reason for wanting to join the expedition
* your relevant skills
* the questions you have

Focus on writing *Formal letter 2*

DESCRIBING OBJECTS

❶ Look at the following expressions and then use them to describe the objects below.

Materials			Patterns		
It's They're	made of	wool (It's woollen) leather cotton wood (It's wooden) silk plastic etc.	It's They're		spotted checked striped plain

See Functions Bank, pages 109–110 for adjectives describing shape.

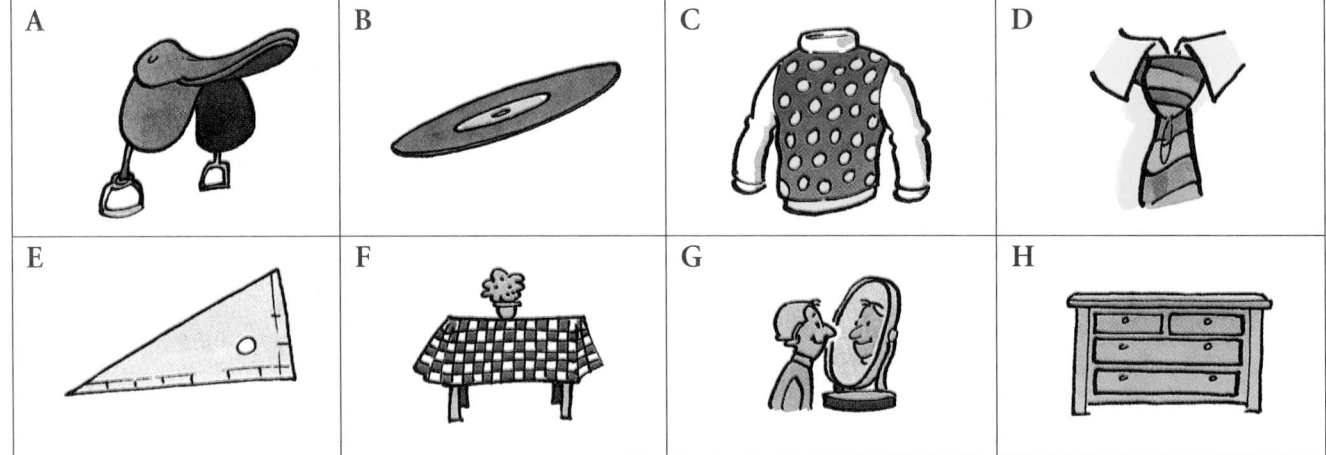

A   B   C   D

E   F   G   H

❷ Fill in the adjectives which have the opposite meaning to the following:

long	....	wide	....	expensive	....
hard	....	full	....	enormous	....
heavy	....	sharp	....	curved	....
thick	....	tight	....	dark (of colours)	....
smooth	....	hollow	....	bright (of colours)	....

WRITING TASK

❸ On a recent journey to Scotland for an adventure training course, one of your suitcases was lost by the airline. The picture below shows the case and some of its contents (but you should be able to remember a few more). Write a formal letter to the airline company (Customer Relations Officer, Beeline Travel Ltd., 26 Kingsway, Edinburgh, Scotland) giving details of the case and the main items it contained so that the company can check to see if it has been found. Write your **letter** in **120–180** words excluding the addresses.

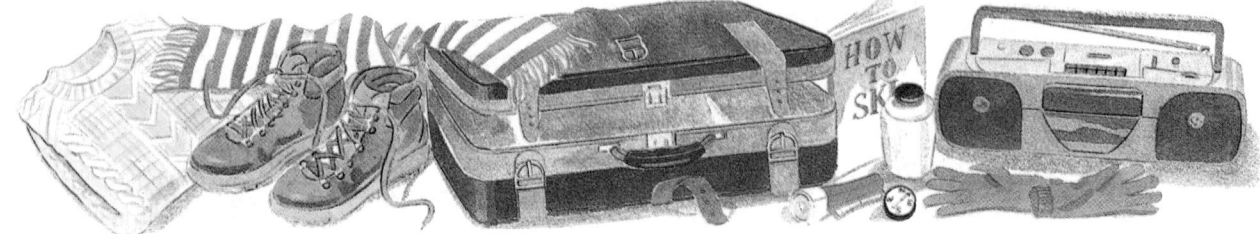

PLAN First paragraph:
Explain why you are writing and give details of the flight (airports of departure and destination, date, time, flight number.

Middle paragraphs:
Describe the suitcase and its contents giving the necessary details to help the company to recognise your belongings (size, colour, material, etc.). Use from one to three paragraphs as necessary.

Last paragraph:
Explain what you would like the airline to do (return your case or pay compensation).

Language review

Choose the word or phrase which best completes each sentence.

1   The first job was to .... the car with the equipment they would need.
    A supply   **B** charge   **C** load   **D** stock

2   It's a good idea to carry a .... pair of shoes in case the ones you're wearing get wet.
    A repeat   **B** final   **C** double   **D** spare

3   Unfortunately the train .... by the time I reached the platform.
    A left   **B** has left   **C** had left   **D** had been leaving

4   The whole team .... a great effort to raise money for the expedition.
    A did   **B** made   **C** put   **D** took

5   Be sure to .... yourself up well if you're going for a walk by the sea.
    A wrap   **B** pack   **C** wind   **D** clothe

6   I've written to the company to complain but so far there's been no ....
    A repeat   **B** receipt   **C** return   **D** response

7   Someone fainted during the lecture and when we couldn't manage to .... him round, we called an ambulance.
    A take   **B** get   **C** bring   **D** pull

8   If you don't pay the fee now, you risk .... your place on the course.
    A of losing   **B** losing   **C** to lose   **D** lose

9   After the assassination of the president, the army .... control of the country.
    A gave   **B** made   **C** led   **D** took

10 Be careful you don't .... on the ice near the door.
    A swing   **B** slide   **C** slip   **D** sink

11 'What's .... ?' she called when she saw our anxious faces.
    A up   **B** on   **C** about   **D** out

12 Working in the midday heat made him .... so much that his shirt stuck to his body.
    A drain   **B** sweat   **C** strain   **D** transpire

13 Riding a horse isn't as difficult as it looks. In fact, there's nothing .... it!
    A to   **B** for   **C** in   **D** by

14 Our wet clothes .... as they dried in front of the fire.

    A smoked   **B** steamed   **C** thawed   **D** streamed

15 I'm really looking forward .... my new job.

    A start   **B** to start   **C** starting   **D** to starting

Odd man out

In each of the following groups of words, there is one which does not fit. Work in pairs to choose the 'odd man out' in each group and say why it doesn't belong there.

NOTE   **There may be more than one correct answer!**

1   steamer   liner   ferry   <u>tram</u>   yacht

2   cart   tractor   wagon   sledge   pram (several possibilities!)

3   lorry   truck   car   van   petrol-tanker

4   taxi   tram   bus   coach   train

5   guard's van   carriage   sleeping car   track   runway

6   pilot   captain   conductor   engine-driver   cyclist

7   anchor   deck   cabin   platform   porthole

8   terminus   station   double-decker   bus-stop   driver

9   horse   ox   camel   dog   goat

10 Rotterdam   Southampton   Cairo   Bombay   Marseilles

Lead-in

❶ Look at the pictures of two different family groups below. Describe each one.

❷ What are the advantages and disadvantages of growing up with several brothers and sisters in the family?

What are the advantages and disadvantages of growing up as an only child?

❸

QUESTIONNAIRE

There are 12 statements below. Read each one carefully and decide if you agree or disagree with it. Then write A (if you agree) or D (if you disagree) in the box on the right.

1   For women, financial support is one of the most important reasons for getting married. □
2   Women should work outside the home and make a financial contribution to the family budget. □
3   A husband should share his earnings fairly with his wife. □
4   A husband should help very little in the home, if the wife stays at home. □
5   If the wife works full-time, housework should be shared equally between both partners. □
6   Women should spend more time than men with children. □
7   Mothers shouldn't go out to work while their children are small. □
8   A husband should have the last word on big decisions. □
9   A woman's career is just as important as a man's. □
10 Both husbands and wives should be free to have interests and friends of their own. □
11 Older children should help with the housework. □
12 Parents should always respect the wishes of their children. □

When you've finished, compare your answers with other students' and discuss the reasons for your opinions.

Text I

❶ Why was teenager Simon Richards arrested? Read the first three paragraphs of the text to find out, then check your answer with another student.

❷ Now read the whole text fairly quickly to find out more about the story.

SCRUFF JUSTICE

Police are called in as teenager refuses to tidy his bedroom

THE NEXT time teenager Simon Richards is told to tidy his room he won't argue … or he might get arrested.

That is what happened when the 18-year-old ignored his mother's requests for him to clear up his mess. First, he locked himself in the garden shed as a protest. Then, after he refused to **budge**, Mrs Richards summoned two police officers.

When Simon popped his head out of the shed an hour later he felt a firm hand on his shoulder. The following day he admitted **disorderly behaviour** in the local magistrate's court and was **bound over** for three months.

The result would win applause in homes throughout the country. It is a tale of the **gulf** between parents who want a tidy bedroom and a teenage rebel who needs his own space.

ORDER

The small room at the back of the Richards' large semi-detached house has always been a source of disagreement between Simon and his mother.

Mrs Richards, a mother of two boys and four girls, and her husband, Desmond, are very strict. Simon must be home at 10.30 **sharp** every night. The children – four still live at home – are expected to help out with household **chores.** Being late for the family evening meal is unforgivable. But above all, everything should be in its place.

Much of it goes back to when Mrs Richards was a girl. 'I was always taught to look after my own property. Simon can have his room as he wants it to a certain extent, but if it gets too untidy, then I get annoyed.'

Once a week, she grabs a bin bag and **puts on a brave face** before she enters Simon's room.

There, among scattered clothes and foot-high piles of newspapers, she sometimes has to empty eight overflowing ashtrays and carry several mugs back to their place on the rack. 'It usually takes me quite a while to **get it straight,**' she complained.

But Simon said: 'I thought it was my own space, and that I could keep it as I wanted. Generally, I think it is tidy, but I know my idea of that is different from my mum's idea. I've always felt very comfortable in it and so I thought it didn't matter.' But last week it did matter.

Mrs Richards said: 'I told him to tidy his room and when he refused I said he might as well sleep in the shed. So he said he would.'

SORRY

Worn down by the battle between them, Carol decided there was only one thing to do – call the police. 'I wanted to give him a sharp shock to make him see my point of view. I didn't want them to arrest him, but they decided they had no choice. I do not regret doing it, although I am sorry for hurting him because I love him very much. Most of the time you could not wish for a better son.'

But has the treatment worked?

Since the incident, Simon has redecorated his room and managed to keep it tidier. He said:

'Going to court was not nice but I know Mum did it to make a point. I'll be keeping the room tidy from now on – at least, as tidy as I know how.'

From *The Evening Standard*

❸ **Discuss these questions with another student.**

1 Do you think Simon's mother did the right thing? Why/Why not?

2 How do you think Simon felt when he was arrested?

3 Do you think he will keep his room tidy in future?

❹ **Nine words or phrases that you may not know appear in bold type in the text. Study them carefully and think about what they could mean in the context. Below are nine explanations but they are not in the same order. Match each explanation to the correct word or phrase.**

1 exactly (of time)   ....

2 ordered by law to cause no more trouble   ....

3 tries not to look as upset as she feels   ....

4 move from a particular place   ....

5 a serious lack of understanding   ....

6 made tired and weak   ....

7 small regular jobs around the house   ....

8 make it tidy   ....

9 causing trouble in public   ....

❺ **Read the text carefully to answer the following questions.**

1 Simon was in the garden shed because

  A his mother had sent him there as a punishment.

  B he didn't want to be arrested by the police.

  C he wanted to show that he was angry with his mother.

  D he had locked the door by accident and couldn't get out.

2 He was arrested

  A when the police broke into the shed.

  B as soon as he looked out of the shed.

  C after he tried to fight with the police.

  D the next day when he admitted that he had behaved badly.

3 How does the writer think that other parents would feel about the incident?

  A They would be shocked by what Mrs Richards did.

  B They would worry about the effect on Simon.

  C They would approve of Mrs Richards' action.

  D They would criticise the police for arresting Simon.

4 Mrs Richards is very concerned about tidiness

  A because of the way she was brought up.

  B because it's important in a house with six children.

  C because otherwise she can never find anything.

  D because she wants to impress the neighbours.

5 How does Simon feel about being arrested?

  A He's ashamed of himself.

  B He's very upset about appearing in court.

  C He thinks it was an exciting experience.

  D He doesn't blame his mother.

Focus on grammar 1 The infinitive

THE INFINITIVE WITH *TO* IS USED:

▶ to express purpose. *For example:*

I know Mum did it to make a point. (Text 1)
It usually takes me quite a while to get it straight. (Text 1)

EXERCISE 1 Complete the following sentences, using an infinitive with **to**.

a He's got to go on a diet ....
b We've decided to employ an architect ....
c They telephoned the police ....
d There's a plumber coming tomorrow ....
e I went to the doctor's ....
f We had to call the Fire Brigade ....
g He joined the army ....
h .... the team will have to play extremely well.

▶ after **adjectives**. *For example:*

He's unlikely to get the job.
You're free to leave whenever you want.

▶ also with **too + adjective**, and **adjective + enough**. *For example:*

This tea is too hot (for me) to drink.
Are you strong enough to lift that by yourself?

EXERCISE 2 To complete the following sentences, choose an adjective from List A and a verb from List B. Don't forget to use **to** with the infinitive.

List A

delighted	certain	simple	important	hard	amazed	anxious	disappointed

List B

meet	check	know	use	believe	be	hear	see

a They told me in the shop that this camera was .... , but I can't get used to it at all!
b I was .... from his mother that he didn't get the job he wanted so much.
c I'm sure you're all very .... what your exam results are.
d You can wait for him if you like – he's .... home before 6 o'clock.
e It's .... it's June when you see all this rain!
f I've learned so much about you and I'm .... you at last.
g We were all .... your picture in the paper. How on earth did that come about?
h It's very .... that the electricity is switched off before you start.

EXERCISE 3 Complete the following sentences:

a This case is too heavy for me ....
b There aren't enough eggs ....
c Is the runway long enough for the plane ....
d The weather is too bad for the ship ....

e   He's too short-sighted ....

f   Have you had enough practice ....

▶   after **main verbs**. *For example*:

He refused to budge. (Text 1)

Simon has managed to keep his room tidier. (Text 1)

Other common verbs which take an infinitive with **to** are:

afford	ask	expect	help	learn	prepare	seem
agree	begin	fail	hope	offer	pretend	
arrange	choose	happen	intend	prefer	promise	

▶   after the **object of a verb**. *For example*:

I told him to tidy his room. (Text 1)

I didn't want them to arrest him. (Text 1)

Other common verbs which take an object followed by an infinitive with *to* are:

advise	encourage	force	intend	order	recommend	warn
allow	expect	get	invite	persuade	remind	
ask	forbid	help	leave	prefer	teach	

EXERCISE 4   Complete the following sentences with suitable verbs from the two lists above. Fill in an object where necessary.

a   We did everything we could to .... come with us, but he refused.

b   Would you .... have tea or coffee?

c   If you .... see him, please give him my regards.

d   Could you .... set the alarm for 6 a.m.? It would be terrible if I overslept.

e   When I was a child, my parents .... play in the street, though I wanted to.

f   Are you sure you can .... buy a new car? Wouldn't a second-hand one be wiser?

g   He .... take a course in typing and said it would be very useful for me.

h   When I leave school, I .... get a job in a television studio.

i   If you take on an assistant, it will .... get through your work more quickly.

j   I .... climb the tree, but you ignored me. Now I don't know how we'll get you down!

▶   after some **auxiliary verbs**. *For example*:

I had to look after Sarah. (Text 2)

You need to take more care.

Other verbs in this group are: *be, ought, used.*

▶   as the **subject of a sentence**. *For example*:

To try to escape would be foolish!

THE INFINITIVE WITHOUT *TO* IS USED:

▶   after **modal verbs**. *For example*:

Simon must be home at 10.30 sharp. (Text 1)

Other verbs in this group are: *will, shall, would, should, can, could, may, might.*

▶ after **make** and **let**. *For example:*

> *You can't make me do anything!*
> *Let the next patient come in now.*

▶ after **would rather, had better** and **why not ...?** *For example:*

> *I'd rather take a train (than fly).*
> *You'd better stay in bed.*
> *Why not come with us?*

EXERCISE 1   The following passage describes the attitudes of two families, one French and one British, towards money. Put the verbs in brackets into the correct form: **infinitive** with **to**, **infinitive** without **to**, or **gerund**.

'What's the point in (worry)[1] too much about the future?' says Francine Beudet. Francine, her husband Hervé, and daughter, Marine, live 100 miles south of Paris. 'We don't save much. We prefer (spend)[2] our money now on (have)[3] a good life.'

In England, Gordon and Fiona Robinson take the same approach to money. Fiona decided (stay)[4] at home (look after)[5] their daughter, Chloe, who is nearly 3. 'I have considered (take)[6] a part-time job, but as it's impossible for Gordon (be)[7] home at a set time each evening, it's too difficult (arrange)[8] at the moment.'

On the other side of the Channel, Francine has found an ideal solution to the problem of (combine)[9] work with (run)[10] a home and (bring up)[11] children. She's a nurse and she works part-time at an old people's home. Although the hospital is close to Francine's home, she needs a car (get)[12] there quickly.

Hervé is expected (buy)[13] his own car but he does receive hotel and petrol expenses for his work, which involves (drive)[14] an enormous distance each year. He organises his work so that when Francine is on night duty, he can (get)[15] home every evening (take)[16] care of Marine.

Gordon's car is provided by his employer and he is lucky enough (get)[17] a new one every two years. He also spends each working day (travel)[18] around his area, but instead of (stay)[19] overnight in hotels, he manages (get)[20] home.

From *'Vive la différence', Mail on Sunday Magazine*

STUDY BOX 1   Phrasal verb *look*

'I was always taught to *look after* my own property.' (Text 1)

look after – take care of.	See example above.
look for – try to find.	I'm **looking for** my keys. Have you seen them?
look in – visit.	I'll **look in** and see you next week.
look into – investigate.	Police are **looking into** several burglaries in the area.
look out – take care (usually imperative).	**Look out!** There's a car coming.
look through – examine.	**Look through** the contract carefully before you sign it.
look up – search for information.	I had to **look** the spelling **up** in the dictionary.
look up to – respect.	He's always **looked up to** his elder brother.

Communication activity

Work in pairs for this activity:

Student A: Look at the instructions below and the picture on page 227.
Student B: Look at the instructions below and the picture on page 229.

INSTRUCTIONS

The pictures are the same except for ten small differences.

You must find the differences by describing your pictures to each other. Do not let your partner see your picture!

Take it in turns to describe a section of the picture in detail. Be prepared to ask each other questions in order to be sure that what you see is exactly the same. When you discover a difference, make a note of it.

Focus on listening 1 *Children speaking*

1 You are going to hear three children being interviewed. As you listen, fill in the missing information in the table below.

	Age	Brothers/ Sisters	Pocket money	Spends money on …	Help in the house	Punishment	Bed Time	
							Earliest	**Latest**
First child		2 brothers		sweets	.... and laying the table.	gets sent to bed or gets a smack.		11 p.m.
Second child	7			sweets	.... wiping up + putting things away.		8 or 9 p.m.	
Third child			£1–£2		.... and bring the knives and forks.			11 p.m.

DISCUSSION POINTS

2 Work with a partner. Tell each other:
1 how much pocket money you got as a child, and what you used to spend it on.
2 what you did to help in the house.
3 what time you went to bed when you were eight or nine years old.
4 how your parents punished you if you were ever naughty!

3 What time should an eight-year-old child go to bed? What exceptions would you make?

4 Should you smack naughty children? What other punishments can be used?

Text 2 *Working mothers: what children say*

In the texts on page 155, four children give their opinions about having a working mother.

❶ Which of the four (A, B, C or D):

found their sister a problem at first?

gets more pocket money for helping in the house?

was a very young child when their mother started working?

plans to be a different kind of parent?

wouldn't mind giving up foreign holidays if their mother stopped working?

sometimes helps to look after smaller children?

didn't feel very close to their mother as a child?

finds it interesting to listen to their mother's experiences?

would like their mother to visit their school more often?

learned to enjoy being independent after a while?

1	A
2	B
3	C
4	D
5	B
6	C
7	D
8	B
9	C
10	A

❷ Debbie and Penny use several colloquial expressions. Choose the best explanation for the examples below:

1 I had enough *on my plate* (Debbie)
   A enough things to deal with   **B** enough food to eat   **C** enough work to do

2 without having Sarah *tagging along* (Debbie)
   A watching   **B** waiting   **C** following

3 she *shrugged us off* (Debbie)
   A behaved violently towards us   **B** made us angry   **C** treated us as unimportant

4 she wouldn't *nag* (Debbie)
   A understand   **B** complain   **C** approve

5 I haven't been *mollycoddled* (Penny)
   A protected too much   **B** given too many toys   **C** allowed too much freedom

6 she *switches off* (Penny)
   A stops watching television   **B** stops paying attention   **C** stops speaking on the telephone

❸ Find words or phrases in the section about Peter Swift which mean the same as:
1 lots   *loads of*
2 cut (with a machine)   *mow the lawn*
3 find time for doing something   *to get round to*
4 spoken angrily to   *getting told of*
5 exchange   *to swap*

Debbie Hollobon   A

Debbie Hollobon, aged 21, comes from Northamptonshire. Her mother has worked full time
5 *since Debbie was aged 13 and her sister, Sarah, was ten.*

'I didn't like it a bit when she took a full-time job and, as the elder sister, I had to
10 look after Sarah. Everything seemed to come at once: we'd just moved to Daventry and I was in my second year at comprehensive school and
15 meeting new people and making new friends. I felt I had enough on my plate without having Sarah tagging along every time I
20 went out. I went through a stage where I couldn't stand her; she seemed to get in the way of everything I wanted to do.'

25 'I never told my mum how I felt. I knew she'd have been miserable sitting at home alone in a town where she didn't know anyone, so the
30 job was very good for her. Once the initial shock wore off, I got to like it, being trusted with my own key and feeling grown up and
35 independent.'

'However much she had to do, coming home to the cooking and cleaning after a day's work, she always had
40 time for us when we wanted to talk. There was never a time when she shrugged us off because she was too tired or too busy.'

45 'I probably helped around the house more than I would have done with a stay-at-home mother, but she never told me to do any chores
50 before she got home. I did

what I felt like when I felt like it and I knew she wouldn't nag if it wasn't done.'

Peter Swift   B

Peter Swift, aged 15, lives near Leeds. His mother has worked as a graphic designer for the last three years.

55 'I hate it; I've always hated it. Mum disappears at 7.30 a.m. and doesn't get home until about 7.30 p.m., so we come home to an empty
60 house. It doesn't worry my sister Elizabeth. She's a year older than me and has loads of homework, so she sits upstairs working and I'm left
65 on my own.'

'Elizabeth and I both have our own chores. I load the dishwasher and I sometimes wash the car or mow the
70 grass. Elizabeth does the ironing – well, she says she does, but she never seems to get round to ironing my shirts. We get extra pocket
75 money because we help out, so I suppose it's fair, but all my friends do absolutely nothing around the house.'

'There is a good side to it.
80 Mum has lots of interesting things to tell us and I like to hear her talk about the people she meets. We probably get more freedom,
85 too – I can make my models on the table without getting told off. We wouldn't have as much money for trips to France or hobbies like
90 photography if she didn't work, but I'd swap all that if it meant she'd be at home like she used to be.'

Michael Hunt   C

Michael Hunt's mother went
95 *back to full-time work when he was 18 months old. Now, at eight, he spends the school holidays with a childminder near his*
100 *Hertfordshire home. In term-time, he goes home with a classmate and waits for his mother to collect him.*

'Mum takes me to
105 Andrew's house before she goes to work and I go to school with him, then I go home with him in the afternoon. I don't like that
110 much because he's not really one of my friends. He's much taller than me and he's rough; he's always sitting on me.'

115 'I go to a better place in the holidays; Aunty Jane takes us swimming and we go walking down to the river. The other children
120 there are younger than me so I help out and make sure the little ones don't fall in the water.'

'It would be much nicer if
125 my Mum wasn't out working. Then she'd be able to take me to the park and come to school for things like the May Day festival and
130 the Christmas assembly, when we sing carols. She can't often manage that now. Some of the mothers come to school on ordinary
135 days to help with things like taking us for walks and it would be good if my Mum could come as well.'

Penny Goldstone   D

Penny Goldstone is 17. Her
140 *mother has worked since she started school.*

'I'm glad, now, that I haven't been mollycoddled, but when I was younger I
145 used to think of an ideal mother as someone who'd be sitting at home waiting for us with tea all ready. I regret not being closer to Mum when I
150 was younger. Because she was out all day, she seemed a bit distant and when I needed support or reassurance I'd turn to Nan or my friends. I
155 think that's why I'm not very good at displaying affection.'

'Now that I'm older I value her more as a friend and I can appreciate what a good job
160 she does keeping this massive house clean. I wouldn't like to have to do it'.

'Nowadays I can always talk to her if I have a
165 problem. There are times when she switches off, and says she has problems of her own, but as long as you give her a chance to get settled
170 when she gets in, instead of trying to pour everything out the minute she comes through the door, it's all right. It's not a bad thing for us to
175 have to consider her feelings as well as our own.'

'All the same, I think I'll probably be the opposite of my mother when I have a
180 family. I'd like to get established in my career and wait until later to start a family. Then, once I had children, I'd like to be
185 thoroughly maternal and enjoy them growing up before I thought about working again.'

Focus on grammar 2   Reporting statements

TENSE CHANGES

EXERCISE 1   Look at the examples below and then complete the tables which follow.

a	I work here on Saturdays.	She said (that) she worked there on Saturdays.
b	I'm going to London tomorrow.	He said (that) he was going to London the next day.
c	I've written a letter today.	He said (that) he'd written a letter that day.
d	I saw an old friend yesterday.	She said (that) she'd seen an old friend the day before.
e	I'd forgotten to tell you.	She said (that) she'd forgotten to tell me.
f	I'll ring you later this week.	He said (that) he'd ring us later that week.

	Direct speech	Reported speech
a	Present simple	
b	Present continuous	
c		Past perfect
d	Simple past	
e	Past perfect	
f		would

Direct speech	Reported speech
now	then
today	
tomorrow	
yesterday	
this	
here	
ago	before

Notes   When the reporting verb is in the present tense, it isn't necessary to change the tense. *For example:*

I'll send you a postcard.   *He says he'll send us a postcard.*

In spoken English, if the original words are still true, the tense is sometimes left unchanged. *For example:*

I'll send you a postcard.   *He said he'll send us a postcard.*

Present modal verbs normally change to past forms. *For example:*

I may join you later.   *He said he might join us later.*
I can't hear you.   *She said she couldn't hear me.*

Past modal verbs normally don't change. *For example:*

He might come.   *She said he might come.*
That could be our train.   *He said that it could be our train.*
You ought to lie down.   *She said that I ought to lie down.*

REPORTING VERBS

There are a number of other verbs apart from **said** which can be used in reported speech with a **that** clause.

EXERCISE 2   Put the sentences which follow into reported speech and choose one of the reporting verbs below for each one.

explained   admitted   complained   argued   promised

a 'You never lift a finger to help me!' His wife …
b 'I'll give you a hand with your homework this evening.' My father …
c 'I'm late because the bus broke down.' I …
d 'I'm afraid I've had an accident with your car.' My friend …
e 'John ought to go first because he's the youngest.' The teacher …

Notes

When the verb **suggest** is used to report advice, it's normally followed by **should**. *For example:*

'Ask in the Post Office for directions.'
He *suggested* that we *should* ask in the Post Office for directions.

▶ The verb **tell** can be used to introduce a reported statement. It is followed by a personal object and a **that** clause. *For example:*

He *told us that* the film was excellent.

Other common verbs like this are: **advise, warn, remind**. *For example:*

They *warned me that* the road was icy.
You *didn't remind me that* the clocks change today.

▶ The verb **tell** is also used to introduce indirect commands. *For example:*

'Go to your room.' He *told me to go* to my room.
'Don't shout.' He *told me not to shout.*

Other common verbs which are used to introduce indirect commands, requests, advice, etc., are: *advise, invite, recommend, forbid, warn, remind, ask.*

EXERCISE 3

Put the following sentences into reported speech and choose one of the reporting verbs above for each one:

a 'Could you shut the door, please?' The interviewer …
b 'Don't forget to switch off the fire.' My mother …
c 'Would you like to sit down and wait?' The receptionist …
d 'I should lie down, if I were you.' My friend …
e 'You mustn't tell anyone about this product.' My boss …
f 'Don't move or I'll shoot!' The gunman …
g 'Try to stay at the Imperial Hotel if you can.' Some friends of mine …

EXERCISE 4

Complete the following sentences with either **to** + infinitive or a **that** clause.

a My neighbour invited me .... her garden.
b The mechanic warned him .... dangerous condition.
c They forbade the children .... in the road.
d Didn't I tell you .... my exam with Grade A?
e I told the children .... too much noise.
f Police warned drivers .... in the fog.
g I had to remind him .... the cat.
h The waiter recommended us .... the salmon.
i Why didn't you remind me .... closed on Saturday?
j The travel agent advised them .... because the weather then would be very hot indeed.

Focus on writing I *Part I Informal letter* WRITING BANK: PAGE 112

An English friend is coming to stay with you and your family and has sent you the letter below. Read the letter and the notes you have made and then write a suitable reply. Write your **answer** in **120–180** words excluding your address.

> Just a note to say how excited I am about coming to stay with you. I'm really looking forward to meeting your family and I was wondering if you could tell me a bit about them – just to put me in the picture. I'm sure your days will be organised rather differently from mine in England – is there anything I should know in advance? Oh, one other thing – I don't know whether you have any trips planned but let me know if I need to bring anything special with me.

send photos?

describe typical day!

swimming? (bring swimming things)

sightseeing? (camera)

other possibilities.

PLAN

First paragraph:
Thank your friend for the letter and express pleasure that she/he is visiting.

Middle paragraphs :
Describe the members of your family briefly. Mention jobs, hobbies, interests, etc. Explain what a typical day in the life of the family is like (mealtimes, household tasks, entertainment, etc.) Think about the things that your friend may find quite different from English family life. Make suggestions about things to see and do during the visit.

Last paragraph:
Explain arrangements for meeting your friend and say how much you're looking forward to the visit.

STUDY BOX 2   Phrasal verb get (2)

'... she never seems to **get round to** ironing my shirts.' (Text 2)

get off – leave (usually a public vehicle).	Ask the conductor when to **get off**.
get on – make progress.	He's **getting on** very well in his new job.
get on with – manage to work/live with.	How do you **get on with** the neighbours?
get out of – avoid (a duty).	I'll do anything to **get out of** the ironing.
get over – recover from (illness/difficulties, etc.).	I haven't **got over** the shock yet.
get round to – find time to do.	See example above.
get through – make contact (usually by telephone).	I couldn't **get through** because the line was engaged.

Focus on listening 2 *Single-parent family*

❶ Listen to the conversation between two old friends, Helen and Gay, who have just met.
For questions 1–8 tick (✓) whether you think the statements are true or false.
For questions 9–12 fill in the missing information by writing short answers in the spaces.

		True	False
1	Gay has just separated from her husband. *False*	☒	☒
2	She has two children. *True*	☒	☐
3	She has several friends who help her look after the children. *True*	☒	☐
4	Her mother pays for some of the children's clothes. *–False*	☐	☒
5	Gay lives in a friendly neighbourhood. *True*	☒	☐
6	She has to nurse her elderly father at his home. *–False*	☐	☒
7	She thinks her ex-husband should do more to help her and the children. *True*	☒	☐
8	The children rarely see their father. *–False*	☐	☒

9 The course Gay has been attending was for .... only. *wood machining   women only*

10 It lasted for ...*6 months*... *6 mnt*

11 It cost ...*free*... *free   child minder   Nothing   independent*

12 One good thing about Gay's situation is that her children have become very ....

DISCUSSION POINTS **❷**

1 Do children need two parents? Why/Why not?

2 What are some of the problems for a single parent?

3 Are the problems greater when the children are younger or when they are older?

4 Should parents stay together for the sake of the children?

5 In what way can children of single-parent families grow up to be more independent?

Focus on grammar 3   Comparatives: *The … the …*

EXERCISE 1   Look at these examples:

The younger the child, the more sleep he needs.
The more children there are, the less peace we'll have!

This is a very convenient and common construction in English. Explain the meaning of the two examples in other words, and see whether your sentence is longer.

Change the words in green type so that the sentences say the opposite.

FORM

> **The** + comparative word …   **the** + comparative word
> (*more/less/-er*)   (*more/less/-er*)

Notes   1 **The** can be followed by both adjectives and adverbs. *For example:*
The more chocolates he ate, the fatter he became. (Adjective)
The more slowly we walk, the longer it will take to get there. (Adverb)

Notes   2 Sometimes, if the meaning is clear, the subject and verb may be left out. What has been left out at the end of the sentence in the following example?
The hotter the weather is, the better.

In the English saying **The more, the merrier,** both subjects and verbs are left out. The meaning is: *The more people who come, the merrier we shall be.*

When would you say **The sooner, the better,** and what would you mean?

EXERCISE 2   Complete the following sentences with suitable comparative words:

a The more exercise you take, the .... you will become.
b The .... the car, the .... it is to hire.
c The .... you speak, the .... it is for me to understand.
d .... you study, ... chance you will have in the exam.
e .... I get to know him, ... I like him, I'm sorry to say.
f The more frightening the film, ...
g The sharper the knife, ...
h .... , the more homesick I felt.

EXERCISE 3   Write sentences to describe the relationship between:

a money and happiness
b age and wisdom

'I was in my second year at comprehensive school' (Text 2)

The following words are used without an article when they are used for their main purpose.
They are used with an article when they are used for some other reason.

NO ARTICLE	**DEFINITE ARTICLE**
He's gone *to bed.* (to sleep)	Stand on *the bed* to reach the shelf.
I'm still *at school/college/university.* (studying)	I'm going to *the school* to interview the headmaster.
They took him *to hospital.* (for treatment)	Will you come to *the hospital* to see me?
He's *in prison.* (for punishment)	I called at *the prison* to deliver some food.
Also: church, dock, court	

Focus on writing 2 *Narrative* WRITING BANK: PAGE 122

A young people's magazine is holding a competition for the best short story written by one of its readers. The theme is childhood and the competition rules say that the story must end with the words: *It was certainly a day I'll never forget.* Write your **story** for the competition in **120–180** words.

❶ Study the section on Narratives in the Writing Bank on page 122 and answer these questions:

1 What's important about beginning and ending a story?
2 What's the easiest kind of story to write?
3 How do you use paragraphs in a narrative?
4 What are the three main tenses usually used in a narrative, and how are they used?
5 What are three ways you can make your story more lively and interesting?

❷ Once you have decided what you want to write about, make a paragraph plan of your narrative: Introduction, Para 1, Para 2, etc.

– First make notes about the different stages of the story for the middle paragraphs.
– Next think about the tenses to use and also how and where you can add interest in the form of reported or direct speech, and adjectives and adverbs to describe actions and feelings.
– Finally, decide how to begin and end your story in an interesting way.

NOTE: You may want to check your plan with your teacher before you begin writing properly.

Language review

Choose the word or phrase which best completes each sentence.

1 Don't you regret ....*C*.... before the end of the course?
   A leave   **B** to leave   **C** leaving   **D** to have left

2 I've sent the children outside to play. They were getting in my ....*D*.... all the time.
   A place   **B** hands   **C** nerves   **D** way

3 You should try to get a good night's sleep ....*B*.... much work you have to do.
   A whatever   **B** however   **C** no matter   **D** although

4 He hates washing up so he usually tries to ....*A*.... doing it.
   A get out of   **B** get away with   **C** get by   **D** get over

5 The doctor recommended me ....*C*.... on a strict diet.
   A go   **B** going   **C** to go   **D** I should go

6 It's only a bruise and the pain will .... after a while.
   A wear out   **B** wear off   **C** clear up   **D** clear off

7 I don't think it's .... ! She does exactly the same job as me but she earns more.
   A even   **B** equal   **C** kind   **D** fair

8 The children have .... lots of new friends since we moved to this town.
   A formed   **B** become   **C** made   **D** got

9 There is a(n) .... training period before you start work.
   A initial   **B** first   **C** primary   **D** beginning

10 I'll buy my ticket on the train if the guard will .... me go through the barrier.
   A allow   **B** let   **C** permit   **D** agree

11 She didn't feel she could .... him to keep a secret.
   A trust   **B** rely   **C** depend   **D** ensure

12 Could you .... me to post this letter? I'm sure to forget otherwise.
   A advise   **B** remember   **C** warn   **D** remind

13 He was extremely disappointed not .... first prize.
   A getting   **B** to get   **C** receiving   **D** to receive

14 The prize money was shared equally .... the two sisters.
   A with   **B** among   **C** for   **D** between

15 I can't afford to buy new clothes but fortunately I don't .... wearing old things.
   A care   **B** complain   **C** mind   **D** object

Lead-in *What is health?*

What are these people doing? Do you do anything like this? Do you do anything special to keep healthy?

❶ Being healthy means different things to different people. What do you mean by health? The following quiz will help you to find out.

Work with one or two other people. First tick the five statements you most agree with. Then compare your results. There will probably be large differences so find out the reasons your partner(s) chose the statements they did and explain the reasons for your choices.

	For me, being healthy is:	You	Other(s)
1	living to be very old.		
2	being able to run for a bus without getting out of breath.		
3	hardly ever taking any pills or medicines.		
4	being the ideal weight for my height.		
5	taking part in lots of games or sports.		
6	never suffering from anything more than a mild cold or stomach upset.		
7	feeling glad to be alive when I wake up in the morning.		
8	being able to touch my toes or run a mile in 10 minutes (a kilometre in about 6 minutes).		
9	having all the bits of my body in perfect working condition.		
10	eating the right foods.		
11	enjoying some form of relaxation or recreation.		
12	never smoking.		
13	hardly ever going to the doctor.		
14	having a clear skin, bright eyes and shiny hair.		

From *The Good Health Guide*

❷ Now read the following paragraphs.

Health is …
BEING FIT

Statements 2, 5, 8 or 11 suggest that, for you, health is something to do with being physically fit. But can you be fit and still be unhealthy? Or unfit and still be healthy?

When you are fit your muscles are so well trained that they can do more work without putting extra strain on the heart. Another benefit of fitness is that blood pressure is lower. This means it is easier for the heart to pump the blood around the body. Being fit is part of being healthy.

Health is …
NOT BEING ILL

If you ticked 3, 6, 9 or 13 you probably think of health as something to do with medicine. Perhaps you think that you can only be healthy with the help of doctors. Unfortunately doctors can do little to help us to be healthy. They usually only help when we are ill. When scientists try to measure how healthy we are as a nation, they look at the amount of disease and death that occurs. *Health* itself is not measured.

Health is …
LIVING TO AN OLD AGE

If you ticked 1, 4, 10 or 12 you probably think being healthy means reducing your chances of dying young.

But is living to 100 really a good measure of health for *you*? Some people live to be very old but don't enjoy their life very much. Living to an old age is only one aspect of health.

Health is …
POSITIVE HEALTH

Statements 7, 10, 11 or 14 see health as something quite different from illness or medicine. Although this is quite an ancient idea, we have only recently begun to take it seriously. Positive health covers all the things we can do to prevent illness plus all the things we can do to become even more well.

Text 1

❶ Before reading the text opposite, work with a partner and say whether you think each of the following statements is true or false.

		True	False
1	Not having the right balance in our diet can damage our health.	☒	☐
2	If other members of our family get fat quite easily, we probably will too.	☒	☐
3	If we like eating sweet things, it's probably a habit we learnt from our parents.	☐	☒
4	Men are just as likely to get fatter as they grow older as women are.	☐	☒
5	Most people don't eat enough protein. (Protein is found in meat, fish, milk, eggs, etc.)	☒	☐
6	It's useless for most people to take vitamin pills.	☒	☐
7	The more calories we eat in food, the more energetic we will feel.	☐	☒
8	We should try to reduce the amount of bread and potatoes we eat.	☒	☐

❷ Now read Text 1 and see how correct you were.

❸ Each sentence below (A–G) is a summary of one section of the article. Choose a summary sentence for each section and write the correct letter in the spaces (1–6). There is one extra sentence which you do not need to use.

A If we eat food with more calories than we need, we get fat.

B Fibre is an important part of a good diet.

C It is better to eat regular meals than to wait for one big feast at the end of the day.

D We all need the right mixture of different types of food in our diet.

E People differ in the food they enjoy and also in the way food affects them.

F We are likely to get all the proteins, vitamins and minerals we need in a good balanced diet.

G A bad diet can damage our health.

1

The average person swallows about half-a-ton of food a year – not counting drink – and though the body is remarkably efficient at extracting just what it needs from this huge mixture, it can only cope up to a point.

If you go on eating too much of some things and not enough of others, you'll eventually get out of condition and your health will suffer.

So think before you start eating. It may look good. It may taste good. Fine! But how much good is it really doing you?

2 E

What you eat and the way it affects your body depend very much on the kind of person you are. For one thing, the genes you inherit from your parents can determine how your body-chemistry (metabolism) copes with particular foods. The tendency to put on weight rather easily, for example, often runs in families – which means that they have to take particular care.

And your parents may shape your future in another way. Your upbringing shapes some basic attitudes to food – like whether you have a sweet tooth, nibble between meals, take big mouthfuls or eat chips with everything.

Eating habits, good or bad, tend to get passed on.

And then there's your *lifestyle*. How much you spend on food (time as well as money), how much exercise you get – these can alter the balance between food and fitness.

And finally, both your *age* and your *sex* may affect this balance. For example, you're more likely to put on weight as you get older, especially if you're a woman.

So, everybody's different and the important thing is to know yourself. Read on and see if you think you are striking the right balance.

3

Your food should balance your body's need for –
NUTRIENTS (proteins, fats, carbohydrates, vitamins, minerals and water) – the raw materials needed to build and repair the body-machine.
ENERGY (calories) – to power the body-machine, all the thousands of different mechanisms that keep you alive and active.
DIETARY FIBRE (a complex mixture of natural plant substances) – the value of which we are just beginning to understand.

4 F

If you're eating a fairly varied diet, it is just about impossible to go short of proteins, vitamins or minerals. It is likely, too, that you have more than enough fats and carbohydrates.

Take *proteins* for instance. On average, we eat about *twice as much* protein as we need.

Vitamin pills aren't likely to help either. A varied diet with plenty of fresh fruit, vegetables and cereals along with some fish, eggs, meat and dairy products will contain more than enough vitamins. Unless you have some special medical reason, it is a waste of time and money to take vitamin pills.

As for *minerals,* there is no shortage in the average diet and it is useless to have more than you need.

5 A

Just about everything you eat contains energy – measured as *calories;* the higher the number of calories, the more energy. But don't make the mistake of thinking that eating extra energy-rich foods will make you more energetic. The amount of energy in your daily diet should exactly balance the energy your body-machine burns up. If you eat more than you use, the extra energy is stored as body fat. And this is the big problem.

6 B

Over hundreds of thousands of years, man's food came mainly from plants.

He ate cereals (like wheat), pulses (like beans and peas), vegetables, fruit and nuts. So our ancestors were used to eating the sort of food that contains a lot of fibre.

In comparison with our ancestors, the sort of food we eat today contains very little fibre. Our main foods are meat, eggs and dairy products, which contain no fibre at all.

Lack of fibre seems to be connected with various disorders of the digestive system. Some experts also believe that lack of fibre may even lead to heart disease.

If you're worried about your weight, eating more fibre may actually help you to slim! Food with plenty of fibre like potatoes or bread can be satisfying without giving you too many calories.

From *The Health Education Council*

❹ **Now look at Sections 1 and 2 again and find the words which mean the same as:**

Section 1		Section 2	
1 able to do a job well	....	6 receive	....
2 taking out	....	7 decide	....
3 very big	....	8 training and caring for a child	....
4 manage successfully	....	9 take small bites	....
5 in the end	....	10 change	....

DESCRIBING FOOD **⑤**

Most people have their own favourite dishes which they prefer to new and unfamiliar foods. A favourite dish may be raw or cooked, very ordinary or quite exotic, simple or complicated to prepare, cheap or expensive.

1   Write down your favourite dish: ....
    Compare your answer with your neighbour's and say why you like your favourite so much.

2   How would you describe the tastes of the foods below? Write the foods under the different taste headings. (You may want to put the same food under more than one heading sometimes.)

FOODS

lemon juice	bananas	beer	vinegar
honey	anchovies	Indian vegetable curry	thick onion soup
butter	ice cream	grapefruit	almonds
peanuts	yoghurt	peaches in syrup	sausages
olives	British fish and chips	black coffee	crisps

TASTES

Spicy	Bitter	Salty	Sweet	Sour	Greasy	Creamy

3   Now decide which kinds of food that you've eaten would fit the following descriptions:

Most attractive to look at	
Simplest to make	
Most difficult to make well	
Most unpleasant	
Most enjoyable foreign	
Most unusual	

Adapted from *'The Good Health Guide' (Open University), Harper & Row*

When you've completed your list, compare it with your neighbour's. Explain why you chose the foods and describe the colour, taste, smell and cost. You may like to check the expressions on page 110 of the Functions Bank before you begin.

Focus on listening I *Old wives' tales?*

An old wives' tale is a traditional belief, or a piece of traditional advice, passed down from generation to generation.

❶   Look at the 5 old wives' tales opposite and decide whether you think they are true, partly true, or false. Then read the questions which follow.

❷   Now listen to the tape and answer the questions by ticking by the correct box.

		True	Partly True	False
1	An apple a day keeps the doctor away.	☐	☒	☐
2	You should always sleep with an open window.	☐	☐	☒
3	If you get soaking wet you're more likely to catch a cold.	☒	☐	☒
4	Feed a cold and starve a fever.	☒	☐	☐
5	Carrots help you to see in the dark.	☒	☐	☐

❸   Write short answers to the following questions.

1   What fruit contains more Vitamin C, according to the doctor?
......*Oranges*..

2   Which two groups of people are most at risk of catching an infection?
......*Older one's and babys*......................................

3   How did the man in Norway get wet?
......*fishing in freezing river*..............................

4   What advice does the doctor give to people with flu?
......*drink liquid.*..

5   What other foods contain Vitamin A, according to the doctor?
......*Green beans, milk butter, fish oil*......

❹   Can you think of any other old wives' tales? Are they true or false?

Focus on grammar 1   Expressing quantity

COUNTABLE AND UNCOUNTABLE NOUNS

Uncountable nouns like **petrol** or **pride** cannot be used with an indefinite article **a/an** and cannot be made plural.

EXERCISE 1   Put the following words in the correct place in the table below:

² *rice*	¹ *apple*	² *news*	¹ *chair*	² *furniture*	¹ *vitamin*	¹ *programme*
² *spaghetti*	¹ *snack*	¹ *coin*	² *information*	¹ *journey*	² *crockery*	² *blood*
¹ *biscuit* ✓	¹ *plate*	² *travel*	² *weather*	² *money*	² *music*	

Countable ①		② Uncountable
biscuit snack.		Rice
apple plate		spaghetti
vitamin coin		

Some words can be either countable or uncountable depending on their meaning.

EXERCISE 2   Give different examples of the words below when they are used as a) countable and b) uncountable. *For example:*

     box of chocolates – countable   *a cake made of chocolate* – uncountable

cheese	*time*	*wood*	*hair*	*iron*	*tin*	*exercise*	*skin*

MUCH/MANY, A LOT OF, ETC.

EXERCISE 1 Many of the following words or phrases occur in Text 1. Put them in the correct column in the table below according to whether they are used only with countable nouns, only with uncountable nouns or with both types.

too much	*no … at all*	*hardly any*	*a large number of*	*very little*
too few	*not enough*	*plenty of*	*a great many*	*a great deal of*
a lot of	*a large amount of*	*a lack of*	*very many*	

Countable ₁	Uncountable ₂	Both ₃

EXERCISE 2 Now complete these sentences with the correct expression of quantity:

a   The quality of the material depends on .... you want to spend.

b   I'm afraid there's very .... I can do to help you.

c   There was .... applause .... after the performance and the conductor looked very uncomfortable.

d   I was worried about one child in the class who seemed to show a complete .... of interest in the subject.

e   We had to cancel the trip to Oxford because .... members wanted to go.

f   I saw a large .... of elephants by the lakeside on that early morning boat ride.

g   Make sure you put .... cheese in the omelette. I love it!

h   I know you spent a great .... money on the carpet but I still think it's rather ugly.

i   The trouble with me is that I take .... exercise apart from walking to the shops.

j   A great .... famous people are said to have stayed at this hotel.

AS … AS

Look at these examples:

> *On average, we eat about twice as much protein as we need.* (Text 1)
> *The club has only got half as many members as it had last year.*
> *Your suitcase is about three times as heavy as mine!*

EXERCISE Now write sentences comparing the two items in each box below.

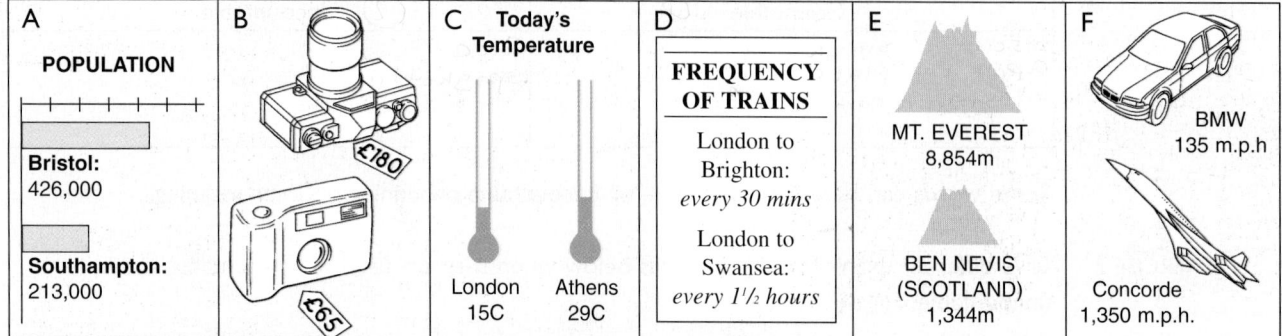

Focus on writing 1 *Article* WRITING BANK: PAGE 124

An international students' magazine is planning to have a special feature on your country in a future edition and you have been asked to write an article on the subject of typical food and drink. Write your **article** for the magazine in **120–180** words.

NOTES 1 It's important to think about the **purpose** of your article before you begin. Is it just to describe and explain or is it also to entertain and persuade?

2 Make notes on every aspect of the subject you can think of, so that there is plenty of **variety** in your article. Think, for example, about:
   – simple dishes and typical home cooking as well as famous specialities
   – customs involved with eating and drinking (e.g. greeting visitors; weddings; feast days)
   – where to eat for good value/traditional cooking/the finest food and drink, etc.
   – what food or drink to take home as a souvenir.

3 Remember the importance of a **heading** and a good **beginning** and **ending**.

4 Look at the notes on writing articles in the Writing Bank (page 124) and also at ways of describing **taste** and **smell** in the Functions Bank (page 110).

Communication activity

You are in a restaurant. A and B are customers and C is the waiter. You each have instructions on different pages. Read and remember your instructions and then turn back to this page. A's instructions are on page 173; B's are on page 176; C's are on page 178.

The Laughing Cook
RESTAURANT
MENU

STARTERS

Potato soup £1.00
Tomato salad £2.00
Spaghetti bolognaise £1.50
Smoked salmon £3.00
Grilled sardines £2.50

MAIN COURSES

Cheese Omelette £2.50
cooked with 3 large eggs and lots of tasty Cheddar cheese

Caldeirada £4.50
a delicious Portuguese seafood stew.

T-Bone Steak £7.00
best quality, tender steak, cooked to perfection.

Moussaka £4.00
the famous Greek dish, made with minced beef, aubergines, potatoes and covered with a creamy cheese sauce

Paella £5.00
an authentic Spanish recipe which includes chicken, prawns, mussels, green peppers, onions and rice.

Chilli con Carne £4.00
a Mexican speciality – spicy beef and red kidney beans on a bed of rice

Grilled Trout £5.50
fresh from the River Wye, served with almonds

Sweet and Sour Chicken £4.00
a Chinese favourite – tender pieces of chicken fried in batter and covered with our famous sweet and sour sauce.

ALL DISHES ARE SERVED WITH A CHOICE OF FRESH VEGETABLES OR SALAD.

DESSERTS

Fresh Strawberries £2.50
Tinned Peaches £1.50
Cheese and Biscuits £1.25p
Vanilla Ice Cream £1.00
Chocolate Cake £2.00
Apple Pie and Cream £1.50

YOUR WAITER WILL BE HAPPY TO ADVISE YOU ON YOUR CHOICE OF DISH.

STUDY BOX 1   Verb + preposition (2)

'... taking part *in* lots of games or sports.' (Lead-in)

accuse (somebody) *of*	believe *in*	discourage (somebody) *from*
(dis)agree *with* (somebody)	compare X *with* Y	distinguish *between*
about (something)	complain *to* (somebody)	look *for*
apologise *for*	*about* (something)	protect (somebody) *from*
apply *for*	concentrate *on*	provide (somebody/something) *with*
argue *with* (somebody)	confuse X *with* Y	spend (time/money) *on*
about (something)	congratulate (somebody) *on*	suffer *from*
	consist *of*	surround (somebody/something) *with*

Focus on grammar 2   Reported questions

Look at this example:

I asked where the post office was.

What were the original words?

'Excuse me, where ....?'

Notes

In reported questions:

1   The **word order is different** from the original question. The verb follows the subject as in an ordinary statement.
2   The auxiliary verb **do** is not used.
3   There is **no question mark**.

QUESTIONS WITH QUESTION WORDS (*When, Where, ...*)

Complete the following examples:

'How are your parents?'   She asked me how my parents ....

'Who did you go home with?'   They wanted to know who I ....

EXERCISE 1

Change the following into reported speech:

a   'How much do you earn?' He wanted to know ....
b   'Where did you buy your watch?' She asked ....
c   'How many kilos have you lost?' The doctor asked ....
d   'When are you coming to stay with me?' My aunt wanted to know ....
e   'Why won't you marry me?' Her boyfriend wanted to know ....
f   'Who on earth gave you my address?' I asked him ....

QUESTIONS WITHOUT QUESTION WORDS

These questions are reported with **if** or **whether**. Complete the following examples:

'Do you like jazz?'   I asked you if *you* ....

'Can I use the telephone, please?'   He asked if *he* ....

171

EXERCISE 1   Change the following into reported speech:

a 'Have you got change of a £5 note?' The man asked me ....
b 'Have you seen Tim today?' They wanted to know ....
c 'Will you be at home this weekend?' I asked if she ....
d 'Does your wife speak any Portuguese?' At the interview, they asked ....
e 'Did you telephone me last night?' She wanted to know ....
f 'Can you lend me £1 till tomorrow?' My friend asked ....

EXERCISE 2   Work in pairs. Student **A** – find out as much as you can about Student **B's** family and childhood by asking direct questions. You will have **three** minutes!

Before you begin, spend a minute or two thinking about the questions you can ask. It may help to make a few notes: *For example:*

  Brothers and sisters? ages? where born? etc.

When you have finished, report your questions and **B's** answers to the class.

Then repeat the exercise with Student **B** asking the questions. (Try to think of some new ones!)

Sometimes we introduce a direct question with a short phrase. For example:

  'Can you tell me who that man is?'
  'Do you know if the bus has gone yet?'

In this case, the word order is the same as in a reported question and the tense remains the same.

EXERCISE 3   Work in pairs. Take it in turns to ask for the following information, using the phrases:

  Can/could you (possibly) tell me …
  I wonder if you could tell me …
  Do you (happen to) know …

Try to answer the questions too!
Ask about …

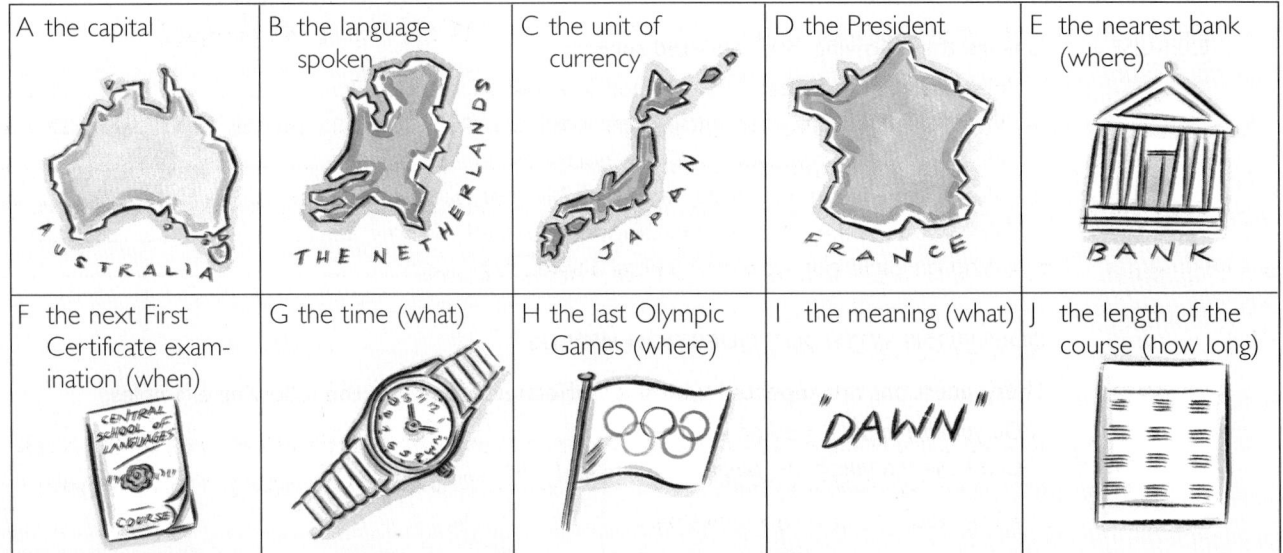

A the capital	B the language spoken	C the unit of currency	D the President	E the nearest bank (where)
F the next First Certificate exam-ination (when)	G the time (what)	H the last Olympic Games (where)	I the meaning (what)	J the length of the course (how long)

Focus on listening 2

For questions 1–8 tick (✓) the correct answers.

1 The course goes on for

   A one day.   **B** two days.   **C** one week.   **D** several weeks.

2 On the subject of bandages, the speaker tells his students that they

   A should practise putting them on at home.   **C** don't need to be able to use them at all.

   B must read about them in first aid books.   **D** can do an extra course to learn about
                  them.

3 He realised that the situation in the restaurant was serious because

   A the man was lying across the table.   **C** the man's face had changed colour.

   B the man had fallen off his chair.   **D** the man hadn't eaten his food.

4 Which picture shows the position he put the man in?

      A   **B**   **C**   **D**

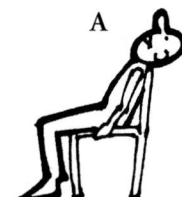 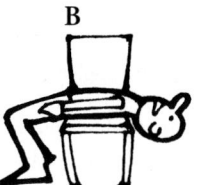  

5 He shouted at the waiter because

   A the waiter didn't believe it was an
       emergency.

   B the waiter was too far away to hear.

   C he thought the waiter might be too
       frightened to act.

   D he was angry with the waiter for
       walking away.

6 The man's problem was that

   A something had stuck in his throat.   **C** he had had a heart attack.

   B the food he had eaten had made him ill.   **D** he had fainted.

7 The ambulance

   A was cancelled.   **C** took the man home.

   B came but wasn't needed.   **D** took the man to hospital.

8 Which is true? In First Aid

   A you must always act very quickly.   **C** you must stop and consider before you
                   act.

   B you must realise when there's an
       emergency.   **D** you must always call an ambulance.

**COMMUNICATION
ACTIVITY:
ROLE A**

Before you begin, talk to B and decide whether you are:

1 boyfriend and girlfriend *or*

2 business colleagues *or*

3 friends who haven't met for a long time.

Now read on: you have invited B to dinner and you really want him/her to enjoy the meal.
Unfortunately you're a bit short of money at the moment (you've only got £12 with you)
but you don't want B to know this.

First, look at the language for Asking for Advice in the Functions Bank (page 106). You
begin speaking.

Text 2

❶ Look at the list of eight words below. Six of them are names of minor injuries and two of them are types of dressings which can be put on injuries.

1 Underline the two words which are not minor injuries.

2 Write each word below the correct picture.

cut   bruise   plaster   bite   burn   bandage   graze   scald

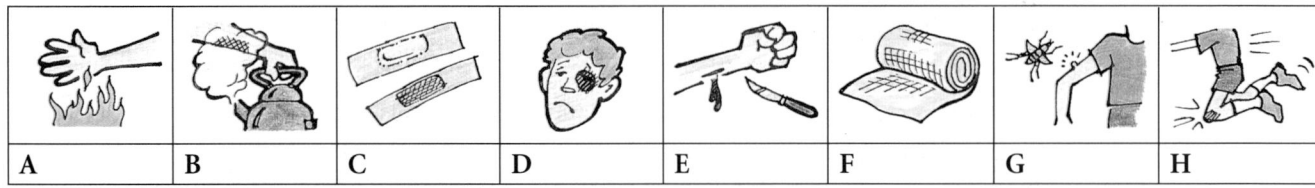

A	B	C	D	E	F	G	H

❷ Now read the following passage from a health education booklet and answer questions 1–5.

From 'Minor Illnesses', Health Education Council

CUTS, BRUISES, BITES AND BURNS

Cuts

Bleeding can usually be stopped by applying pressure to the cut for 2 or 3 minutes. The cut can then be carefully inspected. If it has bled freely any germs will normally have been washed away by the blood.

Apply a plaster dressing firmly, bringing the edges of the cut together so that it knits quickly. Keep dry for 1 to 2 days.

If the cut is deep and the edges cannot be pulled together with a dressing consult the doctor or the practice nurse. A tetanus injection may be needed.

Grazes

Dirt will often enter a graze caused by falling on a hard or rough surface. It must be cleaned out carefully with an antiseptic solution.

After cleaning, leave the graze uncovered. Exposure to the air will cause a scab to form. This will gradually dry and fall off.

It is not a good idea to apply a dressing. This may stick to the graze or make it soggy and infected.

Bruises

Bruises are very common in children. They normally get better in 7 to 10 days. Parents sometimes worry that a bone may be broken. Children's bones are rubbery and rarely break, but if in doubt consult the doctor.

If a child gets up at once after a fall and moves about normally, it is unlikely that a bone has been broken. But the child may be stiff the next day because of the bruising which has occurred.

Severe bruising can be treated by rest for 24 to 48 hours. In the case of a badly bruised leg, the limb should be raised. Lying in bed is the easiest way to do this.

A cold compress may ease a bad bruise if applied at once. This is made by soaking some material in water and applying it to the bruise.

Bruises on the head may cause anxiety. If the patient was not 'knocked out' and can remember the accident it is unlikely that serious injury has resulted.

But if the patient was knocked unconscious and cannot remember what happened, he or she should be taken to a hospital casualty department.

Insect bites

These are common in the summer. They look like spots about 5mm across. They are very itchy and usually appear on exposed parts, e.g. arms and legs.

The itching can be relieved by calamine lotion.

Burns and scalds

Minor burns and scalds cause redness of the skin. Immediate treatment by pouring cold water over a burn is often helpful. If burns cause severe blistering or break the skin, the doctor should be consulted.

Sunburn should, if possible, be prevented by avoiding long exposure and covering exposed areas adequately. It may be treated by calamine lotion and soluble aspirin to relieve the pain.

1 The purpose of the booklet is

 A to tell us what to do until a doctor arrives.

 B to explain what causes minor illnesses.

 C to show that it is unnecessary to call a doctor.

 D to help us to treat minor illnesses at home.

2   The one injury which we are told not to cover is
   A a bruise.
   B sunburn.
   C a graze.
   D an insect bite.

3   When treating a minor cut, we are first told to
   A clean out the wound.
   B press down on the wound.
   C wash the blood away.
   D close up the wound.

4   The injury which we are told how to avoid is
   A sunburn.
   B insect bites.
   C scalds.
   D cuts.

5   Patients with badly bruised legs are advised to go to bed so that
   A they can rest completely.
   B their injured leg can be lifted up.
   C they can soak their leg in water.
   D a cold compress can be applied.

Focus on grammar 3   Expressing number

▶ **Each, both, either, neither** and **all** can be used with a noun (in the same way as **a, the,** etc.). They can also be used as pronouns, **in place of a noun**. *For example:*
   They looked at each house *carefully.* Each *had its advantages.*
   You can ask either waiter *for service.* Either *will serve you.*

▶ **Every** is never used on its own as a pronoun, but always with a noun. (**Everyone/ everything** are pronouns.)

▶ **None of** is also used with a noun, but **none** is always a pronoun. *For example:*
   Every *book on the shelf was a detective story.*
   None of *the books was by Agatha Christie.*
   I looked at them all but none *appeared very interesting.*

The table below shows which words are used to refer to singular nouns (and may take singular verbs), and which refer to plural nouns (and may take plural verbs).

Singular	Plural
each	both
every	all (with countable nouns)
either	
neither	
none*	
all (with uncountable nouns)	

'None sometimes takes a plural verb in informal speech when referring to countable nouns.

Notes

1   **Each** refers to one of a group of two or more.

   Every refers to one of a group of three or more. It cannot refer to two.

The two words have a similar meaning and can sometimes be used interchangeably. *Each,* however, suggests a distinct individual in a group, while every suggests any member of a group. *For example:*

Every actor must learn his words by heart.
Each actor has a different method of learning his lines.

2   **Both** refers to two.   *Both my parents are still working.*

   All refers to more than two.   *I'm lucky enough to have all four grandparents still.*

3   **Either, neither** refer to one of two.

   They're both good. You can have either of them.
   I've got two brothers but neither lives nearby.

   None refers to one of several.

   There are three banks in town but none of them is open.

EXERCISE 1   **Now use words from the table to complete the following sentences:**

a   Near the junction there are shops on .... sides of the road.

b   .... professional musician has to practise regularly.

c   He painted several pictures during his time in Italy but .... of them has been found.

d   The Princess took the time to speak to .... child in the class individually.

e   Before you leave the plane, please make sure that you have .... your belongings with you.

f   .... of my parents has ever been abroad.

g   I've looked in the library and the canteen but there's no sign of her in .... place.

h   Not .... cooks can bake bread as well as you can.

i   He gave me the choice of two insurance policies but .... of them really suited me.

j   You can take .... the motorway or the A38. .... routes are equally fast.

COMMUNICATION ACTIVITY: ROLE B

Before you begin, talk to A and decide whether you are:
1   boyfriend and girlfriend *or*
2   business colleagues *or*
3   friends who haven't met for a long time.

Now read on:

A has invited you to dinner and you're sure you're going to enjoy yourself, especially as A is paying the bill! You especially like fish of all kinds. The only thing you can't eat is cheese, which doesn't agree with you, but you'd prefer not to eat anything too fattening either.

First, have a look at the language for Responding to Advice and to Suggestions in the Functions Bank (page 107).
A will begin speaking.

Focus on writing 2 *Report* WRITING BANK: PAGE 126

You have recently started working in local tourism and you had to visit a leisure facility (for example, a tennis club, a swimming pool, a gymnasium or a riding centre) in your area. Now you must write a report for your boss. Write your **report** in **120–180** words, describing the facility, what it has to offer to tourists, and commenting on its good and bad points.

NOTES

1 Look at the model report and notes in the Writing Bank (pages 126–7)

2 You could mention some (but probably not all!) of the following topics:
   – general atmosphere
   – attitude of staff
   – size
   – range of equipment
   – standard of changing rooms
   – number of members
   – training/supervision
   – restaurant/bar/café?
   – cost of using the facilities (discounts?)
   – busiest/quietest times

   Think about how to group your chosen topics and decide on the subheadings you will use.

3 Remember to introduce your report and to end with a summary and perhaps a recommendation.

STUDY BOX 2 **Phrasal verb *come***

'He was beginning to ***come round***.' (Listening 2)

come across – find or meet by chance.	*I **came across** a very interesting book in the library.*
come across – be understood.	*He didn't **come across** as a very serious person.*
come off – succeed.	*Do you think your plan will really **come off**?*
come out – appear/bloom.	*The garden looks lovely now the roses have **come out**.*
come round – visit.	*Can I **come round** and see you next week?*
come round – regain consciousness.	*See example above.*
come to – regain consciousness.	*When I **came to** after my operation, I couldn't think where I was.*
come up against – be faced with.	*We've **come up** against a serious problem, I'm afraid.*

Language review

Choose the word or phrase which best completes each sentence.

1 I'll try to get in touch with him but he's .... ever at home when I phone.
   A rarely   **B** almost   **C** hardly   **D** occasionally

2 There'll be four of us going camping, not .... the dog!
   A counting   **B** adding   **C** involving   **D** saying

3 After climbing the stairs to the sixth floor, I was completely out of ....
   A breath   **B** air   **C** wind   **D** gasp

4 Experts recommend a .... diet with plenty of fresh vegetables.
   A various   **B** varied   **C** wide   **D** changeable

5 You are unlikely to need vitamin pills .... you have some special medical reason.
   A if   **B** because   **C** while   **D** unless

6 Put your hand in cold water. That will help to .... the pain of the burn.
   A bear   **B** avoid   **C** relieve   **D** resist

7 .... carrots are said to be much better for you than cooked ones.

A Raw   **B** Rare   **C** Crude   **D** Fresh

8 They were all badly .... by mosquitoes on their first night in the tent.

A picked   **B** bitten   **C** stung   **D** scratched

9 He's certainly .... a lot of weight since I last saw him.

A taken on   **B** put on   **C** put up   **D** taken up

10 I didn't feel too bad really. I only had a .... attack of 'flu.

A weak   **B** small   **C** gentle   **D** mild

11 In comparison .... the Japanese, the British eat far more fatty foods.

A from   **B** to   **C** with   **D** of

12 He still suffers .... headaches as a result of the accident.

A of   **B** for   **C** by   **D** from

13 Did you .... my passport while you were clearing out the desk?

A come round   **B** come across   **C** come to   **D** come up against

14 There wasn't .... news in his letter.

A a great many   **B** hardly any   **C** a great deal of   **D** a large number of

15 It costs nearly twice as much to take the train .... it does to go by coach.

A than   **B** for   **C** while   **D** as

Odd man out

In each of the following groups of words, there is one which does not fit. Work in pairs to choose the 'odd man out' in each group and say why it doesn't belong there.

NOTE There may be more than one correct answer!

1 chin   jaw   cheek   thumb   lip

2 bandage   thermometer   plaster   pill   ribbon

3 wrist   ankle   stomach   elbow   shoulder

4 cut   spot   bruise   sting   scratch

5 eggs   milk   cheese   butter   cream

6 grill   fry   boil   bake   roast

7 spaghetti   rice   meat   chips   bread

8 butcher's   grocer's   fishmonger's   ironmonger's   baker's

9 tennis   golf   judo   cricket   football

10 Sydney   Barcelona   Munich   Moscow   Seoul

COMMUNICATION ACTIVITY: ROLE C

There are only 15 minutes left before you go off duty and you don't want to spend too long with these customers. The chef has told you that there's a lot of steak, moussaka and sardines left over and he'd like you to encourage customers to order these. The caldeirada has run out completely. Mark these on your menu, but don't show to your customers.

Let A and B discuss the menu for a few moments before you ask if you can take their order. In the meantime, have a look at the language for Giving Advice and Recommendations, and Persuading in the Functions Bank (page 106).

Lead-in

Newspapers often carry stories of disasters but occasionally they also feature stories of lucky escapes.

❶ Look at the four headlines below and discuss with a partner what you think the story was about in each case.

1
Bouncing boy's car escape

2
MY HOUSE OF HORROR
Now the roof falls in on jinxed family
By Jenny Sneesby

3
Girl saved by sword bearer

4
THE FLAMING MIRROR
Glass starts a blaze in bedroom
BY ALFRED LEE

❷ To find out if you were thinking along the right lines, match the extracts from the articles below to the headlines. There are three extracts for one of the headlines and two each for the rest.

Cause
There were no electrical appliances or wires near the curtain. There was no radiator nearby. The Coxes were non-smokers. The bay windows were shut and no spark could have come from outside. Firemen were mystified at first until they discovered the cause of the fire. On the dressing table, 18 inches from the curtain, was

Mr Robinson, of Grenfell Close, Stanmore, Middlesex, behaved 'magnificently' when he heard Tracey Roke, aged 18, screaming for help outside his home late at night.

A YOUNG mother has branded her council house 'a disaster area' after a second major incident in three months wrecked her home.
An attic tank, containing 60 gallons of water, burst on Friday night, crashed through two floors and landed in the sitting room.

'When I walked in on Friday night I couldn't believe it. The carpet was completely wet and the ceiling was coming down,' said Teresa.
'We were very lucky no one was in at the time.'

Running back down the road she saw an incredible sight. Sam, sobbing but otherwise completely unhurt, was limping to the side of the road. Nearby were several stationary vehicles which had narrowly missed him.

The sun's rays had hit the magnifying mirror and were reflected on to the velvet curtain, causing it to smoulder and burst into flames.
Mrs Cox, of De Vere Road, Thrapston, Northamptonshire, said: 'I hope the accident does not happen to anybody else. If we had not been at home, it would have been disastrous.'

He grabbed a ceremonial sword, ran outside and stopped the car in which she was trapped. He took the weeping girl into his home after noting the number of the car.

In November, Teresa's solid fuel stove exploded, burning husband Joseph's hair and lips and setting fire to the furniture.

WITH her four year-old son Sam playing boisterously with a friend in the back of her Mercedes estate car, Mrs Linda Norton turned into the busy main road and began accelerating.
She was approaching 20 mph when suddenly she heard a loud noise. Glancing in the mirror, she saw the car's tailgate had swung open.
And to her horror she was just in time to catch sight of Sam falling out on to the

❸ Now explain in your own words what each of the narrow escapes was.

❹ Below are dictionary definitions of two of the words in the headlines. Can you explain why they are used?

to bounce – to spring back up again from the ground like a ball.
to be jinxed – to suffer from a lot of bad luck.

Text 1 *Crew saves pilot*

The article opposite tells the story of an emergency aboard an aeroplane. Five paragraphs have been removed from the text.

❶ Read the article fairly quickly, ignoring the gaps for the moment, in order to find answers to these questions:
1 What happened to the pilot?
2 What caused the problem?
3 How did the crew save the pilot?

❷ Choose a paragraph from the list (A–E) below to fill each of the gaps in the text. Write the correct letter in the space.

> **A** 'The pilot looked in a bad way but I reckoned he was conscious because they were talking to him all the time.'
>
> **B** The window, made of 15-cm-thick toughened glass, was found intact on a farm near Wallingford, 88 km west of London.
>
> **C** Mr Rogers and Ms Prince then grabbed the captain as Mr Ogden let go because he had cut his hand badly on broken glass.
>
> **D** Captain Lancaster later sat up in bed at Southampton General Hospital talking to his wife Margaret.
>
> **E** Mr Aitcheson made an emergency landing at Eastleigh airport, near Southampton.

❸ Now say whether the following statements are true or false, and why.

		True	False
1	The captain was not injured.	☒	☒
2	The airline later criticised the crew.	☐	☒
3	The window which caused the problem was a new one.	☒	☐
4	Captain Lancaster is an experienced pilot.	☒	☒ *to yough*
5	One of the stewards managed to fly the plane.	☐	☒ *copilot*
6	The passengers remained calm during the emergency.	☒	☐

No panic

❹ Find words or phrases in the text which mean the same as:
1 team of people who work on an aircraft .....*a crew*.....
2 part of a plane where the pilot sits .....*cockpitt*.....
3 main body of an aircraft ....
4 breaks (in bones) .....*fractures to his ribs*.....
5 injury caused by extreme cold .....*minus 29°C*.....
6 being quick to notice what is happening ....
7 window at the front of cars/aircraft ....

8   was pulled out with great force ....Popped..........

9   held on tightly ....grabbed..him round the waist

10 seized quickly ....

LONDON: A holiday jet crew who saved their captain in a terrifying 15-minute struggle were hailed last night as heroes.

They held on to pilot Tim Lancaster's legs as he dangled helplessly out of his shattered cockpit window at 24,000 ft. Captain Lancaster lay on the nose of the plane after his body was repeatedly slammed against the fuselage.

He has fractures to his ribs, elbow, wrist and thumb and frostbite on one arm. The temperature outside the cockpit was minus 29°C.

1

British Airways said he was in a 'satisfactory' condition yesterday. British Airways spokesman Mr Tony Cocklin said the captain owed his life to quick thinking by the crew. 'We have nothing but praise for them,' he said. 'It was a tremendous example of alertness.'

The drama happened on Sunday 15 minutes after the plane took off from Birmingham carrying 81 passengers to Malaga, Spain. While it was climbing to its cruising height one of the six windscreen panels came out and the aircraft depressurised.

Mr Cocklin said the window had been replaced two days earlier

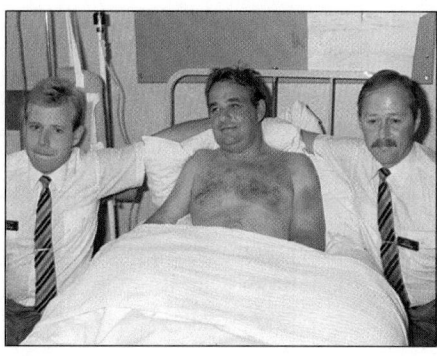

in a routine maintenance check.

2  E

Captain Lancaster, a pilot for 21 years, was sucked out of a single lap belt by decompression. He had removed his full shoulder harness after takeoff.

Stewards Simon Rogers and Nigel Ogden had clung to the captain as co-pilot Alistair Aitcheson took the BAC-111 jet into a dive to get below 10,000ft., where pressure drops to normal.

3  B

The captain was so far out of the port side of the windscreen that firefighters were able to lift him through it.

A BA internal inquiry and an investigation by the Air Accidents Investigation Branch will centre on

how the new windscreen was fitted.

Stewardess Susan Prince said: 'The window popped and Tim went out like a rag doll. Simon grabbed his legs and braced himself against his chair and the fuselage.'

4  C

Next Mr Rogers strapped himself into Captain Lancaster's seat harness, then grabbed him round the waist and held on for 15 minutes.

A passenger, builder David Duncan, 35, of Merseyside, said: 'The stewardesses had just started serving tea and coffee when there was a terrific bang and a rush of air that was so strong it seemed to part my hair.

The cockpit door was blown off its hinges and I was confronted with the horrific sight of the pilot hanging out of the window. There was no panic among the passengers.'

5

'His body was flapping in the wind on the top of the plane's nose and he was still there after the plane had finally landed.'

All the crew members were taken to hospital. Four passengers were treated for shock.

LANGUAGE CHECK: PREPOSITIONS

5 Complete the following sentences with the correct prepositions. (Sometimes two words may be needed.) The prepositions all come from the Lead-in extracts or Text 1.

1   I didn't know what to do ......at......... first, but then I started shouting ......for......... help.

2   There was nearly a major fire .... Friday night when some children set fire .... a pile of rubbish in the street.

3   That's the second accident he's had .... six months.

4   I'd be grateful if you wouldn't make so much noise late .... night when other people are trying to sleep!

5   Before you turn .... a main road, always stop and make sure the road is clear.

6   When I looked .... my mirror, I saw a police car was following me.

7   If you leave now you'll be just .... time to catch the 5.20.

8   Several people had to be treated .... cuts and bruises after the game.

9   There were a number of honeymoon couples .... the ship's passengers.

10 The hospital reported that she is .... a satisfactory condition.

Focus on grammar 1   Expressing time

In telling the story of Captain Lancaster's narrow escape, Text 1 uses a number of link words for time and other time expressions.

EXERCISE 1   Look back at Text 1 and see how many time expressions you can find. Add them to the table below.

Before	Same time	Later	Sequence
before previously	during meanwhile	as soon as immediately once afterwards	first(ly) second(ly), etc. last(ly)

SPECIAL
POINTS

1 **While/during/meanwhile** (complete the second examples)
During is a preposition and is followed by a noun. *For example:*
 I managed to sleep during *the flight.*
 You are not allowed to take photographs during ....

While is a conjunction and introduces a clause. *For example:*
 Did you learn any Spanish while *you were living in Madrid?*
 He likes to sing while ....

Meanwhile is an adverb which means 'during the time between'. *For example:*
 The taxi will be here in five minutes. Meanwhile, *I'll just phone Jim.*
 The rice will take a bit longer to cook. Meanwhile, *could you* ....

2 **First(ly)** v. **At first**
First(ly), as an adverb, means 'before anything else'. It's often used when describing a sequence of actions. *For example:*
 First *check in your mirror that the road is clear, and then pull out.*
 Before they booked a holiday, they first ....

At first means 'at the beginning'. *For example:*
 I made a lot of mistakes at first, *but now my typing's quite accurate.*
 It .... at first, *but later the sun came out.*

3 **Last(ly)** v. **At last**
Lastly, as an adverb, means 'after everything else' or 'finally'. *For example:*
 He gave me my final instructions and lastly *wished me good luck.*

At last means 'in the end' (after a long time). *For example:*
 I spent the whole evening waiting for the call and at last *the phone rang.*
 It had been such a hard winter that we were relieved when ....at last.

4   **After** *v.* **Afterwards**

After is followed by a clause. *For example:*

After we had watched the film we ....

or by a noun. *For example:*

After the film, we ....

Afterwards means 'after that'. *For example:*

We watched the film and afterwards *we had a Chinese meal.*

EXERCISE 2   Choose one of the following time expressions to put in each space below.

before	meanwhile	afterwards	at last	during	finally
at first	first	after	while	then	

I didn't enjoy the course ...at first... (1) but ...after... (2) a few weeks, I began to find it very interesting. We were given a lot of work to do ...during... (3) the holidays, so ...while... (4) my friends were having a good time, I was busy studying! I was terribly nervous ...before... (5) the examination in June. There were three separate sections: ...first... (6) we had a shorthand test; ...then... (7) we had to type a letter and a report; and ...finally... (8) there was a paper on office practice. I felt absolutely exhausted ...afterwards (9) !

We had to wait six weeks for the results and ...meanwhile... (10) I took a temporary job as an office clerk. When the envelope with the results arrived ...at last... (11) I found I had been given a distinction!

TENSES AFTER TIME LINKS

Look at the following sentences:

I'll see him tomorrow. I'll be able to ask him then.
I'll be able to ask him when *I* see *him.*

She's going to see her solicitor. She'll contact you after that.
She'll contact you after *she's* seen *her solicitor.*

before	once
as	as soon as
while	until
after	by the time
when	

When the words in the box are used to introduce a clause of time, they are followed by a verb in the **present** or **present perfect** tense, not the future tense.

EXERCISE 3   Complete the following sentences with a suitable word or phrase. Use the correct form of the present or present perfect tense.

a   By the time he ...comes... home, it'll be dark.

b   You'll have to get used to driving on the left when you ...are in... England.

c   I intend to fly to America as soon as I ...have... my visa.   received

d   He won't stop worrying until he ...get... the train.   catched.

e   Once they ...arrived in... their hotel, there'll be an evening free for sightseeing.

f   I'm hoping to hear the news on my car radio while I ...am at... work.

g   Make sure you get a good night's sleep before you ...go to work...

h   After you ...seen... the film, you'll want to buy the book!

Focus on listening 1 *A survival kit*

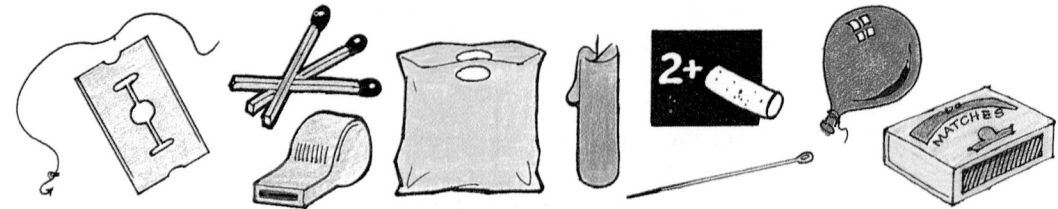

❶ You are going to hear a short talk about making a survival kit. As you listen, complete the table below, and answer questions 2 and 3.

Item	Purpose	Special notes
1 .... (a)	to hold your kit	
2 fishing line	to catch fish	Use only .... (b)
3 .... (c)		
4 razor blade	to gut fish	
5 plastic bag	to .... (d) to cover wounds to trap fish	Make sure .... (e)
6 .... (f)	to give light to make a waterproof seal	
7 balloon	to carry water to cover a wound	Don't .... (g) or it will burst.
8 needle	to sew, to .... (h) to make a compass	
9 matches	to light a fire	Make them .... (i) with wax.
10 chalk	.... (j) to leave a trail	
11 .... (k)	to call for help	

❷ Which item in the survival kit is the most important?   Item number ....

❸ Which item is carried separately from the rest?   Item number ....

Focus on writing 1 *Instructions*

The drawings below show how you can make matches waterproof for a survival kit.

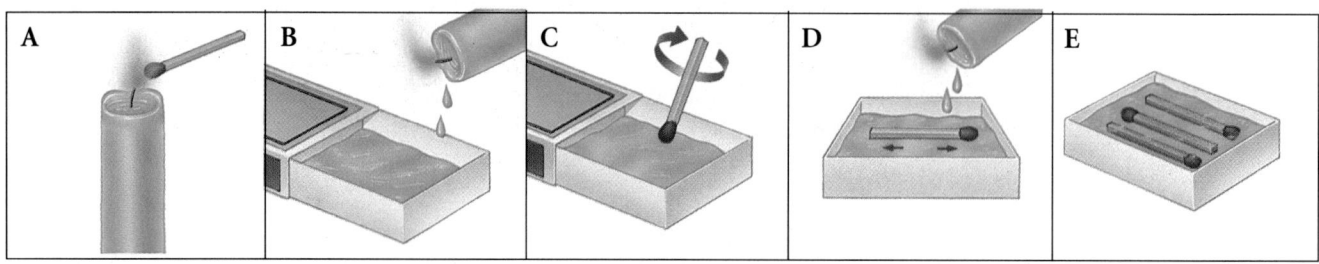

❶ The following instructions are out of order. Write the numbers 1 to 7 in the spaces provided to show the correct order. The first is done for you.

.... Drip the wax along the length of the match.

.... Hold the candle over the base of your matchbox and let some wax drip into the base.

.... Lay the matches end to end so that …

.... Lay the match in the wax.

...*1*... Light a candle.

.... Repeat the process for each match.

.... Place the head of a match in the wax and turn it carefully in order to …

❷ Two of the instructions are unfinished. Decide with another student how they should end.

❸ *Be careful not to …   Make sure you …   Once you …*

Decide what sentences beginning with the above phrases you could add to the instructions, and where.

❹ Now write a paragraph of instructions to go with the drawings above.

NOTES 1 Start with a heading.

2 Instead of the numbers you wrote above, use the words which show sequence from the Focus on grammar 1 section in this unit.

❺ Write a similar set of instructions for making a solar still, using the information from the diagram below.

1 Before you begin, make notes about the different steps which are necessary and decide which order they should come in.

2 You may also find it useful to look at the language for Describing Location in the Functions Bank (page 109).

FACT SHEET MAKING A SOLAR STILL

If you are ever lost in a desert area, you can collect an emergency supply of water by making a solar still. The still should be situated in a low area where there is no shade. It will only work in sunlight. You will need: A large piece of clear plastic, a container, a tool for digging, some stones.

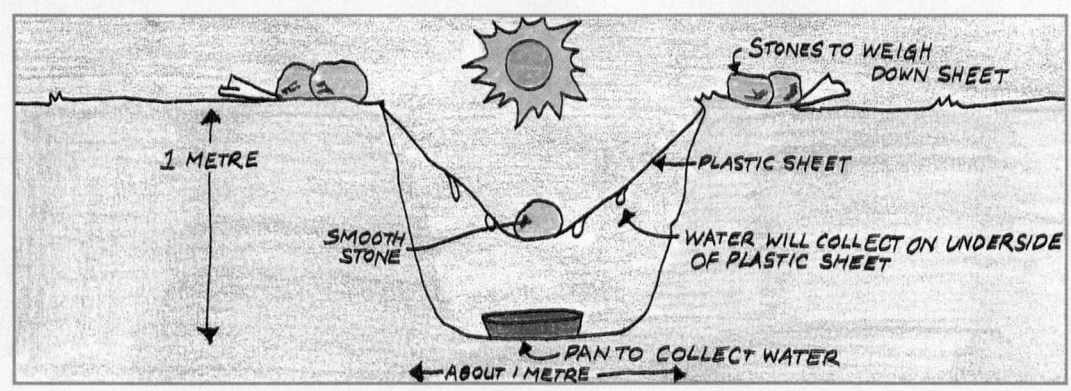

1 METRE

STONES TO WEIGH DOWN SHEET

PLASTIC SHEET

SMOOTH STONE

WATER WILL COLLECT ON UNDERSIDE OF PLASTIC SHEET

PAN TO COLLECT WATER

ABOUT 1 METRE

Text 2 *Rescue from the rapids*

INTRODUCTION In 1983, a natural historian, Redmond O'Hanlon, and a poet, James Fenton, set out on a long river voyage into the interior of the Borneo jungle, hoping to find out whether the Borneo rhinoceros still existed. They travelled with three native trackers, Dana, the local chief, Leon and Inghai, in a canoe Dana had built.

In this extract from the book Redmond O'Hanlon wrote, the travellers are passing through dangerous rapids and the boat has stuck in shallow water, close to a waterfall. While Leon and Inghai clear a channel, Redmond and James are pulling on a rope attached to the boat to keep it straight. At this point, they are told to move a little to their right …

❶ Read the text once, quickly, to answer these questions.
1 Why was James in serious danger?
2 Who rescued him?
3 What condition was James in afterwards?

It was only a stride or two. But the level of the river-bed suddenly dropped. James lost his footing, and, trying to save himself, let go of the rope. I stepped back and across to catch him, the rope bound round my left wrist, snatching his left hand in my right. His legs thudded into mine, tangled and then swung free, into the current, weightless, as if a part of him had been knocked into outer space. His hat came off, hurtled past his shoes, spun round in the water, and disappeared over the edge of the waterfall.

His fingers were very white and slippery. He bites his fingernails; and they could not dig into my palm. He simply looked surprised; his head seemed a long way from me. He was feeling underwater with his free arm, impossibly trying to grip a boulder with his other hand, to get a hold on a smooth and slimy rock, a rock polished smooth for centuries by never-ending tons of rolling water.

His fingers bent straighter, slowly edging out of mine, for hour upon hour, or so it felt, but it must have been seconds. His arm rigid, his fingertips squeezed out of my fist. He turned in the current, his arms and legs extended. Still turning, but much faster, he was sucked under; his right ankle and shoe were strangely visible above the surface; he was lifted slightly, a bundle of clothes, of no particular shape, and then he was gone.

'Boat! Boat!' shouted Dana, dropping the rope, bounding down the rocks.

'Hold the boat! Hold the boat!'

yelled Leon to me.

James's bald head, white and fragile as an owl's egg, was sweeping round in the whirlpool below, spinning, bobbing up and down in the foaming water, each circle of the current carrying him within inches of the black rocks at its edge.

Leon jumped into the boat, climbed on to the raised outboard-motor frame and then, with a loud cry, launched himself in a great curving leap into the centre of the whirlpool. He disappeared, surfaced, shook his head, spotted James, dived again, and caught him. Holding on to him, Leon went once round the whirlpool until, reaching the exit current, he swam out downstream, edging, yard by yard, toward the bank.

Obeying Dana's every sign, I

helped him to position the boat on to a strip of beach. James, when we walked down to him, was sitting on a boulder. Leon sat beside him, an arm around his shoulders. 'You be all right soon, my friend,' said Leon, 'you be all right soon, my very best friend. Soon you be happy.'

James, looking very sick, his white lips an open O in his black beard, was gasping for air, his body shaking.

'You be okay,' said Leon. 'I not let you die my old friend.'

Just then little Inghai appeared, beaming with pride, holding up one very wet hat.

'I save hat!' said Inghai, 'Jams, Jams! I save hat!'

James looked up, smiled, and so stopped his terrible gasps for air. He really was going to be all right.

From 'Into the Heart of Borneo' by Redmond O'Hanlon

❷ **Now read the text again to answer these questions.**

1 James first got into difficulty because
     A the rope he was holding broke.
     B the clothes he was wearing were unsuitable.
     C he couldn't swim.
     D he lost his balance.

2 The writer reacted to the emergency by
     A grasping one of James's hands.
     B shouting for help.
     C handing James a rope.
     D hanging on to James's body.

3 James was swept away by the current because
     A he was too shocked to try to save himself.
     B he resisted his friend's efforts to save him.
     C there was nothing he could hold tightly to.
     D he tried to turn round in the water.

4 Leon went to James's rescue by
     A steering the boat towards him.
     B running along the bank to catch him.
     C jumping into the water near him.
     D throwing him something to hold on to.

5 During the emergency, the rope attached to the boat was held by
     A Dana.   **B** the writer.   **C** Dana and the writer.   **D** nobody.

Communication activity 1

This is an old puzzle. Work in pairs or small groups to solve it.

You will need to use the words which mark sequence from Focus on grammar 1 to work out the answer and explain your solution.

A man lives in a remote house with his only possessions – a fox, a chicken and a bag of grain. One night the nearby river overflows and the house is surrounded by water. There is a rowing boat with enough room for the man and either the fox, or the chicken, or the grain. If he takes the grain, the fox will eat the chicken. If he takes the fox, the chicken will eat the grain.

How does the man carry them all safely to land?

STUDY BOX I	**Purpose clauses**
for + -ing	*You'll need matches **for making** a fire.*
	*You can use the plastic bag **for covering** wounds.*
to	*You use the chalk **to** mark trees.*
in order to + infinitive	*It's best to cover wounds **in order to protect** them from infection.*
so as to	*I've folded it very small **so as to** get it into the box.*
so that + clause	*You mark the trees **so that** you can leave a trail.*

Focus on grammar 2   Modal verbs 4: Certainty / probability / possibility

PRESENT/FUTURE

What do you think this picture shows …?

Sure

↓

Less sure

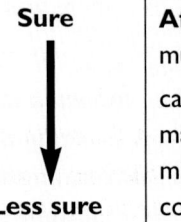

Affirmative
must
can
may   + infinitive
might
could

Negative
can't + infinitive

Interrogative
can
might + subject + infinitive
could

PRACTICE   Work in pairs. Suggest what these pictures show. You'll find the answers on page 226.

A 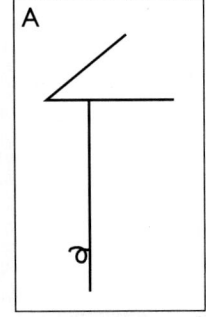   B 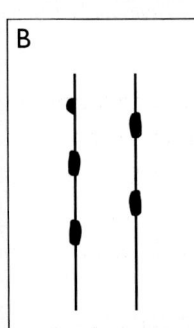   C 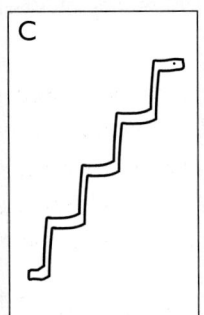   D 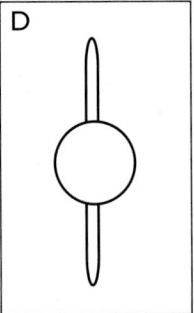   E 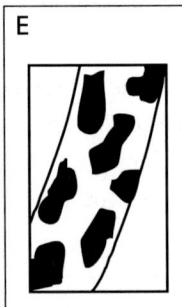   F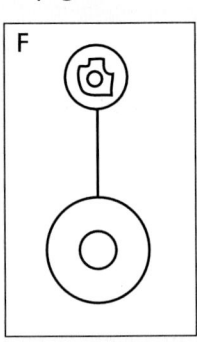

Look at these examples:

a *If that's the 6 o'clock news, my watch must be slow.*
   (The speaker is fairly **sure** that his watch is slow because it seems logical.)

b *Food with plenty of fibre can be satisfying.* (Unit 9)
   (This is **generally possible**, though perhaps not in all cases.)

c *Eating more fibre* may *actually help you to slim.* (Unit 9)
   (This is a **less certain** possibility.)

d *I* might *go away for a few days, but only if the weather improves.*
   (Both *might* and *could* express an **even less certain** possibility than *may*.)

e *It* can't *be John at the door. He's still on holiday in Italy.*
   (*can't* expresses **negative certainty** – the speaker is sure that something is **not** the case.)

PAST

Sure ↓ Less sure

Affirmative	
must	
may	+ have + past participle
might	
could	

Negative	
can't	+ have + past participle
couldn't	

Interrogative
can
might + subject + have + past participle
could

Look at these examples:

a *His fingers bent straighter … for hour upon hour, or so it felt, but it* must have been *seconds.* (Text 2)
   (It's fairly **sure**.)

b *The Yankee Bandit* may have earned *a place in the Guinness Book of Records.* (Unit 4)
   (This is a less certain possibility. *Might have* and *could have* also express this.)

c *They* could have taken *a taxi and got home sooner.*
   (*Could have* and *might have* are also used to talk about an event which was possible but did **not** happen.)

d *I* can't have made *a mistake with the bill because I used a calculator.*
   (*Can't have* and, less commonly, *couldn't have* are used in negative sentences. The speaker is fairly sure that something was **not** the case.)

e *What* can have happened?
   Can and *could* are used in questions when any number of events is possible.

EXERCISE I Rewrite the following sentences using modal verbs from the table above. Be careful to use the correct past participle! You don't need to include all the information.

a There is a possibility that my mother phoned while we were out. My mother ....

b Perhaps Helen saw the film on TV last night. Helen ....

c The most likely reason for your stomach upset is that you ate too much at lunch. You
   ....

d I've just been reading quietly so I certainly didn't wake the baby. I ....

e I wonder where John is. Perhaps he forgot the appointment in his diary. John ....

f Oh no! Look at all the water on the floor. I suppose a pipe burst while we were away. A pipe
   ....

g It's possible that the cleaning lady threw your cheque book away by mistake. The cleaning lady
   ....

Focus on listening 2

You will hear two people discussing an experience they had on holiday in Morocco.

For questions 1–7, tick (✓) one of the answers (A, B, C or D). For question 8, you will have to mark a place on a map.

1 The two travellers got into difficulties because they
   A didn't read the map.
   B took the wrong road.
   C decided to take a short cut.
   D didn't notice the river on the map.

2 They ignored the shepherds who were warning them because
   A they didn't believe them.
   B they didn't notice them.
   C they couldn't understand them.
   D they couldn't hear them.

3 They decided to try to drive through the first river because
   A it didn't look dangerous.
   B it was an adventure for them.
   C they couldn't turn the car round.
   D they didn't want to turn back.

4 The situation became serious when
   A the car got stuck in the mud.
   B the engine stopped working.
   C the river carried the car downstream.
   D the car sank in the river.

5 They didn't expect to get any help because
   A they didn't think that anyone lived nearby.
   B they couldn't speak Arabic.
   C it was too dark for anyone to see them.
   D they thought the local people were unfriendly.

6 After the rescue there was a problem because
   A they didn't have any money.
   B they didn't have the right sort of money.
   C they didn't want to give any money.
   D they didn't know how much money to give.

7 They stopped on their way to Rabat in order to
   A rest for the night.
   B ask for directions.
   C repair the car.
   D empty the water from the car.

8   On the map, mark the place where the car got stuck in the river with a cross (✗).

Communication activity 2 *Brain-teasers*

Work in pairs or small groups to solve the following puzzles.

A   Here is the last page from a statement which was made to the police. The rest of the statement has been lost. Can you tell **what had happened to the man?**

I was very frightened of course. Nothing like this had ever happened to me in my life before. And I was all alone. I just sat in the car, and gripped the wheel tightly.

The car came slowly to a stop. It seemed to take ages, but I could do nothing about it. It was very cold, and very dark. And I could see nothing outside.

Speed was important of course. So I took off my raincoat – not easy inside a car. I knew I had to move fast.

I wound the window down – I remembered you had to do that – and then I got out of the car. I used all my strength to move as quickly as possible.

When I finally saw the city lights, they were a long way off. But I was so glad to see them that I almost cried. I went into the nearest police station, and made this report.

B   Although it was night and there was dense fog, Tom was able to give a warning to deaf Dan, who was in serious danger in a boat two miles offshore. **How did he do it**, without the use of any equipment?

C   There's a place where the railway passes through a narrow tunnel. A single track runs through the tunnel but separates into two tracks again at each end of the tunnel.

One afternoon, a train went into the tunnel at one end, and another train went into the tunnel at the other end. Both trains entered the tunnel at top speed, and they didn't slow down or stop. But there was no crash, and both trains came out safely and went on their way. **How?**

D   A motorist was driving down a narrow country lane. His car lights were not working. There were no street lamps and no moonlight. Yet he still managed to avoid a man dressed all in black walking away from him down the centre of the road. **How?**

STUDY BOX 2	Prepositional phrases				
at first	*at* once	*on* fire	*in* danger	*in* difficulty(ies)	*at* the same time
at last	*at* times	*by* accident	*out of* danger		*in* the end

Focus on grammar 3   Question tags

Look at these examples from the conversation about the holiday in Morocco:

The road had been pretty bad, hadn't it?

It was marked yellow on the map, wasn't it?

They were shepherds coming home, weren't they?

Question tags like these are often used in conversation to invite agreement.

FORM

Question tags consist of an auxiliary verb and a personal pronoun. There are a few basic rules:

1 If there is an auxiliary (*do, be, have*) or modal auxiliary verb in the main clause, this is repeated in the question tag. *For example:*

He hasn't arrived yet, has he?

(NB **Have** can also be used as an ordinary verb)

You should be in bed by now, shouldn't you?

2 If there is an ordinary verb in the main clause, *do* is used in the question tag. *For example:*

You know how to change a wheel, don't you? (Present)

They went to Russia last year, didn't they? (Past)

He had an accident last year, didn't he? (Past – **have** as an ordinary verb)

3 Normally an affirmative statement has a negative question tag, and vice versa:

Statement		Question tag	
Affirmative	+	Negative	*You're coming, aren't you?*
Negative	+	Affirmative	*He doesn't like jazz, does he?*

EXERCISE 1

Match the two halves of the sentences below.

a You usually catch the 9 o'clock train,
b You can't speak Spanish,
c You haven't got change of £1,
d You'd better answer the telephone,
e You could always borrow the money,
f You won't tell anyone,
g You didn't wear that to the party,
h You're going to see him tomorrow,
i You hadn't been to an opera before,
j You've got some time to spare,

1 aren't you?
2 couldn't you?
3 had you?
4 will you?
5 can you?
6 don't you?
7 hadn't you?
8 haven't you?
9 have you?
10 did you?

SPECIAL POINTS

1 *I am* is followed by the question tag *aren't I? For example: I'm lucky, aren't I?*

2 After an imperative, *will you?* or *would you?* are the most common forms. *Will you?* is the only form possible after a negative imperative. *For example:*

> *Pay attention,* will you?　　　*Don't be late,* will you?
> *Shut the door,* would you?

3 Negative expressions like *no, nothing, nowhere* and *nobody* in the main clause are followed by an affirmative question tag. *For example:*

> *He takes no interest in his work,* does he?

4 *Somebody/someone, everybody/everyone* and *nobody/no-one* are followed by *they* in a question tag. *For example:*

> *Nobody called for me,* did they?
> *Everyone was very pleased,* weren't they?

5 *Nothing/anything* in the main clause is followed by *it* in a question tag. *For example:*

> *Nothing could be better,* could it?
> *Anything could happen now,* couldn't it?

EXERCISE 2　Add correct question tags to the following statements.

a We left at dawn, ...
b You've no idea at all what I'm talking about, ...
c You'd rather be staying at home, ...
d Don't tell anyone, ...
e There are some fantastic bargains, ...
f You shouldn't have made such a fuss, ...
g We had some really bad luck, ...
h Nobody heard what you said, ...
i Switch on the light, ...
j I'm managing quite well, ...

STUDY BOX 3　**Phrasal verb go**

The journey seemed to **go on** for ever.

go down with – become ill.	I hope I'm not **going down with** 'flu.
go in for – enter an exam/competition.	Are you **going in for** the race?
go off – explode.	We heard the bomb **go off**.
go off – go bad.	This milk smells as if it's **gone off**.
go on – continue.	How long does this concert **go on**?
go on – happen.	What exactly has been **going on**?
go over/through – examine.	The teacher **went through** our test papers.
go through – search.	**Go through** your pockets to see if you can find it.
go with – match/suit.	That tie doesn't **go with** your shirt.
go without – manage without.	You can't **go without** water for long.

Focus on writing 2 *Narrative* WRITING BANK: PAGE 122

Write a short **story** in **150–180** words for your school/college magazine. It must begin with the following words: *I once had an extremely narrow escape …*

Whether you are telling a story aloud or writing it in a letter, an article or an essay, the most important thing is to hold the listener's or reader's attention so that they want to know what happened next.

NOTES

1 PLAN

Opening paragraph:

Introduce the story and try to catch the reader's attention with a statement which makes him/her want to read on. For example:

'*When we set off on our camping holiday, we had no idea that it was going to turn into a nightmare.*'
or '*I'll never forget 12th September, 19... It was the day …*'

Middle paragraph:

Develop the story clearly, step by step, describing each main stage in a new paragraph.

Closing paragraph(s):

Give the story a definite ending and comment on the experience. You might say what you have learnt from it, for example.

2 TENSES

A good narrative is likely to include a variety of past tenses – past simple, past continuous and past perfect. Look at these examples from Text 1 and discuss why they are used.

1 The plane was climbing to its cruising height when one of six windscreen panels came out.
2 Mr Cocklin said the window had been replaced two days earlier.
3 The stewardesses had just started serving tea and coffee when there was a terrific bang.
4 The pilot looked in a bad way but I reckoned he was conscious because they were talking to him all the time.

Language review

Choose the word or phrase which best completes each sentence.

1 The bank doesn't open for another half an hour so .... I'll do a bit of shopping.
   A previously   **B** during   **C** afterwards   **D** meanwhile

2 He .... of the lead for a moment and the dog ran off.
   A dropped   **B** released   **C** let go   **D** took hold

3 It's dangerous to swim in this part of the river because of the strong ....
   A stream   **B** tide   **C** current   **D** flood

4 You .... have been delighted when you won the competition.
   A can   **B** must   **C** may   **D** could

5 Be careful as you walk. I've just polished the floor and it's rather ....
   A smooth   **B** slippery   **C** sticky   **D** stiff

6 He'd rather look for a different job than move to another city, ... ?
   A doesn't he   **B** hadn't he   **C** isn't he   **D** wouldn't he

7 This is the third cold I've had .... six months!
   A for   **B** during   **C** in   **D** since

8 He looked a bit tired when I met him, but .... well.
   A otherwise   **B** in addition   **C** elsewhere   **D** except

9 The car hit a lamppost, causing it .... over.
   A fall   **B** falling   **C** to fall   **D** fallen

10 He .... have lost his way. He knows the city so well!
   A would   **B** might   **C** mustn't   **D** can't

11 You should clean the cut thoroughly .... prevent any infection.
   A so that   **B** so as to   **C** for   **D** in order

12 I enjoy living alone although I do get lonely .... times.
   A at   **B** for   **C** in   **D** by

13 Look at that smoke. It looks as though the barn is .... fire.
   A at   **B** on   **C** to   **D** in

14 I went to a party last night and .... some friends came back for coffee.
   A after   **B** at last   **C** finally   **D** afterwards

15 I don't feel very well. I'm afraid I may be .... 'flu.
   A going down with   **B** going in for   **C** going off with   **D** going into

Lead-in *Topic vocabulary*

❶ Who is the person who sells:

1 meat
2 bread
3 fish
4 fresh fruit and vegetables

5 newspapers and magazines
6 cigarettes and tobacco
7 medicines, drugs and cosmetics
8 dry and preserved goods, such as rice and coffee

❷ Where do you go to:

1 buy tickets for the theatre
2 buy a railway ticket
3 buy books
4 buy petrol

5 arrange a holiday
6 buy writing paper and pens
7 find a house to buy
8 buy goods for the home or garden, such as tools

❸ Where do you go to:

1 have your hair cut
2 have your shoes repaired

3 have your clothes washed
4 wash your clothes in a coin-operated machine

❹ Some items are usually bought by a particular unit. Choose two items from the list below that you would usually buy by the:

1 slice   ....
2 bar   ....
3 bunch   ....
4 roll   ....
5 pair   ....

chocolate	flowers	cold meat	wallpaper
bandage	gloves	soap	grapes

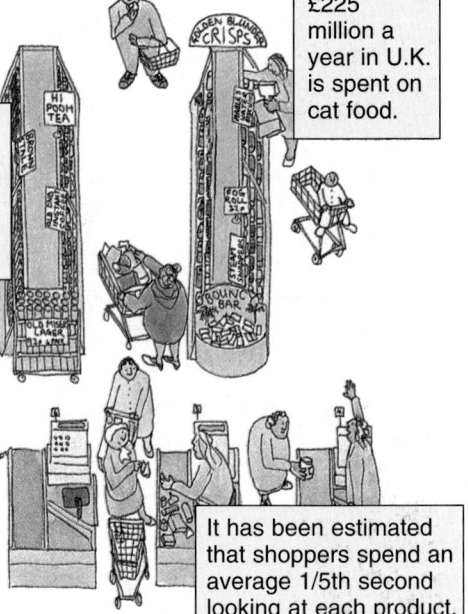

The first self-service groceries were opened in America in 1912.

£225 million a year in U.K. is spent on cat food.

It has been estimated that shoppers spend an average 1/5th second looking at each product.

❺ Choose words from the list to label the picture.

basket	trolley	aisle	check-out	shelf

Text 1 *Down the aisle!*

❶   You are going to read an article about supermarket shopping. Choose from the list (A–H) the sentence which best summarises each section of the article. There is one extra sentence which you do not need to use. The first answer has been given as an example.

> **A** Experts have studied the way we shop.
>
> **B** We notice goods displayed on one side before the other side.
>
> **C** A lot of money is spent on finding out the best place to display goods.
>
> **D** Some places in supermarkets are very bad for selling goods.
>
> **E** Most people buy more in a supermarket than they had intended.
>
> **F** Products sell well in places where people stop for a while.
>
> **G** Shopping is an unpleasant experience for most people.
>
> **H** Products are more likely to catch our attention when they are in certain places.

0 E

When you visit a supermarket you probably think you know exactly what you're going to buy, but the truth is you're very easily persuaded. Over half the decisions you make are made suddenly, on impulse, while you're inside the store, so it's vital that a product is displayed in an eye-catching position if it is to have any chance of success.

1

Today's supermarkets invest millions of pounds in powerful computers which tell them what product sells best and where. 'Space management' is the name given to a highly sophisticated way of influencing the way we shop to make sure that stores make the maximum profit.

2

You walk into a supermarket. You pull out a trolley and stare up and down row after row of packed shelves. You step out into the aisles. You are faced with possibly the widest choice of food and drink in the world. But over the next hour or so you will shop in a completely predictable way. This is what the space management teams who work for supermarkets have found out. They believe that everything depends on the following rules about our behaviour in supermarkets:

3

• The modern supermarket offers too many images for our brains to absorb so we switch off and notice only a fraction of the goods on display. A product will be more noticeable in some parts of the store than others, so manufacturers and retailers must work hard to attract our attention.

• In general products sell best when they are placed at eye level.

4

• Products placed at the beginnings of aisles don't sell well. In tests, secret fixed cameras have filmed shoppers' movements around a store over a seven-day period. When the film is speeded up it clearly shows that we walk straight past these areas on our way to the centre of the aisle. These early shelves are known as 'the graveyard'.

5

• When we finally stop to consider in the centre of an aisle, we look along the length of it. And because we read from left to right, we look from left to right too. So we see products displayed on the left side of the aisle first.

6

• Any spot where the supermarket can be sure we are going to stand still and concentrate for more than a few seconds is good for sales. That's why the shelves at the check-out have long been a favourite for manufacturers of sweets, perhaps the most popular 'impulse' buy of all.

DISCUSSION POINTS   **❷**

1 What are the advantages and disadvantages of shopping in a supermarket?

2 Do you sometimes buy things which aren't on your shopping list when you're in a supermarket? What do you buy? What makes you decide to buy them?

3 Supermarkets prefer people to use a trolley rather than a basket. Why?

4 Supermarkets expect to lose about one in five of their trolleys a year. What do you think happens to them? What could supermarkets do to prevent this loss?

Focus on grammar I   The passive voice

Look at these sentences and answer the questions which follow.

£225 million a year in the UK is spent on cat food. (**Who** spends this amount?)
The first self-service groceries were opened in America in 1912. (**Who** opened them?)

There are at least six examples of the passive voice in Text I. Find as many as you can and underline them. When you have finished, compare your answers with another student's.

MAIN USES OF THE PASSIVE VOICE

1   When the person doing the action (the agent) is not known, or when it is unnecessary to mention the agent. *For example:*
My car's been stolen!   *Milk is often sold in cartons.*

2   To emphasise the action or event rather than the agent. *For example:*
Letters are collected from the boxes, taken to the sorting office, sorted and then sent to the correct part of the country.

3   To avoid using **you** or **one** when making an impersonal statement. *For example:*
Taking photographs in the museum is forbidden.   *Children are not allowed in the bar.*

FORM
1   In the active voice the normal order is Subject – Verb – Object. To make a sentence passive, the object must become the new subject and this must be followed by a passive form:

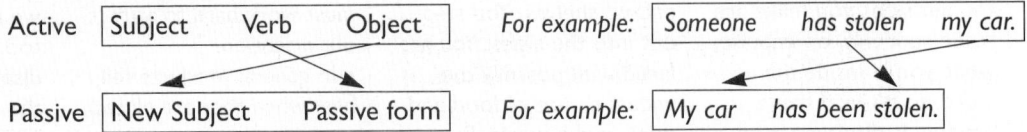

2   The passive is formed with the different tenses of the verb **to be** followed by a past participle.

EXERCISE I
The passive voice can be used in most tenses and also with **going to** and modal verbs. Complete the following table with a partner so that you have a complete record of how the passive voice is formed.

Tense	Subject	Verb **to be**	Past participle
Present simple	Dinner	....	served,
Present continuous	....	is being	built.
....	A stolen car	has been	found.
Past simple	The thief	was	....
Past continuous	The room	....	painted.
....	The decision	had been	taken.
Future simple	Your offer	will be	....
Future perfect	....	will have been	posted.
Other Structures			
Going to	His car	....	serviced.
Modals (Present)	This machine	can	mended.
(Past)	....	shouldn't have been	opened.

EXERCISE 2   The passive voice is often used in signs and labels. There are some examples below but they've been jumbled up. Match the word or phrase in column **A** with the correct ending in column **B**.

Column **A**	Column **B**
1 Rooms	a must not be removed from the library.
2 Shoplifters	b should be addressed to the Registrar.
3 This wine	c will be prosecuted.
4 This dictionary	d must not be left unattended.
5 No goods	e is protected by guard dogs.
6 Applications	f can be exchanged without a receipt.
7 Bags	g must be vacated by 12 noon.
8 This building	h is best served at room temperature.

When you have finished, compare your answers with another student's.

EXERCISE 3   Look at the signs below and write suitable captions for them using the passive voice.

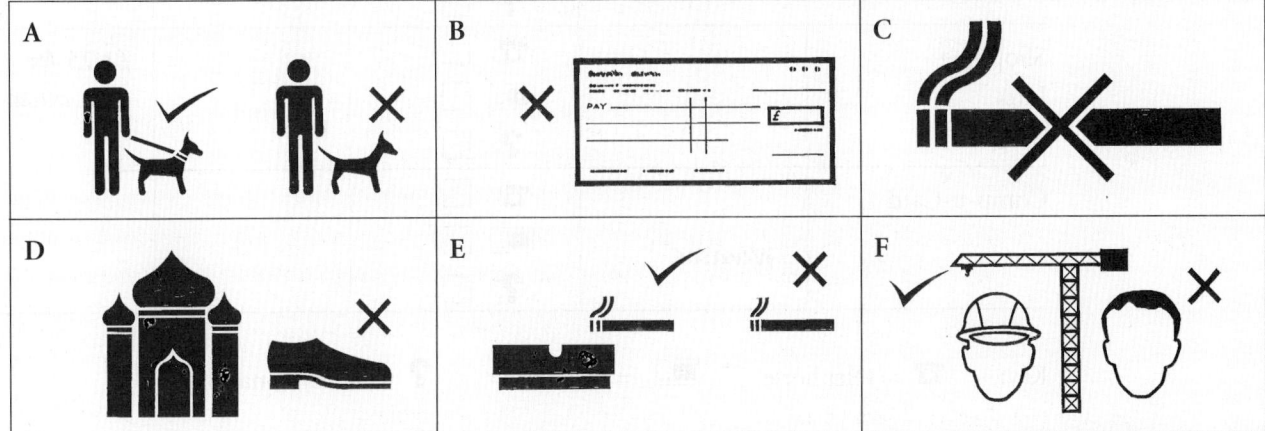

EXERCISE 4   Put the verbs in brackets into a suitable passive form. Don't forget to make any necessary changes in word order. (The first five sentences come from texts in Unit 5.)

a   Every year, a forest the size of Wales (cut down) to make paper for use in Britain.

b   Cycleways should (build) to make cycling safer.

c   Vast amounts of money (spend) on nuclear power each year.

d   Energy could (also/save) if more short journeys (make) by bicycle.

e   Rubbish, with the hard bits removed, can (grind up), (mix) with sewage and (sell) as compost.

f   Our team (only/beat) once so far this year.

g   This painting (probably/paint) by Dali.

h   She's only crying because some soap went into her eye while her hair (wash).

i   A new guidebook to the cathedral (write) at the moment.

j   Women (still/deny) the right to vote in some countries.

k   This strike (not/forget) very quickly.

l   It's not like him to be late. His train must (delay).

m   The wine that (spill) on the carpet during the party has left an awful stain.

n   The votes (count) by midnight?

o   He noticed at once that the safe (break into).

Focus on listening I *Chips with everything*

You are going to hear a short talk about how computers are being used to help to make shopping easier.

The table below gives a summary of the information in the talk. Study it carefully before you begin and, while you listen, fill in the missing information.

System	Town	Equipment needed		Home delivery?	Cost
Over-60s Shopping Line	Gateshead	☎ ✓ ▣ ✓ ? ☐		☐	
	Birmingham	☎ ☐ ▣ ☐ ? ☐		✓	
Shopping Link		☎ ☐ ▣ ☐ ? ☐		☐	£1.73 for each order
Comp-u-Card	Windsor	☎ ☐ ▣ ☐ ? ☐		☐	

Key: ☎ = telephone   ▣ = television   ? = no information

Text 2 *Buying by post*

❶ Read the notices and the advertisements below in order to answer the questions which follow.

A FEW GOLDEN RULES

When you buy by post a little common sense can avoid a lot of trouble.

1 When you see something you like, check that the newspaper, magazine, or catalogue is up to date.
2 Read the advertisement carefully.
3 When you write off (and when you return goods) always include your name and address.
4 Keep a copy of your order and a note of the date it was sent.
5 Keep details of the advertisement – when it appeared, advertiser's address, the main points.
6 Never send cash through the post.
7 Send cheques, postal orders, etc., only if you're asked for payment in advance, and make sure you keep cheque stubs or counterfoils.

IF YOU HAVE TO COMPLAIN

'Postal Bargain' advertisements:
Write to the Advertising Manager of the newspaper or magazine if goods you've ordered haven't arrived within 28 days. Include the following information (tick them off on this checklist):
❑ date of advertisement
❑ date of your order
❑ details of goods ordered
❑ name and address to which goods should be sent
❑ amount paid (cheque, postal order)
❑ if you still have a receipt
❑ trader's full name and address
And anything else you think may be useful.
If the trader has gone bankrupt, you will be told.
You must then send in a formal claim, together with some proof of payment.

From *The Central Office of Information*

BARGAINS from SAVE-A-LOT!

Sweater Dryer [A]

Keep the value and shape of your sweaters. With this incredible dryer you can retain shape without pulling or stretching delicate fibres. Easy to use at home – folds flat for travel or storage. Perfect for Jumpers Cardigans Baby clothes Fine woollens Synthetics etc. No home should be without one.

Only £7.95 incl. p&p

Bright Super Lamp [B]

The lamp that can be fixed almost anywhere – fit in seconds with contact stickers. Use as bedside lamp, in attics, sheds, garages. Completely safe. No wiring. Ideal for power cuts too. Super deluxe model. Do not confuse with inferior models.

Only £6.75 + 80p p&p

Soft Ice Pack [C]

RELIEF TO ALL THOSE ACHES

Now you can relieve those nagging aches and pains caused by bruising, headaches, toothaches etc. – the old-fashioned way. Simply fill the bag with ice, and place over the area of your choice – feel and note the difference! Indispensable for home – car – office. A must in any first-aid box. Try relief the old-fashioned way!

£3.75 + 60p p&p

Wallet Belt [D]

IDEAL!

SAFE!

Money Jewellery Documents Wear this strong 'invisible' belt with the king-size double pockets and your worries are over. Protect yourself from loss, pickpockets and thieves. Order now while stocks last.

£4.50 + 65p p&p

POST TODAY TO SAVE-A-LOT LTD., DEPT. M., 42 WINDSOR GARDENS, LONDON NW3X 6TS

❷ According to the Golden Rules, which of the following mistakes can you make when you buy something by post? Tick the correct boxes.

1 Ordering something old-fashioned. ☐
2 Ordering something which is no longer available. ☐
3 Not keeping a record of the advertiser's address. ☐
4 Sending a cheque before you receive the goods. ☐
5 Putting the wrong date on your cheque. ☐
6 Not giving the newspaper or magazine your address. ☐
7 Sending something back without giving your address. ☐
8 Not keeping a record of your payment. ☐
9 Not making a note of the date of your order. ☐
10 Not keeping the receipt for your goods. ☐

❸ Choose from the four 'small ads' (A–D) to answer these questions and write the letters in the boxes.

Which advertisement suggests that a particular product is very easy to install? [1][ ]

Which advertisement suggests that supplies of a particular product are limited? [2][ ]

Which advertisement suggests that using a particular product will help prevent damage to your clothes? [3][ ]

Which advertisement suggests that a product is copied by other manufacturers? [4][ ]

Which advertisement suggests that a product can give you peace of mind? [5][ ]

Which two advertisements suggest that it is essential to have a particular product? [6][ ] [7][ ]

Focus on writing *Formal letter* WRITING BANK: PAGE 114

You ordered one of the items advertised on page 201 a month ago. It still hasn't arrived and you are beginning to get worried! Following the instructions on the same page, write a formal letter of complaint. Write your **letter** in **120–180** words, excluding addresses.

Before you start, check the notes on Formal Letters in the Writing Bank, page 114.

STUDY BOX 1 Have something done

'They choose when they want to **have** it **delivered**.' (Listening 1)

Have, used with an object and a past participle, means 'to cause something to be done'.
You might go to the dentist's surgery to **have** a tooth **pulled out**.

Why might you …   go to the shoe-mender's?
                     go to the hairdresser's?
                     go to an optician's?
                     take your car to a garage?
                     call a plumber?
                     employ a carpenter?

Focus on listening 2 *The auctioneer*

In this conversation you are going to hear Mr Ewing, an auctioneer, talking about his work.

NOTES   'An auction' is a public sale where goods are sold to the person who offers the most money.
'A bid' is the money which is offered: *I made a bid of £5 for the mirror.*
'A lot' is an item, or a group of items, sold at an auction: *I'm interested in Lot 59, the four dining chairs.*
'An auctioneer' is the person who conducts the sale.

For questions 1–4 tick (✓) which you think is the correct answer in each case (A, B, C or D).

1 Mr Ewing became an auctioneer when
   A he completed a training course in auction selling.
   B his family started up an auction business.
   C his firm gave him the chance to work in its auction room.
   D he failed his Polytechnic course in surveying.

2 One of the most usual ways of making a bid at an auction is to
   A wave your arms.
   B raise your voice.
   C make a secret signal.
   D lift your catalogue.

3 When auctioneers take a bid from someone who was only signalling to a friend, it's usually
   A a genuine mistake.
   B an arrangement which has been made in advance.
   C a way of entertaining the audience.
   D a way of selling unpopular goods.

4 Auction fever happens when people get very
   A excited.
   B frightened.
   C ill.
   D angry.

For questions 5–9 tick (✓) whether you think the statements are true or false.

	True	False
5 Country house sales are always well attended because the prices tend to be reasonable.	☐	☐
6 When the painting was found it was in a very poor state.	☐	☐
7 Mr Ewing was very surprised by the price the painting was sold for.	☐	☐
8 The four-poster bed was found in several pieces.	☐	☐
9 As a provincial auctioneer, Mr Ewing is only expected to give expert advice on a limited number of items.	☐	☐

For questions 10–12 fill in the missing information in the spaces.

10 Mr Ewing is especially interested in ....

11 His problem is that he .... the items he would like to own.

12 His advice is not to be .... about going to an auction for the first time.

STUDY BOX 2	Prepositional phrases followed by a noun or a gerund			
according **to**	except **for**	**as** regards	in addition **to**	instead **of**
on account **of**	as far **as**	in spite **of**	apart **from**	by means **of**

Communication activity *Selling pets*

NOTE   Before you begin, check the Functions Bank (page 106) for the language of Asking for and Giving Advice, and of Persuading.

INSTRUCTIONS ❶

1 Work in pairs. If numbers are uneven, two students may work together in one of the roles. Alternatively, one student may act as an observer, noting language used.

2 **Role A:** You have one of the animals in List A. Your job is to persuade your partner(s) to buy it. Before you begin, tell your partner what the first letter following your animal is. Give him/her time to read through the role. Your partner will begin.

3 **Role B:** Your partner will tell you which role you have from List B. You want to buy a pet and you go to your partner for advice on what animal to choose. Look through your role quickly and then be prepared to begin the conversation.

4 After five minutes, change round so the buyer is now selling, and the seller is buying. You should have a new animal and, this time, Role B is the second letter after the animal.

List A				List B
snake	a	b	a	You live in a small flat and you want a pet that's not too much trouble to look after.
tortoise	d	f		
canary	c	e	b	You live alone and would like a pet for protection.
white mouse	e	a	c	You want a pet that will keep you active.
goldfish	f	d	d	You are a teenager. You want a pet that you can have fun with.
cat	b	c		
			e	You are a filmstar. You want a pet as a mascot.
			f	You are an elderly person. You want a pet to keep you company.

DISCUSSION POINTS ❷

1 Were any of the sellers successful? If so, what techniques of persuasion did they use?

2 If you were unsuccessful in selling your animal, how and why did the buyer reject your advice?

Text 3 ❶ Read these four short extracts and answer the following questions.

Beware supermarket selling **A**

Much research has been done by supermarket chains to find out how to persuade shoppers to buy more. Supermarkets are arranged to take advantage of the impulses of the people shopping in them – for example by putting sweets at checkouts in racks at children's eye-level. In general, you are likely to spend less shopping if you leave the children behind, if you have eaten recently and if you shop infrequently.

Use your oven sparingly **B**

Ovens are expensive to heat (particularly electric ovens), and can be costly to run for any length of time. Try to plan your cooking to have a full oven, so minimising the number of times it is used. An asbestos mat will let you cook things slowly on top of the cooker to avoid using the oven to heat one thing only.

Do you need a car at all? **C**

Your car could be costing you more than you think. The cost of just owning a car (i.e. tax, insurance, depreciation and loss of interest on capital) can be at least £15 a week for the cheapest car – before you have put any petrol into it or paid for servicing. Using public transport, taxis or minicabs, and hiring a self-drive car for trips further afield could save money. Think particularly carefully about running a second car – you might find that you can get by with one car by taking a few taxi rides each week (almost certainly saving money).

Buy in bulk **D**

Buying food in large packets and bulk quantities can knock up to 10 per cent off your food bills. If you form a bulk-buying cooperative with friends and neighbours, you could afford to buy food in wholesale quantities and make even bigger savings.

From *The Consumers' Association*

❷ 1 The four extracts all
   A warn against going to certain shops.
   B recommend buying particular products.
   C suggest different ways of saving money.
   D explain the best way to do your shopping.

2 Extract A suggests that if you take your children to the supermarket
   A it will take you longer to do your shopping.
   B you will forget what you wanted to buy.
   C they will encourage you to buy more.
   D they will get in other shoppers' way.

3 Extract B recommends
   A cooking several things at once in the oven.
   B putting an asbestos mat in the oven.
   C only using the top of the cooker.
   D cooking food slowly in the oven.

4 Extract C warns about the high cost of
   A hiring a car.
   B owning two cars.
   C travelling by taxi.
   D replacing your car.

5 Extract D advises you
   A not to buy more food than you need.
   B not to ask shopkeepers for a discount.
   C to share your food with other people.
   D to buy food in large amounts.

Focus on grammar 2   Gerund and infinitive

USE Ⅰ

Some verbs can be followed by either the gerund or the infinitive with no difference, or only a small difference in meaning.

Ⅰ **like, love, hate, prefer**. *For example:*

Do you watch much TV? Well, I *like* | *watching* / *to watch* | the breakfast show | (= enjoy) **no difference**

I like to be early when I'm catching a train. (= prefer/choose)

After **would**, the infinitive is normally used.

Would you like to go for a walk?
I'd hate to miss the chance.
We'd love to hear from you.

2 **begin, start**. *For example:*

It's started | *snowing.* / *to snow.* | **no difference**

After the continuous form of a verb, only the infinitive is used. *For example:*

It's beginning to get dark.

USE 2

Some verbs can be followed by either the gerund or the infinitive, but with a difference of meaning.

Ⅰ **remember/forget**

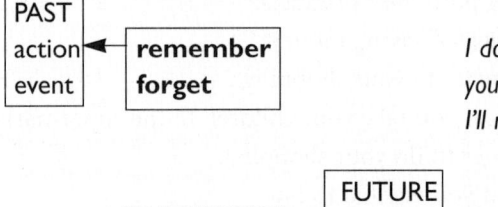

I don't remember seeing you at the party. Were you there?
I'll never forget flying over the Alps for the first time.

Don't forget to feed the cat, will you?
Did you remember to post that letter while you were out?

2 **regret**

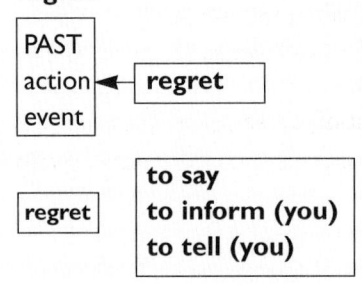

He regrets stealing the money now.
I'll always regret not going to university.

I regret to say I lost my temper.
We regret to inform you that your flight has been delayed.
Mr Brown regrets to tell you that he is unable to see you today.

3 try

(You've lost your keys.) *Try emptying your pockets.*

(possible action – see if it succeeds)

Try to remember when you last had them.

(action may not be possible – see if you can do it.)

4 need

The windows need cleaning. (Passive meaning: need to be cleaned)

I need to call at the post office. (Active meaning: have to call)

5 stop

When **stop** is followed by a gerund it means 'to finish an action'.

Could you stop shouting?

When stop is followed by an infinitive, it means 'to interrupt one action **in order to** do something else'.

We had to stop (walking, driving, etc.) to look at the map.

EXERCISE 1 Put the verb in brackets in the correct form, gerund or infinitive.

a You must remember (call) at the bank on your way home because we need (order) some traveller's cheques.

b Could you stop (type) for a moment? I need (concentrate) on this letter.

c I hope you haven't forgotten (telephone) the garage because the car badly needs (service).

d We could try (make) a dash for the car if it would only stop (rain) for a moment.

e I'm sure you won't regret (buy) the house, even though it needs (paint) and (decorate).

f I regret (say) that he's forgotten ever (promise) you a job.

g I don't remember (take) my wallet out of my bag, but I must have done when I stopped (buy) petrol.

h As I told you, he's rather deaf, so don't forget (try) (shout) if he doesn't answer the door at first.

EXERCISE 2 Gerund and infinitive revision

a I've considered (ask) him (raise) my salary, but I don't think he can afford (do) it.

b If the machine happens (stop) (work), just telephone and arrange for the service engineer (call).

c I can't help (think) that we shouldn't have agreed (lend) him our car.

d If you've finished (use) the typewriter, I'd like (borrow) it for a while, so that I can get used to (type) with that machine.

e He denied (take) the money and warned us (not/call) the police.

f I'm delighted (hear) that you are intending (visit) us and I look forward to (see) you when you come.

Language review

Choose the word or phrase which best completes each sentence.

1 My washing machine has been so useful that I don't know how I managed to .... without it before.
   A get by   **B** get over   **C** get away   **D** get across

2 I'm afraid I can't give you your money back unless you have a(n) .... for the pullover.
   A bill   **B** invoice   **C** ticket   **D** receipt

3 They're going to .... central heating in the office.
   A include   **B** install   **C** connect   **D** conduct

4 There's a .... of silk scarves in the shop window.
   A scene   **B** view   **C** sight   **D** display

5 Look at that man waving. I think he's trying to .... our attention.
   A call   **B** bring   **C** attract   **D** signal

6 The special offer in the magazine looked so good that I .... for it straight away.
   A wrote out   **B** wrote off   **C** wrote up   **D** wrote down

7 We're not sure if we can hold the barbecue yet. It depends .... the weather.
   A of   **B** from   **C** on   **D** for

8 I was very worried about the examination and it was a great .... to hear that I had passed.
   A news   **B** relief   **C** reward   **D** escape

9 He wore thick gloves and a scarf to protect him .... the cold.
   A for   **B** by   **C** from   **D** at

10 I asked the assistant if he had any football boots in ....
   A store   **B** shop   **C** stock   **D** sale

11 Those gloves are much too small for you. Don't try to put them on or you'll .... them.
   A stretch   **B** spread   **C** extend   **D** swell

12 I want to .... advantage of the sale at the shoe shop while it's on.
   A make   **B** have   **C** get   **D** take

13 The bank clerk asked for some .... of my identity, such as a passport or driver's licence.
   A card   **B** signal   **C** notice   **D** proof

14 He doesn't know anybody in London, apart .... his sister.
   A from   **B** for   **C** than   **D** of

15 We regret .... you that the 12.20 to Bristol has been cancelled.
   A inform   **B** to inform   **C** informing   **D** for informing

Lead-in 1

Look at the photographs below. Each one shows an event which marks a turning point in a person's life.

❶ Discuss what is happening in each picture and what changes the event will lead to.

❷ Which of the four events is likely to be the most important turning point, in your opinion?

❸ What other possible turning points in a person's life can you think of?

❹ Have you ever experienced a particular turning point in your life? Describe it.

Lead-in 2

❶ In the quotations (A–E) below five different people are talking about a particular experience. Read what they each say and decide what the experience was.

A It has changed my life considerably in that it has given me more scope and opportunity; it hasn't changed me myself, my outlook, my personality, one little bit.

B My friends did not react very well. The majority of them became embarrassed. Before, when we used to go out, everyone had the same sort of money in their pocket; so now I really don't have the same sort of friends.

C After the win you think 'That's it, I'll never do any work again, just finish'. It doesn't last very long, you've got to have something to do if your mind is active, you've got to make your mind active as well.

D Some of my relatives were jealous. My brother hasn't spoken to me since, although I gave his son £800. I've given up worrying about it now.

E I'm beginning to wish I had never won the money. I am fed up with all the begging letters, the proposals and all the friends I have suddenly found. All I want is a bit of peace and quiet and the only way I shall get it is to leave the country.

❷ Now answer these questions:

1 Some people mention rather negative reactions. Which one is more positive?

2 Which person changed his mind about what he was going to do after the win?

3 Why do you think the friends mentioned in B felt embarrassed? Explain in your own words why that winner lost his friends?

4 Why do you think one winner's brother stopped speaking to him?

5 In E, what were the begging letters and proposals? Who were the winner's new friends, and why was she fed up with them?

6 How might a person's personality change as a result of winning a lot of money?

7 Imagine that a close friend of yours won £100,000. Would it make any difference to your friendship? What difficulties could it cause?

Focus on grammar 1	Expressing wishes and regrets

I WISH …/IF ONLY …

1   When referring to the **present** or **future**, these expressions are followed by a **past tense**.
For example:

I wish | *I had a car!* (I haven't got a car.)
| *he didn't have to go.* (He does have to go.)

If only | *I knew the answer!* (I don't know the answer.)
| *you weren't working tomorrow.* (You are working then.)

Note   The correct form of the verb *to be* after these expressions is **were**. *For example:*

If only | *I were rich!*
| *he weren't so lazy!*

was is also possible, however, and is often heard in conversation.

EXERCISE 1 What would you say in these situations? Use **I wish** and **If only**.

a   You planned to play tennis but it's pouring with rain.

b   A friend has offered to lend you a car while you're in England but you can't drive.

c   There's a party this evening but you've got an awful headache.

d   You're staying in a Youth Hostel but the person in the bed next to you snores very loudly all night.

e   You're only half-way through the last question on an examination paper and there's one minute to go before the end.

f   You're out walking in New York and you're completely lost!

2   When referring to the **past**, **I wish** and **if only** are followed by a **past perfect** tense. *For example:*

*I wish I hadn't won **the money.***

*If only I had listened **to your advice.***

EXERCISE 2   Imagine you are the people in the pictures below. What would you say? Use **I wish** and **If only** and think of one positive and one negative statement for each situation.

3   Other expressions which are followed by a past tense:

would rather + object	*I'd rather you didn't say anything about it.*
as if/as though	*You talk as though you knew a lot on the subject.* (You don't!)
suppose/supposing	*Suppose somebody saw/had seen you.*
It's (about/high) time	*It's high time we left.*

EXERCISE 3   Complete the following sentences.

a   Your car is absolutely filthy! It's high time you ....

b   It's stupid of you not to take out travel insurance for your holiday. Suppose ....

c   I'm grown up now. Why do you still treat me as if ....

d   Don't take her any more chocolates while she's in hospital. She'd rather you ....

Text 1 *Just a normal day?*

❶ Read the text and answer these questions:

1 How did Mrs Barrett win £1 million?

2 When did she discover that she had won?

3 What is worrying her about her win?

FRIDAY, Sept 28. Alice Maude Barrett, 67, got up at 7.30 a.m. as usual. She had her usual breakfast – a cup of tea and a bread roll.

She browsed through her Mirror as usual. Then she did her washing. Not a lot of it to do – only her bits and pieces.

She did it by hand. She only uses the machine once a fortnight to save on electricity.

She hung the washing out to dry in the yard behind her council maisonette. 'Gives the sheets a nice airing.'

Then she took Thumper the dog out for his walkies and popped into the Co-op as usual to do her shopping.

Most mornings she pops into the Co-op. On this particular Friday she bought half a dozen eggs and half a pound of lard.

Back at her flat she dusted around and made her bed and fried up sausages and chips for her dinner.

Then she and Thumper had an afternoon snooze in the armchair until it was time for him to have another walk.

Home then to do the ironing. Daughter Annie came round to bring her mum cabbages and carrots. Annie works on a farm.

BINGO

Then, as usual on a Friday, Alice Maude Barrett, who prefers to be called Maudie, washed and dressed and went to bingo, her favourite thing next to watching snooker on TV.

Back home just after 10 p.m., watch telly for an hour and bed at 11.15.

That's how last Friday ended for Maudie.

Alice Maude Barrett will never again in her life have a normal, ordinary Friday.

On Saturday morning Alice Maude Barrett, aged 67, divorced, mother of five daughters, grandmother of ten great kids, stared

at her Mirror and it began to dawn on her that she might, just might, have got the numbers right on her Who Dares Wins Win a £Million card.

She took a swallow of tea and rang Annie. Annie yawned and went back to sleep.

But by six on Saturday evening there wasn't any doubt. Maudie was a millionaire.

Alice Maude Barrett lives in a council flat on £37.01 a week social security.

The new millionaire came round to my place yesterday for a nice little talk and a cuppa to celebrate.

Tea is what she prefers. She is a very quiet person. Shy. A bit nervous. 'Well you would be, wouldn't you?' she said. 'You can't take it in, can you?

'I'm only worried about one thing; how will I be able to go to bingo now?

'What'll they all think? Suppose I won. I don't want to give up the bingo and all my friends.'

From The Daily Mirror

❷ Now answer these questions:

1 From the article we learn that Mrs Barrett normally led

A a very hard life.

B a very lonely life.

C a very unexciting life.

D a very unhappy life.

2 We understand that Mrs Barrett didn't have much money from the fact that

   A she only did her washing twice a month.

   B she had to worry about fuel bills.

   C she had very little to eat.

   D she couldn't afford to go out.

3 Mrs Barrett explained that she seemed nervous because it was difficult for her

   A to believe what had happened.

   B to decide how to spend the money.

   C to talk to people she didn't know well.

   D to agree to accept the money.

4 Mrs Barrett probably telephoned her daughter that Saturday morning

   A to tell her what vegetables to bring that day.

   B to let her know it was time to get up.

   C to ask her to help check the numbers on her card.

   D to tell her that her mother was a millionaire.

5 Bingo was important to Mrs Barrett because

   A it was her only chance to get out of the house.

   B it gave her the chance to win a million pounds.

   C she had no other entertainment.

   D she enjoyed the company it provided.

DISCUSSION POINTS A ❸

1 Judging from the information in the article, what do you think Mrs Barrett is likely to spend some of her money on?

2 Will Mrs Barrett be able to continue going to her bingo evenings? Why/Why not?

3 Do you think she'll have a happier life as a result of her win? Why/Why not?

DISCUSSION POINTS B ❹

1 **Do this short exercise first, to remind you of the Conditional 2. Make complete sentences from these notes:**

   1 I/probably (feel) better/if I (take) more exercise.

   2 If she (not have) a dog for company, she (be) quite lonely.

   3 If you (win) £1,000, how/(spend)/money?

2 **Look at the three questions below and decide on your answers. Do this alone. (5 minutes)**

   • **If you won £100,000, how much of it would you**

     a spend?   b invest?   c give away?

   • **Which charity organisations would you give part of your winnings to, if any? Choose from the following (or add your own ideas):**

   A society which:

     a looks after orphans (children with no parents)

     b prevents cruelty to animals

     c helps blind people

> d is trying to find a cure for cancer
>
> e fights pollution and protects the countryside
>
> f helps old people
>
> g ....

- Imagine that you have won £10,000 but you can only have it if you can say exactly how you would spend it (and you must spend it all!).
  Make a list of things you would buy, with approximate costs.

5 Now discuss your answers with a partner. Give reasons for your decisions and make sure your partner explains his/her reasons.

THE SEQUEL TO THE STORY

Since Mrs Barrett's win, she has quietly moved out of her council maisonette to an ordinary-looking bungalow. Apart from investing money for her family, her only spending has been on a new bed and a remote-control colour television – which she has still not learnt how to work.

'She has a solicitor and a tax expert at the bank to help her out with financial matters but for a lady of her age and background, she has shown tremendous common sense in the way she's adjusted to her new wealth,' says the man from the newspaper who looks after their big prize-winners.

'It's not changed her at all and I'd be surprised if any of her neighbours even realise who she is. She's just like any other little old lady next door.'

FINAL FOOTNOTE

Fourteen years ago Father James Curtin, a 65-year-old Catholic priest, won £109,000 on the football pools and promptly gave it all away – the only thing he bought himself was a new Mini. The rest went on church repairs and to various charities.

'My life is no different,' says Father James, 'I was completely content then and I'm the same now. It was a wonderful feeling writing all those cheques. In fact, I'd recommend it for all people who win large amounts of money. It will make them feel better, believe me.'

by Mervyn Edgecombe in Woman Magazine

Focus on writing 1 *Exam practice* WRITING BANK: PAGE 114 and 126

1 FORMAL LETTER (PART 1)

You are interested in taking one of the painting courses at the Manor Art Centre but you only have the advertisement shown opposite and need more information. Read carefully the advertisement and the notes which you have made. Then write a letter to the Manor Art Centre, covering the points in your notes and adding any other relevant information about yourself. Write your **letter** in **120–180** words in an appropriate style. Do not include addresses.

NOTES
1 Don't forget to say which course you are interested in (and perhaps why) and to include all the other points in the notes.
2 Make a paragraph plan before you start and include a suitable beginning and ending.
3 Follow the layout for a formal letter shown in the Writing Bank (page 114) but don't include addresses for an exam letter.

Manor Art Centre

Uphill, Somerset, UK

2, 5, 7 day courses. (All abilities.)
Personal Tuition. Choose from:
- *Drawing,*
- *Wild Flower painting,*
- *Portrait painting.*

(Good food) and (accommodation)
in beautiful (unspoilt village.)

OK for complete beginner?
– price?
– are painting materials supplied?

vegetarian dishes?

What?

– nearest station?

❷ REPORT

A small English tour company wants to offer a new holiday destination in your country and has asked you to write a report on a particular town, city or region, describing the main attractions and also any negative points. Write your **report** in **120–180** words in an appropriate style.

NOTES

1 Choose somewhere that you know to write about, if possible, but don't be afraid to invent details if necessary!

2 Think about the kind of things tourists would be interested in and make a list of possible topics to cover. Decide how to group these under **subheadings**.

3 Don't forget to **introduce** your report and to end with a **summary** and **recommendation**. See notes on reports in the Writing Bank (page 127).

Focus on listening 1 *Is there life after redundancy?*

❶ **Can you explain the words in bold type in the sentences below?**
150 workers have been made **redundant** at a factory in Manchester.
They will receive **golden handshakes** of between £200 and £2,000.

(If not, check the explanations on page 226.)

❷ You are going to hear about several people who were made redundant, but who started new careers. As you listen, complete the table below.

	Previous career	Length of time (years)	Redundancy pay	New career	Where?	Success? Yes/No/ Too early to say
A Brian Collins	1. Electrical Industry 2. Teaching sailing	a. 4	b. £350.00	c. Boat repair firm	Scotland	Yes
B William Rudd	Chemical company	d. 20	£70,000	e. Butcher's shop	f. Central London	g. Yes
C Patricia and Rex Pole	h. Banking	33	i. £30,000	j. Pub	South Coast	k. No
D Graham Clarke	l. Sales man	m. 27	n. £2000	Magician	Colchester	o. Too early to say

---

STUDY BOX 1 **Phrasal verb** *give*

'I've **given up** worrying about it now.' (Lead-in 2)

give away – give as a present.	*Father Curtin won £109,000 and **gave** it all **away**.*
give away – reveal.	*The author refused to **give away** any secrets about the ending of his book.*
give back – return.	*Please make sure you **give** me my pen **back**.*
give in – hand in.	*This is the end of the test. Please **give in** your papers now.*
give in – surrender.	*The government refuses to **give in** to terrorism.*
give out – distribute.	*Children helped to **give out** presents to the old people.*
give up – stop.	*My doctor has told me to **give up** eating cakes and sweets.*
give up – surrender/abandon.	*I had to **give up** my flat when I got married.*

Communication activity *Turning points in history*

❶ Work with another student to answer the questions below. If you're not sure what an answer is, choose the answer you and your partner think is most likely.

1   Which of the following was invented first?
   A radio   **B** aeroplane   **C** submarine

2   The first dictionary appeared in
   A China in 1100 BC.   **B** France in 1697.   **C** England in 1755.

3   1961 was the year of
   A the first automatic digital computer.   **B** the first man in space.   **C** the first robot.

4   Paper was first produced in the 1st century BC in
   A Egypt.   **B** China.   **C** Rome.

5   The first journey by hot air balloon took place over Paris in
   A 1783.   **B** 1867.   **C** 1903.

6   Which of the following great shipping canals was opened first?
   A Panama   **B** Suez   **C** Corinth

7   Television was invented in 1926 by
   A an Italian.   **B** an American.   **C** a Scotsman.

8   Which of the following was invented in China in 1000?
   A the wheel   **B** the watch   **C** gunpowder

9   Tobacco was first brought to Europe from
   A Mexico in 1490.   **B** America in 1553.   **C** Africa in 1840.

10   The first printed book was produced in 1456 in
   A Spain.   **B** Germany.   **C** England.

To see how well you've done, check the answers on page 226.

❷ Which of the ten inventions or developments above was the most important turning point in your opinion, and which the least?

❸ What other invention, discovery or achievement can you think of which was more important than any of those above?

Focus on grammar 2 Conditional 3

FORM

| If | had(n't) had(n't) been | + past participle. | would(n't) have would(n't) have been | + past participle. |

For example:

If I *had (I'd) told* **you the truth, you** *wouldn't have believed* **me!**

I would (I'd) have taken **you to the station if my car** *hadn't broken down.*

The Conditional 3 refers to the past. The **if** event is therefore impossible since we cannot change the past.

If a result is **not sure**, we can express this element of doubt with **would probably, might,** and **could**. *For example:*

| *If you* *had driven* **that car, you** | *would probably* *might* *could* | *have had* **an accident.** |

EXERCISE 1   Put the verbs in the following sentences into the correct form to make Conditional 3 sentences.

a   If Mrs Barrett (not buy) the Daily Mirror, she (not take part) in the competition.

b   If she (forget) to check the numbers on her card, she (not win) a million pounds.

c   She (not ring) her daughter if she (not be) so excited.

d   If Annie (not be) so tired, she (not go) back to sleep.

e   She (not be interviewed) if she (not become) a millionairess.

f   If she (not win) so much money, she ....

EXERCISE 2   Using the information in each question below, write Conditional 3 sentences. (There may be more than one possibility.)

a   The Incas of Peru had no paper. Their architects had to make models in clay for the builders to follow.
    If the Incas ....

b   The first photograph was taken in 1826. Napoleon, who died in 1821, never had his photograph taken.
    If Napoleon ....
    or If the camera ....

c   Penicillin was discovered in 1928. It helped to save many lives in World War II.
    Many lives ....

d   The mariner's compass was invented in the twelfth century. Christopher Columbus reached the West Indies in 1492.
    Christopher Columbus ....

e   Tobacco was imported to Europe in 1553.
    If tobacco ....

MIXED CONDITIONALS

When we want to talk about the present result of a past event, we can use a mixed conditional. *For example:*

> *If I hadn't been invited, I wouldn't be here.*
> *I wouldn't be surprised if he had been delayed.*

FORM

If	had(n't) had(n't) been	+ past participle	would/could/might + infinitive

EXERCISE

The Suez Canal was opened in 1869. Before that, ships had to travel round Africa to reach India. Complete the following sentences, putting the verbs into the correct form so that they describe the present result of a past action.

a If the Suez Canal hadn't been opened in 1869, ships (have to) travel ....

b If/Panama Canal (complete)/1914, ships/(sail)/South America/Pacific.

c Ships (go)/Peloponnese/Aegean Sea/if/Corinth Canal/(not build)/1893.

Text 2

❶ You are going to read a text about some opportunities to get married abroad.
To answer the questions below, choose from the countries or states (**A–G**). You may need to choose some of the countries or states more than once.

A Australia   **E** Bali
B Barbados   **F** Florida
C Italy   **G** Grenada
D St Lucia

❷ In which country or state are the following statements true?

It is forbidden to get married in the evening.   1 | B

You have to stay there for more than a month before your wedding.   2 | C

You have to apply several weeks before the wedding.   3 | A

You can have an unusual wedding but you have to learn to dive first.   4 | E

You have to stay there for one week before the wedding.   5 | G   6 | E

You can get married on the day you arrive.   7 | F   8 | B

A special church has been built for some visitors' weddings.   9 | A

It is forbidden to get married on the sand.   10 | D

You can get married just before going up in the air.   11 | F

You can get a free information sheet about weddings.   12 |

The bride and groom have just got married on a Mauritian beach. The congregation was a group of complete strangers – hotel guests in their swimsuits who laid their detective novels on their sunbeds and strolled over to listen to the pastor brief the couple on their new responsibilities.

Each year about 12,000 Britons go abroad to get married, as well as to honeymoon. This has as much to do with economics as romance and sunshine. With the average wedding

seven-day stay and the need to spend a day in Jakarta to deal with the paperwork.

Australia is another possibility. On the island of Hamilton they have even built a church, not for westerners but for Japanese who like

arrive, obtain the licence and marry, all on the same day.

There are several slightly crazy wedding possibilities available in **Florida.** You can get married aboard the Riverside Romance while cruising on the St John's River, for example, or in the basket of a hot-air balloon, with the pilot performing the ceremony just before lift-off, followed by breakfast. Underwater marriages are also conducted in Key Largo, Florida, where the engaged couple

Love
in a strange climate

at home costing about £8,000, a ceremony in paradise will bring significant savings.

Fly to the Dominican Republic, for example, and a couple can have a two-week honeymoon at a luxury hotel for £1,799 for two, including all wedding arrangements, while a three-day package to Gibraltar costs just £600.

An important consideration is the legal requirement concerning residency – the time you have to stay in the country before you can get married. EC countries are among the most difficult. In **Italy**, for example, you have to be there for six weeks. In the Caribbean, the most popular place for overseas weddings, the rules vary from island to island. In **Barbados**, you can marry the day you arrive; in Jamaica, weddings usually take a minimum of three days; in **Grenada**, a week.

Bali is the most popular destination in the Far East, despite the additional complication of a

to follow up their traditional wedding with a white church wedding. You need to apply at least six weeks ahead of your trip. The Australian Tourist Commission publishes a useful free fact sheet.

America leads the way in terms of speed. In Las Vegas a wedding licence is easier to acquire than a television. All you need is your passport and US$45. Then you find a chapel, such as the Elvis Experience, one of several open 24 hours a day, or one in the hotel where you are staying. In **Florida** you can also

are taken on a one-day diving course before undertaking the ceremony.

Many travel companies employ wedding co-ordinators who are well informed about the legal requirements in different countries. There is a rule in **Barbados**, for example, that forbids marriages after 6 p.m., and in the Seychelles marriages have to take place in a permanent building, never a temporary building or tent in the hotel grounds. On **St Lucia**, you cannot marry on the beach but the hotel grass is perfectly fine. ♥

❸ **Find words or phrases in the first two paragraphs which mean the same as:**

1 a group of people at a religious ceremony ...... *Congration* ......
2 walked in a relaxed way ...... *Strolled* ......
3 a leader or minister in a church ...... *Pastor* ......
4 give instructions to ...... *to Brief* ......
5 a short holiday after a marriage ...... *honeymoon* ......
6 financial considerations ...... *economic* ......
7 important/large ...... *Significant* ......

DISCUSSION POINTS **❹**

1 If you could choose anywhere in the world to get married, where would you go, and why?
2 Can you think of any disadvantages to having a wedding in a faraway place?

TOPIC VOCABULARY **❺**

1 *Marriage* is usually used to describe the relationship between two married people.
For example:
They have had a long and happy marriage.

2 A *wedding* is the marriage ceremony and any celebrations such as a party afterwards.
For example:
Have you decided on the date of your wedding yet?
white wedding, wedding ring, wedding present, wedding anniversary, etc.

3 After you *marry* another person or *get married* to them, you *are married.*

❻ **Complete the following sentences with the correct word or phrase.**

1 I've saved you a piece of the .... cake.
2 Her first .... only lasted a year.
3 They ran away to Scotland to ....
4 A third of all .... in the UK now end in divorce.
5 We've decided to have a quiet .... with just a few friends.
6 She .... Alec for thirty years.
7 John's parents didn't approve of his .... to Jackie.
8 I've still got my .... dress. I can't imagine why I've kept it all this time.

STUDY BOX 2 **Phrasal verb *take***

'You can't **take** it **in**, can you?' (Text 1)

take after – resemble.	He **takes after** his father as far as his interest in sport is concerned.
take in – understand, absorb.	When I heard the news, I didn't **take** it **in** at first.
take off – remove.	You look so hot – why don't you **take** your pullover **off**?
take off – leave the ground.	The plane **took off** half an hour late.
take on – accept.	You mustn't **take on** more work than you can manage.
take over – assume control of.	While the Principal is away the Vice-Principal will **take over** his duties.
take to – develop a liking for.	I really **took to** Spanish food while I was in Spain.
take up – adopt as a pastime.	I feel much fitter since I've **taken up** jogging.

Focus on grammar 3   Review of tenses

EXERCISE 1   **Put the verbs in brackets into a suitable tense.**

a Don't worry, I (give) Mr Brown your message as soon as he (come) in.

b He (run) to the bus stop but when he (get) there, the bus (already/go).

c Of course I trust you! Look, I (not/offer) to lend you the money if I (think) you (not/pay) me back.

d Oh no! You (break) my best plate. Now you (have to) buy me a new one.

e What time (this train/get) to Edinburgh?

f It (say) in today's paper that a number of valuable paintings (steal) from the Tate Gallery.

g I (tell) my boss yesterday that I (want) to give in my notice because I (find) a better job.

h If you (not/stop) making that awful noise, I (call) the police.

i We (go) to America this year for our holiday. We think it (be) a complete change because we (usually/tour) in Europe.

j I hope you (not/wait) too long. I'm afraid the lift (break down) and I (must) walk down the stairs from the 24th floor!

k While we (wait) to take off at Hong Kong airport, the pilot (announce) that we (fly) through a thunderstorm.

l I (work) hard on my novel all day and when this page (finish), I (write) three whole chapters.

m We (buy) tickets for the film in advance, but as the cinema is half empty, we (not/need/do) so.

n It was extraordinary! In fact, if I (not/see) it with my own eyes, I (never/believe) it.

o I'd rather you (not/smoke) if you (not mind). Cigarette smoke (always/make) me feel ill.

EXERCISE 2   **In the following conversation, put the verbs in brackets into a suitable tense (active or passive).**

A Hello Jim, I (not/see) you for ages! What (you/do)?

B I (work) abroad, actually. I (have) a 6-month contract with the British Council to teach English in China. I only (get) back two days ago.

A China! How marvellous. Where (you/live)?

B Well, I (spend) four months in Beijing, and then I (go) to Shanghai and Xian.

A And (you/manage) to see the Great Wall?

B Oh yes, and I (climb) it too! I also (see) the Forbidden City, or the Palace Museum as it (call) nowadays. That's fantastic. And lots more.

A And (you/take) many photographs?

B Hundreds! Unfortunately some of them (not/come) out too well because the camera I (use) (not/have) a flash. I really wish I (take) better equipment.

A Well, I hope you (show) them to me one day soon. If I (know) you (go) to China, I (ask) you to bring me some silk.

B I (invite) to go at very short notice, in fact. I'm afraid I (not/have) time to let anyone know.

A Don't worry, I (only/joke)! Look, what (you/do) on Saturday evening?

B This Saturday? My parents (come) in the afternoon but they (leave) by 6 o'clock.

A Well, why (you/not/come) to supper in the evening? Then you (be able to) show me your photographs and tell me all about your trip.

B Thank you, I'd like to. I (even/bring) a bottle of Chinese wine with me to go with the meal!

EXERCISE 3   Put the verbs in brackets into a suitable tense (active or passive) or into an infinitive or *-ing* form.

After I (leave) college, I (find) it very difficult (get) a job. I (must/write) fifty or sixty letters of application but all the replies (say) the same thing: 'We are sorry (tell) you that the post you (apply) for (now/fill).' I only (have) one interview and they (tell) me that there (be) over 200 applications. Needless to say, I (not/get) the job!

In the end I (decide/take) a part-time job as a waitress just (earn) enough money (pay) the rent. Then, while I (serve) meals one day, I overheard two customers (talk). One (explain) that his secretary (leave) at very short notice and that he (not/know) what (do). I (stop/serve) at once and (ask) the man if he (consider) me for the job because I (have) all the necessary qualifications. He (must/be) very surprised but he (agree/interview) me the next day. To cut a long story short, I (give) the job and I (work) as a secretary for a year now. I expect I (still/serve) meals in a cafe, if I (not/have) the courage to interrupt that conversation!

Focus on listening 2 *A new direction*

You are going to hear an interview with a man who left the Merchant Navy and became a nurse. Listen to the interview and answer the questions which follow.

For questions 1–10, tick (✓) whether you think the statements are true or false.

		True	False
1	John decided to go into nursing while he was a patient in hospital.	☑	☐
2	There was no job he could do when he left the Merchant Navy.	☑	☐
3	You need certain qualifications before you can train to be a nurse.	☑	☑
4	He has worked in several hospitals during his career.	☐	☑
5	He did more than three years' training.	☑	☐
6	He joined a special course for male nurses.	☐	☑
7	The working hours for nurses have decreased slightly since John started.	☑	☐
8	He earned far less as a trainee nurse than he had before.	☑	☐
9	Most of the other students on his course were younger than him.	☑	☐
10	While he was training, he had to live in the nurses' home.	☑	☑

For questions 11–13 put a tick (✓) next to the correct answer, (A, B, C or D).

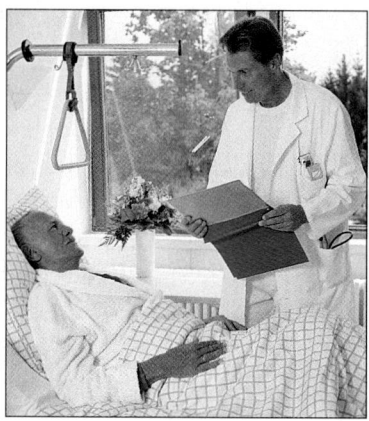

11 John's training course reminded him of his life in the Merchant Navy because in both
   A there was very strict discipline.
   B there were frequent changes of scene.
   C there was a lot of travelling involved.
   ✓ **D** there was a lot of hard work and not much money.

12 He decided to become a nurse teacher because
   A he was bored with working on the wards.
   ✓ **B** he wanted to earn more money.
   C he wanted to develop his career.
   D he had always been interested in teaching.

13 Looking back on his life, John feels that
    A he should have left the Merchant Navy sooner.
    B he should have stayed on at school longer.
    C he regrets the bad things that happened.
    D he wouldn't want to change anything.

Focus on writing 2 *Exam practice*   WRITING BANK: PAGE 113. 123. 121

❶   **INFORMAL LETTER**

You had arranged to spend a holiday with an English friend and you know he/she has made a lot of preparations for your visit. Very recently, however, you have been offered an extremely good job and you have decided to accept even though this will mean missing your holiday. Write a **letter** in **120–180** words to your friend to explain the situation. Do not include addresses.

NOTES   1   Look back at the notes on Informal letters in the Writing Bank (page 113).
          2   Make a plan of your paragraphs before you start. After a short introduction, write separate paragraphs to explain the situation and apologise, to give details about your new job, and to suggest another time when you can see each other. Finish with a short closing sentence.

USEFUL LANGUAGE

Result Links
so …
as a result …
This means …

❷   **NARRATIVE**

Your school/college magazine is planning to have a section called 'Turning Points' in its next edition and readers have been invited to send in suitable stories. Tell the story of an event which marked a turning point in your life. Write your **story** in **120–180** words.

NOTES   1   Make a plan of paragraphs before you start.
          2   Look at the notes on Narratives in the Writing Bank (page 123).
          3   You are likely to need to use the past simple, past continuous and past perfect tenses. Check these in Units 2 and 7 if necessary.

❸   **DISCUSSION**

An international magazine is investigating the question *Do we watch too much television?* and has asked readers to write in with their opinions. Write a short article for the magazine, mentioning the advantages and disadvantages of television. Write your **article** in **120–180** words in an appropriate style.

NOTES   1   Make a list of the main points beforehand. Consider:
- the main advantages of television
- the main disadvantages
- what alternative forms of information/entertainment there are.

2   Include a balance of advantages and disadvantages even if you intend to argue that one outweighs the other in the end.

3   Look at the notes on Articles and also on Discussions in the Writing Bank (pages 125 and 121). Divide your article into paragraphs and make sure you finish with a clear conclusion, giving your considered opinion as to whether we do or don't watch too much television.

Language review

Choose the word or phrase which best completes each sentence.

1   I don't know how he'll .... to the news when you tell him.
   A act   **B** answer   **C** react   **D** behave

2   We were given a lot of information at the start of the course but I didn't .... very well.
   A take it up   **B** take it in   **C** take it on   **D** take it over

3   A very important battle took .... here in the fourteenth century.
   A part   **B** charge   **C** hold   **D** place

4   If it .... , I'd have gone for a walk.
   A didn't rain   **B** wouldn't have rained   **C** hadn't rained   **D** wasn't raining

5   A large number of people have stopped smoking .... recent years.
   A in   **B** for   **C** since   **D** from

6   As far as .... there's only one solution to the problem.
   A I think   **B** I see   **C** I'm sure   **D** I'm concerned

7   I've .... trying to lose weight because it never seems to work.
   A given in   **B** given out   **C** given up   **D** given back

8   You'll need to apply for a visa at least two months .... of your trip.
   A ahead   **B** in front   **C** before   **D** earlier

9   We thoroughly enjoyed our holiday .... the poor weather.
   A in spite of   **B** although   **C** even   **D** despite

10   Today's match has been cancelled .....on..... account of the heavy rain.
   A by   **B** on   **C** for   **D** from

11   Nobody's accusing you .... the watch.
   A from stealing   **B** to steal   **C** of stealing   **D** with stealing

12 I'd rather you .... anything about this to anyone, please.

    A don't say   **B** won't say   **C** hadn't said   **D** didn't say

13 I missed my flight .... of delays on the motorway.

    A by means   **B** as a result   **C** owing   **D** in case

14 I'd like to congratulate you .... your recent engagement.

    A on   **B** about   **C** for   **D** of

15 Could you .... me to the railway station, please?

    A show   **B** direct   **C** lead   **D** indicate

ANSWERS

UNIT 10 ▶

FOCUS ON GRAMMAR 2

Answer to puzzle on page 188

Martha is an orang-utan.

Answer to puzzle on page 188

A A pig going round the corner of a barn.
B A bear climbing a tree. (The top 'paw' is an ear.)
C A snake going upstairs.

D A Chinese person riding a bicycle.
E A giraffe going past a window.
F A Mexican frying an egg.

Answer to question on page 215

redundancy: A worker becomes redundant when he or she is no longer needed by a firm.
golden handshake: A large amount of money given to somebody when they leave a firm, when they retire or when they are made redundant.

UNIT 12 ▶

COMMUNICATION ACTIVITY

page 216

Answers

1 C Built in about 1620 by a Dutchman. (radio – 1901; aeroplane – 1903)
2 A Produced almost 2000 years before the great French and English works.
3 B The Russian, Yuri Gagarin, made a complete circuit of the earth in Vostok 1 before landing safely. (automatic digital computer – 1944; robot – 1928)
4 B Paper, made from wood ash and cloth pulp, was one of the great technological achievements of the Han Dynasty.
5 A The two Montgolfier brothers built and flew their balloon 8 km across Paris. (1903 was the year of the first aeroplane flight.)
6 B 1869. (Corinth – 1893; Panama – 1914)
7 C John Logie Baird.
8 C (the wheel – 4000 BC in Mesopotamia; the watch – 1502 in Germany)
9 B
10 B A Latin bible produced by Johannes Gutenberg in Mainz.

Answer to question on page 269

The photograph in Interview 5, Part 2, is from an advertisement for hair conditioner.

UNIT 5 ►

COMMUNICATION
ACTIVITY
Page 77

STUDENT B

UNIT 8 ►

COMMUNICATION
ACTIVITY
Page 153

STUDENT A

UNIT 2 ►

COMMUNICATION
ACTIVITY
Page 30

THE STRESS LEAGUE

Rating is from 10 to zero. The higher the rate, the greater the pressure.

Miner	8.3	Manager (commerce)	5.8
Police officer	7.7	Professional footballer	5.8
Journalist	7.5	Salesperson, shop assistant	5.7
Pilot (civil)	7.5	Bus driver	5.4
Dentist	7.3	Farmer	4.8
Actor	7.2	Soldier	4.7
Politician	7.0	Engineer	4.3
Doctor	6.8	Hairdresser	4.3
Film producer	6.5	Secretary	4.3
Nurse	6.5	Architect	4.0
Firefighter	6.3	Postman/woman	4.0
Pop musician	6.3	Museum worker	2.8
Teacher	6.2	Librarian	2.0

UNIT 7 ►

COMMUNICATION
ACTIVITY
Page 137

How did you score?

1   **a**   1   **b**   3   **c**   0.   *The ideal age is 29.*

2   **a**   3   **b**   0   **c**   1.   *Long-term emotional stability is essential. Distant fiancées can cause big problems.*

3   **a**   0   **b**   0   **c**   3.   *You have to be genuinely sociable if high seas are going to make your neighbours spill their puddings in your lap – or worse!*

4   **a**   3   **b**   0   **c**   1.   *A personality test. People who push forward are more likely to succeed.*

5   **a**   3   **b**   1   **c**   0.   *A test of honesty and respect for other people's property.*

6   **a**   3   **b**   1   **c**   0.   *A test of honesty again.*

7   **a**   0   **b**   1   **c**   3.   *Testing how practical and economical you can be.*

8   **a**   0   **b**   3   **c**   1.   *Smoking was forbidden on John's trip. Musicians were very popular.*

9   **a**   1   **b**   0   **c**   3.   *Peacemakers are like gold on a long voyage.*

10   **a**   1   **b**   0   **c**   3.   *It's important to have a long-term goal in mind.*

11   **a**   0   **b**   0   **c**   3.   *You must be able to take a joke against yourself.*

12   **a**   0   **b**   1   **c**   3.   *A loyalty test.*

13   *Score one point for each year. People who have already made a constant effort in their studies are likely to do so in other areas.*

14   *Subtract one point for each day. Weaklings with more than a fortnight's illness should drop out here!*

If you scored 40 or more, you can start getting ready tomorrow. You're an ideal candidate for a long and difficult voyage, living with others in limited space.

If you managed 20 or more, you have some of the qualities needed in a long-distance traveller, but don't start packing yet! You'll need to change some of those bad habits!

If you scored less than 20, you should look for a nice steady job with a pension. Wear warm clothes in case you catch a cold on the way to the office, and stay away from travellers of all sorts!

UNIT 6 ▷

COMMUNICATION
ACTIVITY 2
Page 102

STUDENT B

UNIT 8 ▷

COMMUNICATION
ACTIVITY
Page 153

STUDENT B

TEST I

PART I   Read the text below and decide which answer **A, B, C** or **D** best fits each space. There is an example at the beginning (**0**).

Example:
0   A to   (**B**) at   **C** in   **D** by

MICHELLE'S STORY

When Michelle was (**0**) a̲t̲ school her friends and teachers would never have (**1**) .... how she'd (**2**) .... out. The (**3**) .... daughter of a postman, she (**4**) .... up in a small village near Lyons in France. When she (**5**) .... a place at Bordeaux University to study Humanities, her parents were delighted that she was to have the educational opportunities they had (**6**) .... . They hoped she would be a school teacher but (**7**) .... didn't happen quite as they had (**8**) .... . When she finished her studies, Michelle (**9**) .... her driving test, bought an old car and became (**10**) .... with engines. She decided to take a course (**11**) .... car maintenance which (**12**) .... thirteen weeks. At the end of the course, she was told that (**13**) .... all the students she had made the most (**14**) .... . She now works in a local garage as a mechanic and, in a few years, would like to (**15**) .... a garage of her own.

1	**A** hoped	**B** guessed	**C** wondered	**D** told
2	**A** come	**B** carry	**C** show	**D** turn
3	**A** singular	**B** only	**C** individual	**D** lonely
4	**A** came	**B** raised	**C** grew	**D** started
5	**A** won	**B** arrived	**C** applied	**D** entered
6	**A** failed	**B** avoided	**C** lacked	**D** dreamed
7	**A** things	**B** matters	**C** future	**D** life
8	**A** liked	**B** expected	**C** claimed	**D** pretended
9	**A** made	**B** gave	**C** presented	**D** took
10	**A** fascinated	**B** interested	**C** enthusiastic	**D** excited
11	**A** from	**B** for	**C** of	**D** in
12	**A** spent	**B** covered	**C** lasted	**D** passed

13 **A** of   **B** from   **C** beside   **D** by

14 **A** success   **B** advance   **C** achievement   **D** progress

15 **A** begin   **B** open   **C** introduce   **D** make

PART 2

Read the text below and think of the word which best fits each space. Use only one word in each space. There is an example at the beginning (**0**).

FIRST READ THE SMALL PRINT

When you take out travel insurance, you usually just accept the little form which the clerk pushes (**0**) .....*across*..... the counter. You fill it all (**1**) .... , make out a cheque and, (**2**) .... return, you receive a thin sheet of paper with very small print. But nobody ever expects that anything could really (**3**) .... wrong. It always (**4**) .... to someone else! Well, my family is that someone else!

I (**5**) .... never forget the phone call from my daughter who was (**6**) .... holiday abroad. It began: 'Mummy, something awful's happened.' Her hotel room (**7**) .... been burgled and all her luggage stolen. Fortunately, she was insured and she reported the matter (**8**) .... the police at the time. The insurance company, however, wanted not only the police report, (**9**) .... also receipts for everything stolen (**10**) .... they would recognise her claim. (**11**) .... nearly all her clothes were from a chain store, we had no receipts. Other items stolen had (**12**) .... gifts – a camera from her grandparents two years (**13**) .... , a necklace from her boyfriend. It took (**14**) .... nearly three months of writing letters to get any offer from the company at all.

A fight like this teaches you one very important lesson – before you take out insurance, make (**15**) .... you read the small print!

PART 3

For questions **1–10**, complete the second sentence so that it has a similar meaning to the first sentence. Use the word given and other words to complete each sentence. You must use between two and five words. **Do not change the word given.** There is an example at the beginning (**0**).

Example:

0 I haven't enjoyed myself so much for years.

since

It's years ....*since I've enjoyed*........... myself so much.

---

1 He's an enthusiastic football player.

keen

He's very .... football.

2 The remark was so unexpected that she didn't know what to say.

such

It .... that she didn't know what to say.

3 A local shop sold fresh fish at one time. It closed down years ago.

used

There was a local shop .... fresh fish.

4 You use a saw to cut wood.

tool

A saw .... wood.

5 It's often quicker to go by underground than by bus.

takes

The bus .... the underground.

6 No one in the world drives as badly as you do!

driver

You're .... in the world.

7 I tried as hard as I could to make him change his mind.

best

I .... make him change his mind.

8 It will be nice to hear from you.

forward

I'm .... you.

9 Could you connect me to the Information Office, please?

put

Could you .... the Information Office, please?

10 We all moved up so that one person could sit down.

room

We all moved up to .... one more person.

PART 4 For questions **1–15**, read the text below and look carefully at each line. Some of the lines are correct and some have a word which should not be there. If a line is correct put a tick (✓) in the space on the right. If a line has a word which should not be there, write the word in the space on the right. There are two examples at the beginning (**0** and **00**).

YOUNG DRIVER
Oliver Niesewand, 22

0	I passed through my test three weeks ago, so I	*through*
00	still drive with a certain amount of caution. My mother	✓
1	gave to me her car, and I get some help with tax and	....
2	insurance because it's so much expensive. I think	....
3	cost and crime are the most negative aspects of	....
4	owning a car, and you have to realise about how	....
5	powerful and possibly dangerous a car can be. I	....
6	enjoyed the learning to drive and my instructor was	....
7	very patient and uncritical. I've been noticed that	....
8	other drivers are not as patient as when you don't	....
9	have L-plates* any more. I haven't had any accidents	....
10	or near misses yet – the worst thing that could happened	....
11	was when I broke out a wing mirror during a lesson.	....
12	A near miss is probably a good thing because it	....
13	makes you to be more careful. Safe driving has a lot to	....
14	do with attitude. In my opinion, 17 is too young to	....
15	begin learn to drive. Perhaps 20 would be a better age.	....

*L-plates: signs with a large red letter L on them which are fixed to a car to show that the driver is a learner.

233

PART 5

For questions **1–10**, read the text below. Use the word given in capitals at the end of each line to form a word which fits in the space on the same line. There is an example at the beginning (**0**).

EXERCISE

Exercise is essential in promoting general good (**0**) ....*health*.... .	**HEALTHY**
It helps in controlling or losing (**1**) .... and also in	**WEIGH**
stress (**2**) .... and preventing illness. Through regular	**MANAGE**
exercise we (**3**) .... not only our external muscles but	**STRONG**
also our heart and lungs. Exercise (**4**) .... the risk	**LESS**
of heart disease which is a threat to men over 50 and,	
(**5**) .... , to younger men and women.	**INCREASE**

Regular exercise also affects our (**6**) .... on life. It	**LOOK**
allows us to get rid of (**7**) .... , anxiety and frustration.	**TENSE**
During exercise the brain releases (**8**) .... chemicals	**POWER**
called endorphins, which are associated with (**9**)	**HAPPY**
and relaxation, so exercise taken regularly improves the	
(**10**) .... of your body and of your mind.	**FIT**

TEST 2

PART I

Read the text below and decide which answer **A**, **B**, **C** or **D** best fits each space. There is an example at the beginning (**0**).

Example:

0 Ⓐ belief   **B** idea   **C** view   **D** thought

HOME SECURITY

Contrary to popular **(0)** .... most burglaries take **(1)** .... during the day. The quick dash you **(2)** .... to the shops before they close or to **(3)** .... the children from school are ideal opportunities. Burglars know about these things and what time they are **(4)** .... to occur. The garage door which you **(5)** .... open because you didn't have time to shut it before you drove away is as **(6)** .... as an invitation card.

Your best protection is to make **(7)** .... that when the burglar does come to your house, he decides it is not worth the **(8)** .... of breaking in. Your precautions have to be good enough to put him **(9)** .... .

For most people the first **(10)** .... to better security is to frighten themselves **(11)** .... really believing that their house could be burgled. And **(12)** .... , if it happened, would be pretty unpleasant. Anyone who has suffered the **(13)** .... can tell you that the shock of finding your **(14)** .... home vandalised is at least as painful as the actual financial **(15)** .... you suffer.

1	**A** part	**B** way	Ⓒ place	**D** action
2	**A** do	**B** take	**C** go	Ⓓ make
3	Ⓐ collect	**B** pick	**C** take	**D** catch
4	**A** probable	**B** surely	Ⓒ possible	**D** likely
5	**A** forgot	Ⓑ left	**C** let	**D** put
6	**A** well	~~**B** much~~	Ⓒ good	**D** fine
7	**A** clear	Ⓑ sure	**C** safe	**D** care
8	**A** alarm	**B** trap	Ⓒ risk	**D** threat
9	**A** off	**B** out	**C** up	Ⓓ away
10	**A** lesson	**B** point	**C** part	Ⓓ step
11	Ⓐ into	**B** to	**C** with	**D** of
12	**A** which	**B** that	**C** what	Ⓓ then

13 **A** state   **B** fact   **C** knowledge   **D** experience

14 **A** well-known   **B** usual   **C** familiar   **D** regular

15 **A** price   **B** loss   **C** lack   **D** cut

PART 2

Read the text below and think of the word which best fits each space. Use only one word in each space. There is an example at the beginning (**0**).

YOUNG SKATER

I was born and brought (**0**) ....*up*.......... just outside Bristol and (**1**) ....*reached*.... the ages of seven and fourteen, I spent far more of my waking hours on the ice rink (**2**) ....*than*...... I did at home.

(handwritten: between / at.)

When I was six, we went to Bournemouth on holiday and saw an ice show and from (**3**) ....~~Hence~~ *then*...... on I was hooked. (**4**) ....*It*........ was on that same holiday that we met a man who told us that an ice rink was (**5**) .....~~Soon~~ *opened*.... built in Bristol. As soon as it was opened, I (**6**) ....*took*...... skating lessons and I never looked back.

(handwritten left margin: 5, being)

Within a couple of years, I was skating (**7**) ....~~every~~ *during*.... three hours before school, (**8**) ....~~during~~ *at*... lunchtime and then (**9**) ......*in*........ the evening again. (**10**) ....~~At~~ *By*. the time I was nine, I was doing this at (**11**) ....*least*...... three or four times a week.

Mum and Dad used to (**12**) ....*take*...... it in turns to (**13**) ....*wake*...... me up at 5 a.m. with a cup of tea. Fortunately I wasn't the (**14**) ...*only*....... one in the family needing all this attention because I had two elder brothers (**15**) ....*who*..... were already doing their own thing. One was a musician and both were sportsmen.

PART 3

For questions **1–10**, complete the second sentence so that it has a similar meaning to the first sentence. Use the word given and other words to complete each sentence. You must use between two and five words. **Do not change the word given.** There is an example at the beginning (**0**).

Example:

0 I haven't enjoyed myself so much for years.

    since

    It's years ....*since I've enjoyed*............ myself so much.

1 We couldn't sleep because of the noise from the discotheque.

→ **prevented**

The noise from the discotheque .....*prevented* ~~mine~~ *our* ....
was not prevented enough for.
sleeping.

2 She's never been to the circus before.
time

It's the ...~~time to be~~ ... ~~in~~ .... to the circus.

3 The accident made it impossible for him to work.
able

Since the accident he ..... ~~was not able to~~ .... work.

4 When she heard that she'd won, she began to cry.
broke

When she heard that she'd won, she .....*broke* ~~out~~ *into* ....
tears.

5 My parents don't like me to stay out late at night.
disapprove

My parents ......*disapprove* ~~night~~ *staying*. out late at night.
my

6 It was a waste of time writing that letter.
needn't

have written
I .....*needn't* ~~writing~~ ~~write~~ .... that letter.

7 There is room for five passengers in our car.
big

Our car ....*is big enough for*... five passengers.

8 He was very lucky that he wasn't punished for what he did.
get
He was very lucky to .... what he did.

9 He was like my father in many ways.
reminded

He .... my father in many ways.

10 He was good enough to be a professional player but he gave up the game.
could

He .... a professional player but he gave
up the game.

PART 4

For questions **1–15**, read the text below and look carefully at each line. Some of the lines are correct and some have a word which should not be there. If a line is correct put a tick (✓) in the space on the right. If a line has a word which should not be there, write the word in the space on the right. There are two examples at the beginning (**0** and **00**).

TIME OFF
Sandy Murray, 29, air stewardess

0	Working when everyone else has got time off is all	✓
00	part of the job. I never mind if I must have to work on	*must*
1	a Saturday night because of I know I'll have time off	of
2	later in the week when I will get back. I've been flying	✓
3	on long-haul routes for six years now, so I don't	So
4	really get excited about the going away. I know I'm	the
5	going to feel tired when I get up to the other end	✓
6	after a busy night's flight and very little sleep. It's	✓
7	not as difficult work, but it's hard to keep smiling for	as
8	so long. Still, the passengers have been paid a lot of	been
9	money for the flight so they deserve it, and I know I'll	✓
10	have a good time once after we've landed. I'm fortunate	✓
11	because I don't have too much of trouble with jet-lag.	of
12	I have a few hours' sleep when I get to our destination,	✓
13	then I get up, have got a full day out and about, and after	got
14	another night's sleep I'm fine. Soon I've got four nights	✓
15	in Rio. I hope that to go up Sugar Loaf Mountain and	that
	the rest of the time I'll probably sit by the pool.	

PART 5

For questions **1–10**, read the text below. Use the word given in capitals at the end of each line to form a word which fits in the space on the same line. There is an example at the beginning (**0**).

AMELIA EARHART

The **(0)** *disappearance* of Amelia Earhart, the American   APPEAR ⁻

airwoman, is one of the world's **(1)** .... mysteries.   SOLVE

After Amelia made the first solo **(2)** .... across the   FLY

Pacific in 1934, she made frequent public **(3)** .... and   APPEAR

even received **(4)** .... to the White House.   INVITE

When she was at the **(5)** .... of her fame, she came   HIGH

under increasing **(6)** .... from the public to go on to   PRESS *Pressure*

even greater **(7)** .... and, in 1937, she decided to try to   ACHIEVE

fly around the equator. Her first attempt was **(8)** ....   SUCCESS

but two months later she tried again, **(9)** .... by her   COMPANY

navigator, Fred Noonan. Soon after their **(10)** ....   DEPART

from Papua New Guinea, near the end of their journey, the plane

vanished without trace.

TEST 3

PART I   Read the text below and decide which answer **A**, **B**, **C** or **D** best fits each space. There is an example at the beginning (**0**).

Example:
0   **A** desiring   **B** trying   **C** hoping   **D** expecting

---

ROBOTS

Ever since it was first possible to make a real robot, people have been (**0**) .... for the invention of a machine that would do all the necessary jobs (**1**) .... the house. If boring and repetitive factory work could be (**2**) .... by robots, why not boring and repetitive household chores too?

For a long time the only people who really (**3**) .... the problem their attention were amateur inventors. And they came up (**4**) .... a major difficulty. That is, housework is (**5**) .... very complex. It has never been one job, it has always been many. A factory robot (**6**) .... one task endlessly (**7**) .... it is reprogrammed to do something else. It doesn't run the (**8**) .... factory. A housework robot, on the other (**9**) .... , has to do several different (**10**) .... of cleaning and carrying jobs and also has to cope (**11**) .... all the different shapes and positions of rooms, furniture, ornaments, cats and dogs.

(**12**) .... , there have been some developments recently. Sensors are available to (**13**) .... the robot locate objects and avoid obstacles. We have the technology to produce the hardware. All that is (**14**) .... is the software – the programs that will (**15**) .... the machine.

1	**A** around	**B** through	**C** for	**D** over
2	**A** made	**B** managed	**C** succeeded	**D** given
3	**A** took	**B** gave	**C** did	**D** showed
4	**A** to	**B** for	**C** against	**D** on
5	**A** hardly	**B** seriously	**C** surely	**D** actually
6	**A** carries out	**B** carries over	**C** carries away	**D** carries off
7	**A** since	**B** while	**C** when	**D** until
8	**A** total	**B** whole	**C** full	**D** all
9	**A** side	**B** part	**C** hand	**D** view

10	**A** types	**B** ways	**C** methods	**D** systems
11	**A** for	**B** from	**C** by	**D** with
12	**A** Moreover	**B** However	**C** Besides	**D** Therefore
13	**A** assist	**B** allow	**C** help	**D** enable
14	**A** missing	**B** short	**C** left	**D** needing
15	**A** order	**B** practise	**C** perform	**D** operate

PART 2 Read the text below and think of the word which best fits each space. Use only one word in each space. There is an example at the beginning (**0**).

SHIPWRECK

On 19th March 1967, (**0**) ....*the*.... oil tanker 'Torrey Canyon' ran aground on Seven Stones Reef, off the coast of Cornwall, England. Days later, the wreck was blown (**1**) .... in an airstrike by the Royal Airforce. (**2**) .... that time, the cargo of 50,000 tonnes of oil (**3**) .... spilled into the sea, making a gigantic oil slick. The oil killed at (**4**) .... 25,000 birds and damaged hundreds of beaches. (**5**) .... 1975, the 'Showa Maru' ran aground near Singapore. (**6**) .... salvage ships could reach her she had lost 3,000 tonnes of oil – and that was only a small (**7**) .... of the oil she was carrying! The 'Showa Maru' is not one of the world's largest tankers. What (**8**) .... happen if the 'Globtik Tokyo' broke (**9**) .... ? There are lots of other ways that small amounts of oil (**10**) .... get into the sea – from the engines of pleasure boats, for (**11**) ....

The search (**12**) .... oil can make our surroundings (**13**) .... pleasant in other ways too. Construction yards and oil rigs can (**14**) .... a beautiful view. The fuel for cars is made (**15**) .... the oil in refineries and unfortunately refineries are difficult to hide!

PART 3

For questions **1–10**, complete the second sentence so that it has a similar meaning to the first sentence. Use the word given and other words to complete each sentence. You must use between two and five words. **Do not change the word given.** There is an example at the beginning (**0**).

Example:

0 I haven't enjoyed myself so much for years.

since

It's years .... *since I've enjoyed* .... myself so much.

---

1 We all enjoyed the walk even though it rained heavily.

spite

We all enjoyed the walk .... rain.

2 If no one mends the roof, it will collapse.

unless

The roof will collapse .... it.

3 The reason for the delay was a signal box failure.

result

There was a delay .... a signal box failure.

4 I'll give you a door key because I may not be in when you get home.

case

I'll give you a door key .... in when you get home.

5 I think the rain will go on all day.

set

I think the rain .... for the day.

6 The exam starts at 9 a.m. Don't be late.

will

Don't come later than 9 a.m. because the exam .... by then.

7 You should really try to smoke fewer cigarettes.

cut

You should really try to .... smoking.

8   I'm leaving at 6 o'clock so you'll have to phone before that.
use

I'm leaving at 6 o'clock so it .... after that.

9   Switch on the machine and then you can press the 'Start' button.
once

You can press the 'Start' button .... the machine.

10   It's possible that John could help you but he doesn't know about your problem.
might

If John knew about your problem, ... help you.

PART 4

For questions **1–15**, read the text below and look carefully at each line. Some of the lines are correct and some have a word which should not be there. If a line is correct put a tick (✓) in the space on the right. If a line has a word which should not be there, write the word in the space on the right. There are two examples at the beginning (**0** and **00**).

A YEAR IN SOUTH AMERICA

Nicola spent the year between leaving school and going to university teaching English and helping in an orphanage in Ecuador.

0	I was met at the airport by my host family. There was	✓
00	a girl, Christina, who was at my age, and a son who	at
1	was away at the university, so I slept in his room.	....
2	My week was varied. On Mondays and Wednesdays	....
3	I taught English at a college where my first pupil who was	....
4	a man of 35 years. On Thursdays I taught children at a	....
5	private school. Some of the classes got really noisy	....
6	but I used a whistle which it was very effective in	....
7	keeping them more quiet. On Tuesdays and Fridays,	....
8	I worked at an orphanage where I had played with the	....
9	children and helped with the cooking. It was a nice place	....
10	and the children all were beautifully looked after.	....
11	Language wasn't much of a problem since I had been	....

12 learning Spanish for five years ago, which helped me	....
13 get around on buses and go for shopping. Coming	....
14 home was strange. The first week was wonderful but	....
15 then I began to be miss South America. Now I'm looking	....

forward to my university course in Latin American

studies.

PART 5

For questions **1–10**, read the text below. Use the word given in capitals at the end of each line to form a word which fits in the space on the same line. There is an example at the beginning (**0**).

PREPARING FOR EXAMS

The most important rule of exam **(0)** ...*preparation*... is to start your   **PREPARE**

(1) .... early – don't leave it until the last few days   **REVISE**

before the exam.

Revise regularly and use a **(2)** .... of methods to   **VARY**

help you learn and remember. Read your lesson notes

(3) .... and highlight any points which are   **CARE**

(4) .... important.   **SPECIAL**

Be aware of your **(5)** .... and weaknesses and ask   **STRONG**

your teacher to suggest **(6)** .... practice exercises in   **ADDITION**

areas of the language where you lack **(7)** ....   **CONFIDENT**

You could ask a friend to test you **(8)** .... – on your   **OCCASION**

vocabulary or on your **(9)** .... verbs, for example. As   **REGULAR**

the exam approaches, you might also find it **(10)** ....   **HELP**

to answer some questions under exam conditions.

TEST 4

PART I

Read the text below and decide which answer **A**, **B**, **C** or **D** best fits each space. There is an example at the beginning (**0**).

Example:

0 A desire   **B** cause   **C** reason   **D** dream

ADVENTURE TRAVEL

The traditional (**0**) .... for exploration – to boldly go where no man has gone before – has become a little out of (**1**) .... now. Corners of the world which have not been explored are rare indeed. They do (**2**) .... , however, and – from polar regions to tropical rainforest, from 8,000 m. (**3**) .... in the Himalayas to submarine caves in the Caribbean – the attempts to discover them continue.

The increasing (**4**) .... in exploration is reflected in the growth of companies which (**5**) .... in holiday-length expeditions to the foothills of the Himalayas, Africa and South America. Such tours are unlikely to (**6**) .... real danger but they offer (**7**) .... challenge to allow the traveller some of the achievement of full-scale exploration.

The line (**8**) .... exploration from vacation is difficult to draw now. Expeditions may (**9**) .... from packaged adventures along well-known (**10**) .... to a demanding assault on some remote mountain face where survival (**11**) .... on good training, technical (**12**) .... , judgement and good luck. As one climbing enthusiast (**13**) .... it: 'Some people can get full satisfaction (**14**) .... admiring a mountain from a safe distance (**15**) .... others might only be satisfied by actually climbing the mountain.'

1	**A** question	**B** date	**C** order	**D** practice
2	**A** appear	**B** occur	**C** arise	**D** exist
3	**A** peaks	**B** tops	**C** points	**D** crowns
4	**A** popularity	**B** enthusiasm	**C** interest	**D** success
5	**A** specialise	**B** feature	**C** advertise	**D** arrange
6	**A** consist	**B** suffer	**C** involve	**D** propose
7	**A** sufficient	**B** slight	**C** certain	**D** some
8	**A** cutting	**B** dividing	**C** parting	**D** connecting
9	**A** stretch	**B** reach	**C** include	**D** range

10	**A** sites	**B** ways	**C** routes	**D** resorts
11	**A** requires	**B** relies	**C** stands	**D** results
12	**A** method	**B** art	**C** practice	**D** skill
13	**A** put	**B** said	**C** told	**D** mentioned
14	**A** for	**B** from	**C** at	**D** in
15	**A** however	**B** otherwise	**C** despite	**D** while

PART 2

Read the text below and think of the word which best fits each space. Use only one word in each space. There is an example at the beginning (**0**).

VILLAGE LIFE

The land around their village is rocky and the soil is poor. Julia and her husband worked hard in the fields but they could not produce (**0**) ....*enough*.... food to feed their family or buy the things they (**1**) .... Julia's husband was forced to look (**2**) .... work in South Africa. There was no work in Lesotho because there were so (**3**) .... factories and businesses. Many families in Lesotho are (**4**) .... the same situation. (**5**) .... a man has a lot of land or animals, he has no choice (**6**) .... to leave his wife and children and get a job (**7**) .... from home.

Julia's husband (**8**) .... to get home and see his family about once a year but the children are growing up fast and they (**9**) .... recognise their father. Their mother has to (**10**) .... all the family decisions. She is the one who keeps them (**11**) .... order, makes sure they do not go hungry and comforts them when they are sick or unhappy. Julia's parents help (**12**) .... looking after the youngest children and (**13**) .... some of the housework but they are (**14**) .... weak to work in the fields now. Julia has to plough, sow, weed and harvest the land (**15**) .... herself, while she waits anxiously for the next envelope containing money from her husband.

PART 3

For questions **1–10**, complete the second sentence so that it has a similar meaning to the first sentence. Use the word given and other words to complete each sentence. You must use between two and five words. **Do not change the word given.** There is an example at the beginning (**0**).

Example:

0 I haven't enjoyed myself so much for years.
since

It's years .... *since I've enjoyed* .... myself so much.

---

1 It wasn't easy to persuade her to come.
difficulty

I had some .... *difficulty to persuade* .... her to come.

2 Could you please put that cigarette out?
mind

I wonder ..... *do you mind to put* ..... that cigarette out?

3 I like travelling by train more than going by air.
rather

I ..... *would rather travelling go by train* ..... than by air.

4 If you work carefully, you won't make so many mistakes.
more

The ..... *more you work carefully* ..... fewer mistakes you will make.

5 He said he was sorry that he had kept us waiting.
apologised

He ..... *apologised to kept* ..... us waiting.

6 The train left on time and we arrived just after that.
already

When we ..... *already the train had already* ..... left.
already arrived the tain had

7 'I wouldn't take the coach, if I were you', the travel agent said.
advised

The travel agent ..... *advised us do not to* ..... take the coach.

8 I can't swim in that water – it's so cold!
too

The water is ..... *too cold to* ..... swim in.

9 Why not check the meaning of the word in a dictionary?
look

Why not ......look the word...................... up in a dictionary?

10 It would be a good idea if you booked the tickets in advance.
better

You ......~~should~~ better booked... the tickets in advance.
(had)

PART 4

For questions **1–15**, read the text below and look carefully at each line. Some of the lines are correct and some have a word which should not be there. If a line is correct put a tick (✓) in the space on the right. If a line has a word which should not be there, write the word in the space on the right. There are two examples at the beginning (**0** and **00**).

WEATHER FORECASTER

0	Isobel is 23 years old and works as a weather	✓
00	forecaster. She left the school with three A levels and	*the*
1	then took up a maths degree at Exeter University.	✓
2	After graduating, she was accepted on a training course	....
3	at the London Weather Centre and from two years ago	....
4	she became a duty forecaster in there. On a day shift	....
5	she arrives for work at 7.30 a.m. and spends about an hour	....
6	studying about the weather charts to get a picture of what	....
7	the weather is going to be like over the next 48 hours long.	....
8	Isobel's work can also includes writing the scripts for	....
9	presenters to read on the radio and drawing up the charts	....
10	that are appear in the national papers. She sometimes	....
11	answers queries from the Gas Board who want to know	....
12	how much power the public will be use, according to the	....
13	temperature, or from the Buckingham Palace wanting to	....
14	know whether the Queen should go out in an open carriage.	....
15	On night shifts, it's a lot more quieter. She loves watching the	....

sun rise but says it's strange going to sleep when everyone

else is getting up.

PART 5

For questions **1–10**, read the text below. Use the word given in capitals at the end of each line to form a word which fits in the space on the same line. There is an example at the beginning (**0**).

PHOTOGRAPHIC SPORT

With landscape (**0**) *photography* , you can take your time to set	**PHOTOGRAPH**
up your (**1**) .... Shooting sports pictures, on the	**COMPOSE**
other hand, requires quick (**2**) .... and fast reactions.	**DECIDE**
It may seem a difficult technique to master but it just	
takes (**3**) .... and lots of film to become	**PRACTISE**
(**4**) .... The secret is a good position,	**SKILL**
(**5**) .... , and a tripod to support a long lens.	**PATIENT**
(**6**) .... photographers use telephoto lenses to	**PROFESSION**
home in on the action without getting too close to it and you	
can (**7**) .... this lesson yourself. A long lens is a	**APPLICATION**
good (**8**) .... but you may need to move closer	**INVEST**
(**9**) .... if you've only got a compact camera.	**PHYSICAL**
Remember, in many sports there are set plays which	
(**10**) .... you to compose and focus your camera at the	**ABLE**
peak of the action.	

TEST 5

PART I

Read the text below and decide which answer **A**, **B**, **C** or **D** best fits each space. There is an example at the beginning (**0**).

Example:

0 A duties   **B** services   **C** repairs   **D** works

MINOR ILLNESSES

Most people can do minor (**0**) .... in the home – such as mending a fuse or (**1**) .... on a button. Most car owners know how to change a wheel (**2**) .... they have a puncture.

This booklet will help you to (**3**) .... with minor illnesses at home. Helping yourself will help the doctor at the same time. It explains simple (**4**) .... for minor illnesses and accidents which are (**5**) .... to occur (**6**) .... time to time. In some (**7**) .... there is nothing a doctor can do that the patient cannot do (**8**) .... as well.

This booklet will help you to know when you can treat yourself and (**9**) .... the doctor valuable time to help patients who are more (**10**) .... ill, and when you really need to (**11**) .... the doctor.

We hope you will find this booklet useful. At the back there is a list of simple medicines which (**12**) .... will be helpful to have (**13**) .... hand.

And remember, whenever you are really anxious or ill, advice can be (**14**) .... over the telephone. (**15**) .... you need do is ring the practice number.

1	**A** stitching	**B** fitting	**C** fixing	**D** knitting
2	**A** while	**B** if	**C** unless	**D** until
3	**A** react	**B** manage	**C** handle	**D** cope
4	**A** solutions	**B** drugs	**C** treatments	**D** operations
5	**A** normal	**B** likely	**C** expected	**D** possible
6	**A** on	**B** by	**C** from	**D** at
7	**A** cases	**B** occasions	**C** events	**D** types
8	**A** quite	**B** thoroughly	**C** fully	**D** just
9	**A** save	**B** spare	**C** free	**D** make

10 **A** badly   **B** urgently   **C** fatally   **D** seriously

11 **A** command   **B** call   **C** insist   **D** require

12 **A** they   **B** there   **C** it   **D** you

13 **A** at   **B** in   **C** by   **D** from

14 **A** told   **B** sent   **C** passed   **D** given

15 **A** Only   **B** All   **C** That   **D** Simply

PART 2

Read the text below and think of the word which best fits each space. Use only one word in each space. There is an example at the beginning (**0**).

BALLOON RIDE

Larry Walters intended to (**0**) ......*make*...... only a short trip when he took off from Long Beach, California, (**1**) ....*Sitting*.... in a garden chair which was attached (**2**) ......*to*...... 45 balloons filled (**3**) ....*with*.... helium. Instead, the ropes (**4**) ......*that*...... secured his chair to the ground broke and he shot up to 16,000 feet. (**5**) ....*The*...... startled airline pilots eyed the strange flying machine, Larry began to (**6**) ....*feel*.... a little chilly. He shot at several of the balloons (**7**) .....*with*... an airgun he (**8**) ....*had*.... taken with him and began to descend. When the balloon ropes became entangled in a power line, Larry was finally (**9**) ..*ready*... *able* to return to earth after more than an hour.

Larry (**10**) ...*was*....... rescued, uninjured, as his chair hung from the power lines. 'The part that was frightening (**11**) ....*was*...... the last 300 feet, with the rooftops coming up so fast', he said afterwards. 'I fulfilled my dream but I wouldn't do this again (**12**) ....*for*........ anything.'

The US Federal Aviation Administration is determined to see that he does not. An inspector said, 'We know that he broke some part of the law. As (**13**) ...*soon*.... as we decide which part it is, some charge (**14**) ....*will*....... be filed. If he (**15**) ...*had*...... a pilot's licence, we'd suspend that, but he hasn't.'

PART 3

For questions **1–10**, complete the second sentence so that it has a similar meaning to the first sentence. Use the word given and other words to complete each sentence. You must use between two and five words. **Do not change the word given**. There is an example at the beginning (**0**).

Example:

0 I haven't enjoyed myself so much for years.
since

It's years .... *since I've enjoyed* .... myself so much.

---

1 They expected twenty guests but forty turned up!
twice

There were .... they had expected.

2 People gave a lot of money to the Earthquake Disaster Fund.
deal

A .... was given to the Earthquake Disaster Fund.

3 It's possible that the robber hid his gun in a litter bin.
may

The robber .... his gun in a litter bin.

4 The road ran between steep hills.
either

There were .... of the road.

5 There are many ways in which he's like his father.
takes

He .... his father in many ways.

6 They showed two films while we were flying to Hong Kong.
during

They showed two films .... to Hong Kong.

7 I didn't go because I wasn't invited.
if

I would .... been invited.

8 'Did Sylvia attend the meeting?' he asked.

know

He wanted .... attended the meeting.

9 A local garage repaired my car.

had

I .... at a local garage.

10 Who else is entering the competition?

going

Who else is .... the competition?

PART 4

For questions **1–15**, read the text below and look carefully at each line. Some of the lines are correct and some have a word which should not be there. If a line is correct put a tick (✓) in the space on the right. If a line has a word which should not be there, write the word in the space on the right. There are two examples at the beginning (**0** and **00**).

INTERVIEW

0	I was invited to an interview for a place at a big London	✓
00	college for to do a maths degree. I hadn't been for an	*for*
1	interview before so as I was a bit unsure exactly what to	....
2	expect. There were about 20 of us being interviewed	....
3	that day and we were all arrived at the same time. Everyone	....
4	was smartly dressed and some of people were wearing suits.	....
5	First of all we were being led to a lecture theatre where the	....
6	admissions tutor gave us a talk about the college and the	....
7	courses. He also told to us they were interviewing 300 people	....
8	for 100 places. I had the last interview of the day so I went	....
9	with some others to have tea. My interviewer who was very	....
10	friendly as we walked towards his room. He asked about	....
11	my journey and of the weather. But it was more formal when	....
12	we got to his room. He gave me a sort of maths test, which I	....
13	wasn't expecting, but fortunately it wasn't too much difficult.	....

14 I could think he was trying to find out how my mind worked. ....

15 He made it easy to speak because he seemed to interested ....
in what I was saying.

PART 5

For questions **1–10**, read the text below. Use the word given in capitals at the end of each line to form a word which fits in the space on the same line. There is an example at the beginning (**0**).

MARCONI

Guglielmo Marconi (1874 – 1937) was an Italian (**0**) *scientist* ....   **SCIENCE**

and the (**1**) .... of the first practical system of radio   **INVENT**

telegraphy. In 1895 he (**2**) .... in transmitting radio   **SUCCESS**

signals over a (**3**) .... of over two kilometres.   **DISTANT**

The next year he came to London and was given (**4**) ....   **ENCOURAGE**

by William Preece, chief (**5**) .... of the post office.   **ENGINE**

1897 saw the (**6**) .... of Marconi's Wireless Telegraph   **FOUND**

Company and the beginning of his (**7**) .... In 1899 he   **FAMOUS**

made the first telegraphic (**8**) .... between England   **CONNECT**

and France. The (**9**) .... telegraph which he sent on   **HISTORY**

that occasion is preserved in the museum of Radio France in

Paris.

Marconi's greatest triumph was in 1901 when he

(**10**) .... transmitted the first radio signals across the   **SUCCESS**

Atlantic Ocean.

PART 1

You are going to hear people talking in eight different situations. For questions **1–8**, choose the best answer **A**, **B**, or **C**.

SITUATIONS 1

1 Listen to these two people. What's happened?
  A There's been an accident.
  B Someone has broken into their car.
  C Their house has been burgled.

[ ] **1**

2 Listen to this man trying to explain something. Where is he?
  A in a library
  B in a video shop
  C in a bookshop

[ ] **2**

3 You hear this airline representative speaking on the radio. Why did the plane make an emergency landing?
  A It ran out of fuel.
  B It was struck by lightning.
  C Part of its equipment failed.

[ ] **3**

4 Listen to these two women. Where are they?
  A in a dry cleaner's shop
  B in a clothes shop
  C in the cloakroom of a theatre

[ ] **4**

5 Listen to this man. What is he doing?
  A giving someone a driving lesson
  B playing a game
  C taking a photograph

[ ] **5**

6 You overhear this woman speaking on the telephone. What is she apologising about?
  A She's going to be late for a meeting.
  B She can't come to a meeting.
  C She's forgotten about a meeting.

[ ] **6**

7 Two friends of yours are having a problem with a piece of equipment. What is the equipment?
  A a television
  B a computer
  C a tape recorder

[ ] **7**

8 You are staying with a friend. What does she ask you to do?
  A take a message
  B take delivery of a parcel
  C take a package to the post office

[ ] **8**

PART 2

WILDLIFE ARTIST

You are going to hear a wildlife artist being interviewed about his work.

For questions **1–10**, complete the notes about what the speaker says.

His age when he began drawing:	_____ **1**
What he does before he begins drawing:	_____ **2**
What he especially enjoys about drawing:	_____ **3**
The country where he saw wolves:	_____ **4**
How long he spent with the wolves:	_____ **5**
How the wolves showed they were friendly:	_____ **6**
What he uses to draw with:	_____ **7**
Pets he had as a child:	_____ **8**
Who looked after them:	_____ **9**
What upsets him about animals in zoos:	_____ **10**

PART 3

TRANSPORT

You are going to hear five people talking about different forms of transport.

For questions **1–5**, choose from the list **A–F** what each speaker is describing. Use the letters only once. There is one extra letter which you do not need to use.

A boat
B motorbike
C bus
D car
E plane
F bicycle

Speaker 1	1
Speaker 2	2
Speaker 3	3
Speaker 4	4
Speaker 5	5

PART 4

BUDDY DOGS

You are going to hear an interview about a special scheme called 'Buddy Dogs'.

For questions **1–7**, decide which of the choices **A**, **B** or **C** is the correct answer.

1 Andrew decided to join the scheme when
  A he retired from work.
  B he first got Dan.
  C Dan was being trained.

    _____ **1**

2 How long has Dan been a Buddy Dog?

    A three months

    B eighteen months

    C four years   **2**

3 Andrew feels sorry for the old people because

    A they're not allowed to have their pets with them.

    B they've never had pets of their own.

    C they can't afford to keep a pet.   **3**

4 To be suitable for the Buddy Dogs scheme a dog needs to have

    A special training.

    B the right nature.

    C a medical check.   **4**

5 How does Dan behave with other animals?

    A He's friendly with them.

    B He keeps away from them.

    C He chases them.   **5**

6 One difficulty he has is that all the old people

    A are afraid of Dan.

    B want to keep Dan with them.

    C want to give Dan things to eat.   **6**

7 Where does he think the scheme would be useful?

    A with homeless people

    B with young criminals

    C with sick children   **7**

PART I

You are going to hear people talking in eight different situations. For questions **1-8**, choose the best answer, **A**, **B**, or **C**.

SITUATIONS 2

1 This message is on your telephone answering machine when you come in. What does your friend ask you to help her to do?

    A organise a party

    B cook a meal

    C choose a present   **1**

2 You are in a multi-storey car park when you hear these two people talking. What is their problem?

    A They've discovered their car has been stolen.

    B They've lost their car-parking ticket.

    C They can't remember where they parked their car.   **2**

3 Listen to this woman talking about the skiing instruction she received on holiday. What didn't she like about it?
   A The instructor was too young.
   B The instruction wasn't enjoyable.
   C She didn't improve her skiing at all.

| | 3 |

4 A friend is talking to you. What does he want you to do?
   A to lend him something
   B to speak to someone for him
   C to go somewhere with him

| | 4 |

5 Listen to this radio travel report. What is the subject?
   A roads
   B railways
   C flights

| | 5 |

6 You hear one side of a telephone conversation. What is the problem?
   A He telephoned the wrong number.
   B He asked for the wrong department.
   C He was put through to the wrong department.

| | 6 |

7 You hear this conversation in a shop. What kind of shop is it?
   A a hairdresser's shop
   B a clothes shop
   C a furniture shop

| | 7 |

8 Listen to this woman describing how she made a big change in her life. What did she decide to do?
   A to take an educational course
   B to get a job
   C to leave her home and family

| | 8 |

PART 2

EXTRAS

An *extra* is a person who plays a very small part in a film, as a member of a crowd, for example. You are going to hear part of a radio interview about an opportunity for extras to appear in a film.

For questions **1–10**, complete the notes on the information which is given.

The film is not only tragic but also

| | 1 |

The number of extras needed is

| | 2 |

One particular type of person needed is | **3**

This person will also need to have | **4**

They prefer people who are interested in | **5**

The pay will be | **6**

Extras will also receive | **7**

Two places where scenes will be set are | **8**

The filming will last for | **9**

When interviews will take place: | **10**

PART 3

MEMORIES

You are going to hear five people talking about their memories of their youth.

For questions **1–5**, choose from the list of topics **A–F** what each speaker is describing. Use each letter only once. There is one extra letter which you do not need to use.

A a visit to the seaside	Speaker 1 1
B restaurants	Speaker 2 2
C schooldays	Speaker 3 3
D kitchen equipment	Speaker 4 4
E shopping	Speaker 5 5
F a football match	

PART 4

COMPETITION

You are going to hear an interview with two young people, Colin Scott and Jennie Pullen, who have reached the final in a competition to find the Young Waiter or Waitress of the Year.

Answer questions **1–7** by writing **P** (for Presenter), **C** (for Colin) or **J** (for Jennie) in the boxes provided.

Who mentions each of the following points?

1 the number of people who have reached the final | **1**

2 where the final will take place | **2**

3 the number of people who entered the competition | **3**

4 the prize | **4**

5 what people have to do during the competition | **5**

6 ways of preparing for the final | **6**

7 the date of the final | **7**

INTERVIEW I

Work in pairs.

I Each student must talk about two photographs for about a minute.

Student 1: Compare and contrast these pictures and say which of the two rooms appeals to you more.

Student 2: When Student 1 has finished, say which of the rooms you prefer, and why.

Student 2: Now compare and contrast these pictures and say which kitchen you find more attractive.

Student 1: When Student 2 has finished, say which of the kitchens you prefer, and why.

2   Imagine that you and your partner are on holiday in Hawaii. One of the special trips below is included in the price of the holiday. Talk together about the advantages of each trip and decide which one to choose.

You have about three minutes for this.

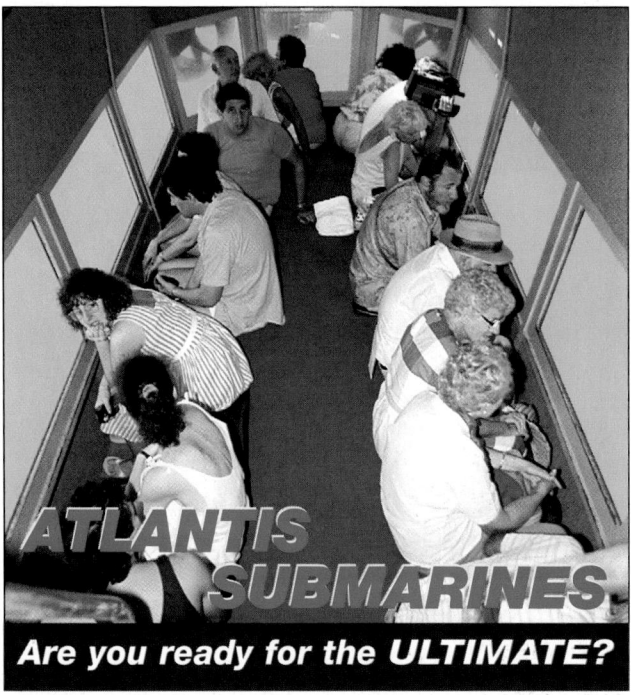

3   Now discuss the questions below.

1   When you are visiting a new place, is it better to go on an organised tour or to explore on your own?
2   Which is more enjoyable – to relax on the beach or to visit places of interest?
3   How do you manage if you don't speak the language of the country you are visiting?
4   What is it useful to find out before you visit a new place on holiday?

INTERVIEW 2

Work in pairs.

I   Each student must talk about two photographs for about a minute.

Student 1: Compare and contrast these pictures and say how you feel about games like these.

Student 2: When Student 1 has finished, say which type of game you prefer to play, and why.

Student 2: Now compare and contrast these pictures and say which way of spending an evening appeals to you more.

Student 1: When Student 2 has finished, say which activity you prefer, and why.

2   The students in your class have collected money to buy a present for a teacher who is leaving the school. Talk about the items below and decide which would be the most suitable gift. They all cost about the same.

You have about three minutes for this.

3   Now discuss the questions below.

1 In a situation like the above, is it better to ask the person what they would like? Why/Why not?
2 In your country what would be a suitable present to take when you visit someone's house?
3 How would you choose a present for a child you didn't know well?
4 What do you do if you receive a present which you don't like or which is unsuitable in some way?

INTERVIEW 3

Work in pairs.

I   Each student must talk about two photographs for about a minute.

Student 1: Compare and contrast these pictures and say which place you would prefer to study in.

Student 2: When Student 1 has finished, say which of the two places you would prefer to study in, and why.

Student 2: Now compare and contrast these pictures and say which you think is the best way to learn and why.

Student 1: When Student 2 has finished, say which of the two ways you would prefer to learn.

2   You and your partner have been asked to make suggestions about what to put in a new magazine for English language students. Talk about the ideas below and decide which three would be most popular and which, if any, would not be suitable.

You have about three minutes to do this.

3   Now discuss the questions below.

1 Can you suggest any other interesting ideas for the magazine?
2 How popular do you think a magazine like this would be? Why?
3 What other ways are there to improve your English outside class?
4 What competitions do you enter? Have you ever won a prize?

INTERVIEW 4

Work in pairs.

I Each student must talk about two photographs for about a minute.

Student 1: Compare and contrast these pictures and say where you would prefer to stay.

Student 2: When Student 1 has finished, say which holiday you would prefer to go on.

Student 2: Now compare and contrast these pictures and say which of the two means of travel you prefer and why.

Student 1: When Student 2 has finished, say how you prefer to travel, and why.

2   You and your partner belong to a local youth club and you have been asked to make arrangements for club members to attend some sporting events. Discuss how interesting the events below would be for members to watch and then put them in order of preference 1–7.

You have about three minutes for this.

3   Now discuss the questions below.

1 What other sporting events might club members like to attend?
2 What sports could the club organise for members to take part in?
3 What kind of person do you need to be to become successful in a sport?
4 What do young children learn from taking part in a sport?

INTERVIEW 5

Work in pairs.

I   Each student must talk about two photographs for about a minute.

Student 1: Compare and contrast these pictures and say which form of exercise would appeal to you more.

Student 2: When Student 1 has finished, say how you would prefer to exercise, and why.

Student 2: Now compare and contrast these pictures and say which situation you would prefer and why.

Student 1: When Student 2 has finished, say which situation looks more attractive to you.

2   The photograph below comes from an advertisement. Discuss the picture and try to decide what product or service is being advertised.

You have about three minutes for this.

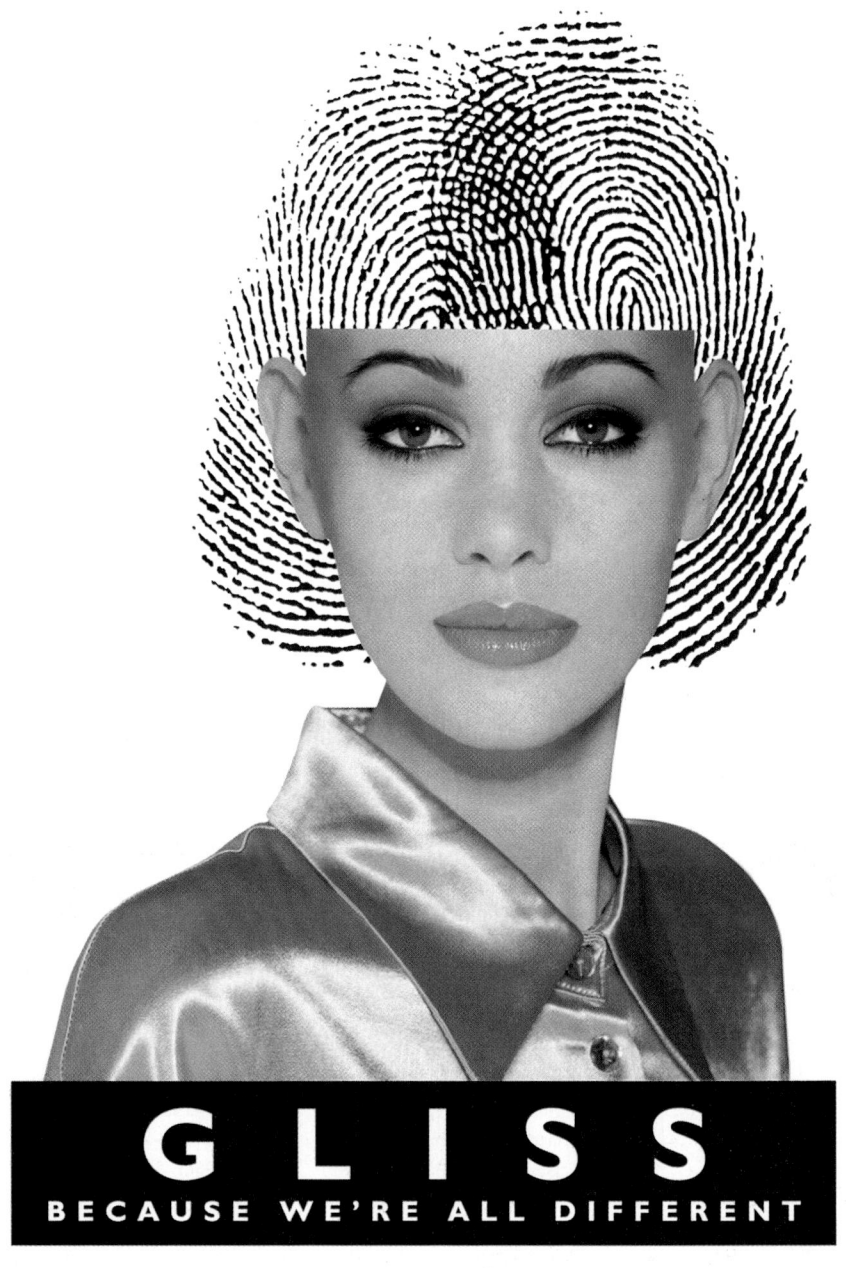

3   Now discuss the questions below.

1   When you watch TV, how much attention do you pay to the advertisements?
2   Which adverts do you like most and which least? Why?
3   How do advertisements try to make you remember a product?
4   How would you advertise something you wanted to sell – a bicycle, a computer or some books, for example.

To find out what is being advertised in the photograph above, look at the bottom of page 226.

269

Index of Structures

This index lists all the structural items covered in *Focus on First Certificate*. Each entry gives the page number and type of coverage. It is followed by an index of Functions.

Key: SB – Study Box; FB – Functions Bank; FG – Focus on Grammar; FW – Focus on Writing

Index of Functions

Key: CA – Communication Activity; FB – Functions Bank; FG – Focus on Grammar; FW – Focus on Writing; LI – Lead-in; SB – Study Box; T – Text; WB – Writing Bank